COMMON CORE

ELA EXEMPLAR RESOURCE

Instruction with Performance Assessment

Grades 9-10

Printed in the U.S.A.

ISBN 978-0-544-02790-9

 6 7 8 9 10   0928   21 20 19 18 17 16

4500604908   A B C D E F G

40000000000030

Table of Contents

About the Common Core ELA Exemplar Resource

9–10 TEXT EXEMPLARS

Stories

Informational Text (continued)

Informational Text (continued)	Page	Suggested Pacing

Overview

The *Common Core ELA Exemplar Resource* was developed to provide instruction for the Grades 9–10 text exemplars listed in Appendix B of the *Common Core State Standards for English Language Arts*.

Use this guide to complement the reading instruction of exemplars within your literature program or use it separately to provide students with questions and activities that deepen their comprehension of text exemplars selected for independent reading or group discussion.

Text Exemplars

The list of text exemplars provided in Appendix B of the *Common Core State Standards for English Language Arts* was compiled based on the texts' quantitative and qualitative complexity, quality, and range.

The text exemplars are presented in bands of two grade levels each (9–10 and 11–12) and are meant to suggest "the breadth of texts that students should encounter in the text types required by the Standards." The works listed were never intended to serve as a partial or complete reading list but rather as a guide to the types of reading materials that will help students successfully meet the Standards.

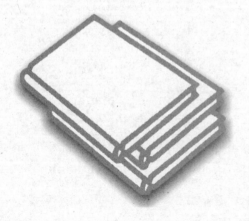

Organization of This Guide

This guide is organized into three parts.

CONTENTS WITH SUGGESTED PACING
The table of contents lists all the exemplars in the order given in Appendix B, along with the page references for where to find each exemplar in this resource. You will need to select and obtain the texts separately. This section also includes suggested pacing for reading each exemplar and teaching its lesson.

EXEMPLAR LESSONS
Most lessons for stories and informational texts are four pages, while most lessons for poetry are two pages. See **Lesson Setup** on p. vii for more information.

ENDMATTER RESOURCES

- **Copying Masters** In the back of this guide, you will find copying masters for several public-domain text exemplars, provided for your convenience.

- **Student Performance Checklists** These checklists will help students assess their writing and speaking and listening.

- **Academic Vocabulary** This compilation lists all the academic vocabulary, or Tier 2 words, introduced and defined in each lesson.

- **Bibliography and Exemplar Websites** These sections include the bibliographic information for each exemplar included in this guide, as well as a list of useful websites that offer additional information for teaching the exemplars and implementing the Standards.

Lesson Setup

Here is the basic setup of a four-page lesson.

PAGE 1 The first part of each lesson provides background information about the text and guidance for introducing the lesson to the class. The following features are included:

- Objectives

- Suggested Instructional Segments

- Options for Reading

- Summary

- About the Author

- Discuss Genre and Set Purpose

- Text Complexity Rubric

- Common Core State Standards met

PAGES 2–4 Each lesson includes two sets of questions that correspond to a "First Read" and a "Second Read" of the text.

- **First-Read Questions** Use these questions during and after an initial reading of the text to help students think through the text and learn to cite text evidence in their responses.

- **Second-Read Questions** Use these questions to guide students through a deeper analysis of the text. These questions give students opportunities for close reading and ask them to make deeper connections between ideas. Here, too, students must cite text evidence to support their ideas.

PERFORMANCE TASK Each lesson culminates in a performance task in which students are asked to demonstrate understanding of the exemplar text. Within each task, students are expected to complete a short writing assignment as well as engage in a speaking and listening activity. Where applicable, the performance task matches the performance-task suggestion provided in Appendix B.

Additional Lesson Features

TEXT COMPLEXITY RUBRIC To help you assess text complexity at a glance, a rubric is provided in every lesson. It identifies the overall complexity as Accessible, Complex, or More Complex. The rubric also includes quantitative measures for the Lexile and shows qualitative measures on a four-point continuum with text-specific rationales.

DOMAIN SPECIFIC VOCABULARY These content-area Tier 3 words are included only for texts with heavy discipline-specific content. Students are likely to use these words only within a specific discipline, such as *centrifugal* in science.

INDEPENDENT/SELF-SELECTED READING This feature, included on the last page of every lesson, suggests two on-level developmentally and age appropriate books students might use for independent reading and additional application of the Standards addressed in the lesson.

RESPOND TO SEGMENT—Classroom Collaboration These activities are aimed to help students wrap up each segment of text. Students summarize what they've already learned and address any questions they have before moving on.

Tips for Getting Started

- **Review the list of text exemplars for your grade span.** The exemplars include a variety of classic and contemporary complex texts. Many of the texts will likely relate to cross-curricular topics already present in your current curriculum and can be used as supplementary material to further discuss a given topic.

- **Consider the needs and the reading levels of the students in your classroom.** Each list of exemplars covers a two-grade span, so some titles may not be at the right level for your class at a given point in the year. Use the text complexity rubric to help you select the exemplars that best suit your students' reading or listening comprehension abilities throughout the school year.

- **Work with your school librarian.** Your librarian can help you find copies of the exemplar texts, online magazine articles, and any poems and stories that are in the public domain.

- **Preview the exemplars.** As you prepare for a lesson, make notes to help you consider additional connections that students can make to the text and how you might best prepare them for reading and discussion.

Literature Discussion Groups

The *Common Core ELA Exemplar Resource* can be effectively implemented with literature discussion groups. You can support students in collaborative discussion to further explore the text exemplars in ways that can foster higher-level thinking and the use of comprehension strategies, vocabulary acquisition, and speaking and listening skills—all essential for meeting the Common Core State Standards for English Language Arts. Use the following tips.

Before Reading

Divide students into small mixed-proficiency groups and schedule a time for the groups to meet each day. Assign roles to students or allow them to choose their own. Possible roles include the following:

- **Discussion Director** moderates the discussion by asking questions provided by the teacher or by creating original questions to pose to the group.

- **Passage Finder** chooses passages that are particularly interesting, revealing, or challenging for the group to focus on.

- **Vocabulary Detective** identifies and records unknown words for the group to look up and discuss.

- **Connector** makes connections between the text and other texts and aspects of real life, either in general terms or in relation to the students' experiences.

- **Summarizer** summarizes the segment of text read by the group or the teacher prior to the group's discussion and describes major characters, settings, and events, or main ideas and details.

Discuss Genre and Set Purpose As groups begin to discuss the text, encourage them to

- identify elements of the text's genre and name other texts in that genre.

- consider the author's purpose in writing.

- review their purpose for reading.

First Read

Have groups read a segment of the text.

- Ask students to take notes or flag sections of the text to later discuss and cite as text evidence.

- Have each group's Summarizer offer a summary of what was read. Others can add missing information as needed.

- Provide Discussion Directors with questions from the lesson or have them make up their own questions.

- Guide students to use the context of the text to understand academic vocabulary.

- Monitor discussions to ensure groups stay focused and cite text evidence to support responses.

Second Read

Have each group reread portions of the text to further analyze ideas and concepts.

- Guide groups to connect a segment to previous segments. Ensure they understand how the segments and ideas build throughout the text.

- Help groups focus on figurative language and literary elements, such as theme.

- Have groups support their responses with evidence from the text.

- Wrap up the discussion by having students summarize what they've learned.

OBJECTIVES

- Describe how characters respond to major events
- Identify the theme of a story
- Interpret symbols and figurative language in fiction
- Analyze text using text evidence

This excerpt from *The Odyssey* is broken into three instructional segments.

Options for Reading

Independent Students read the book independently or with a partner and then answer questions posed by the teacher.

Supported Students read a segment and answer questions with teacher support.

 Common Core Connection

RL 1 cite textual evidence to support analysis of what the text says explicitly as well as inferences drawn; **RL 3** analyze how characters develop and interact with others; **RL 4** determine the meaning of words and phrases, including figurative and connotative meanings

 # from *The Odyssey*

by Homer, translated by Robert Fagles

SUMMARY *The Odyssey* tells the story of Odysseus, a Greek king and hero of the ten-year Trojan War, and his many adventures trying to return home to Ithaca after the war. In the poem, he is called the "man of twists and turns" because he was fated to take so many detours during his ten-year voyage home. This excerpt describes a few of these adventures.

ABOUT THE AUTHOR Homer is the most famous of ancient Greek epic poets, the author of both *The Iliad* (the story of the Trojan War) and *The Odyssey*. However, no one is actually sure if Homer ever existed. The Greeks believe he was a blind storyteller from the island of Chios.

Discuss Genre and Set Purpose

EPIC POEM Point out that *The Odyssey* is an epic poem, which is a type of story that includes heroic characters, exotic settings, and grandiose events. Discuss how elements of this story are mythical and imaginary, but add that even though realism is not the goal of an epic poem, the characters' motives and behavior are very realistic.

SET PURPOSE Help students set a purpose for reading, such as to consider the character of Odysseus and what kind of a hero he makes.

TEXT COMPLEXITY RUBRIC

Overall Text Complexity		from *The Odyssey* FICTION
		MORE COMPLEX
Quantitative Measure	Lexile	1050L
Qualitative Measures	Text Structure	complex, unfamiliar story concepts
	Language Conventionality and Clarity	some figurative language and unfamiliar words
	Knowledge Demands	multiple themes, cultural and literary knowledge useful
	Purpose/Levels of Meaning	multiple levels of meaning

Academic Vocabulary

Read each word with students and discuss its meaning.

chided (p. 169) • scolded

assail (p. 169) • attack

beguiled (p. 170) • charmed or pleasantly distracted

staunchly (p. 174) • firmly or with confidence

suppliants (p. 174) • people who ask humbly for help

flouting (p. 177) • disregarding or treating with disdain

ELL ENGLISH LANGUAGE LEARNERS

Use Descriptive Words

Guide students to generate adjectives that could describe Odysseus. Then have them orally complete lists of descriptors such as the following:

Odysseus can be described as _____. Sample answers: crafty, sneaky, strong, well-spoken, lordly, hardy, cunning, emotional, brave, fierce

FIRST READ ## Think Through the Text

Have students use text evidence and draw inferences to answer questions.

pp. 152–153 • *Who is discussing Odysseus at the beginning of Book Five? The gods, including Zeus and Athena, are discussing Odysseus. Which god is most on the side of Odysseus? Athena* ◼RL 1

pp. 155–157 • *What is Odysseus doing when Hermes finds him? In line 93 on page 155, we see Odysseus weeping. What does this tell you about Odysseus? Odysseus desperately wants to be back home.* ◼RL 3

pp. 161–175 • *How does Odysseus first react when he is offered salvation from the waves Poseidon has sent against him? After line 390, on page 163, Odysseus is initially suspicious of Leucothea's motives. How is his reaction different when he meets Princess Nausicaa near the Phaeacians' city? In lines 154–161 of Book Six, Odysseus is not sure what to do, but he is not suspicious of the girls when he sees them.* ◼RL 3

SECOND READ ## Analyze the Text

- Review page 159. Ask: *How does the text describe Odysseus when he first answers Calypso in this scene? In line 237, Homer calls Odysseus "worldly." Why do you think Homer used that word at this point? Sample answer: Odysseus is trying to flatter Calypso in the hope of winning his release from her island; in this instance, "worldly" can mean that Odysseus is experienced in ways to manipulate others.* ◼RL 4

- Review pages 171–175 with students. Then ask: *What approach does Odysseus decide to take with the princess? What does this reveal about his character? Sample answer: Odysseus decides to approach with subtlety rather than an outright plea for help. This reveals how crafty and calculating he is.* ◼RL 3

- Ask: *What text examples from this section show that Odysseus is tactful and diplomatic? At line 239 of Book Five, he is careful not to make his wife sound better than Calypso. Starting at line 164 of Book Six, he flatters Nausicaa by pretending to confuse her with a goddess. He compliments both women to persuade them to help him.* ◼RL 3

RESPOND TO SEGMENT 1

Classroom Collaboration

Have partners create a summary of the plot events in this segment. Encourage them to write out a list of the characters, including Olympic gods, who have influenced the story so far. Then have students predict what might happen next in the poem.

Domain Specific Vocabulary

nymph (p. 187) • lesser deity in Greek mythology, typically a beautiful woman living in a natural setting and attending the gods

oracle (p. 194) • in ancient Greece, the person at a god's shrine who gives the god's response to questions asked by individuals

 ENGLISH LANGUAGE LEARNERS

Use Comprehensible Input

Ensure students understand the plot events and the characters by asking questions such as: *How does Odysseus get help from others?*

RESPOND TO SEGMENT 2

 Classroom Collaboration

Have small groups work together to summarize the adventures of Odysseus so far. Have them work together to answer questions about things they don't understand.

 Common Core Connection

RL 1 cite textual evidence to support analysis of what the text says explicitly as well as inferences drawn; **RL 2** determine a theme or central idea of a text and analyze its development; **RL 3** analyze how characters develop and interact with others; **RL 10** read and comprehend literature; **W 2** write informative/explanatory texts; **W 5** develop and strengthen writing by planning, revising, editing, rewriting, or trying a new approach; **SL 4** present information, findings, and supporting evidence clearly, concisely, and logically

Academic Vocabulary

Read each word with students and discuss its meaning.

ramparts (p. 181) • wall-like barriers raised to protect a settlement
overweening (p. 181) • conceited or proudly overconfident
libations (p. 184) • wine or other liquids poured out to honor a god
burnished (p. 185) • smooth and polished
slander (p. 197) • false or malicious statement

FIRST READ   Think Through the Text

Have students use text evidence and draw inferences to answer questions.

pp. 179–182 • *Who helps Odysseus find his way to the palace of Alcinous?* Athena helps him, disguised as a girl. *How does Odysseus behave toward the "girl"?* He is respectful and thankful. ▬ RL 1

pp. 185–186 • *How is Odysseus received at the Phaeacian court?* He is greeted as a stranger but treated grandly. *How does the text describe Odysseus's response when he is asked if he is a god?* In lines 243–246, Odysseus immediately denies being a god and is described as "wary" during this denial. ▬ RL 3

pp. 195–199 • *What does Odysseus do when the young athlete Broadsea mocks him?* Odysseus responds angrily in lines 190–215, and he then demonstrates that he is a greater athlete than the young men who have challenged him. ▬ RL 3

SECOND READ   Analyze the Text

• Review Odysseus's difficult journey so far. *What details in this section reinforce the idea that Odysseus is a "man of twists and turns"?* Sample answer: In lines 247–249, he refers to the hardships he has endured, and then from line 278 through line 331, he tells of the journey that brought him to Alcinous's palace. ▬ RL 2

• Revisit pages 186–189 with students. Ask: *What other examples of Odysseus's tact and diplomacy are found in this section?* Sample answer: In line 246, he makes it clear that he is a mortal man so that he will not anger the gods. Beginning at line 346, he diplomatically defends Nausicaa's actions to her father. ▬ RL 3

• Point out that the main theme of *The Odyssey* revolves around Odysseus's endless effort to get home. Ask: *What examples from Books Seven and Eight support this message?* At line 168 of Book Seven, Odysseus throws himself on Arete's mercy; at line 248, he refers to his woes in trying to get home and again beginning at line 277; Book Eight begins with the Phaeacians outfitting a ship, and Odysseus is overjoyed to set out; beginning at line 560 of Book Eight, he is heartbroken when the tale of the Trojan War is told. ▬ RL 2

Academic Vocabulary

Read each word with students and discuss its meaning.

unscathed (p. 214) • unharmed

brandish (p. 221) • shake or wave as a weapon

waft (p. 231) • carry lightly and smoothly on air or on water

muster (p. 236) • a meeting or gathering of troops

malinger (p. 244) • pretend to be ill or injured in order to avoid work

FIRST READ ## Think Through the Text

Have students use text evidence and draw inferences to answer questions.

p. 211 • *How is Odysseus described at the beginning of Book Nine? In the first line, he is called a good story teller. What are other words that have been used in the text to describe him? Sample answer: crafty, wary, diplomatic* ◼RL 1

pp. 223–227 • *What name for himself does Odysseus first give to Polyphemus? In line 410 of Book Nine, Odysseus calls himself "Nobody." Why does Odysseus later tell the Cyclops his real name? He is angry at the Cyclops for killing and eating his men and wants to claim credit for tricking him.* ◼RL 3

SECOND READ ## Analyze the Text

• Review Book Ten with students. Compare it with Book Five. Ask: *How does Odysseus's near capture by Circe compare to his time with Calypso in Book Five? Sample answer: In both cases, an immortal woman tries to trap Odysseus, and he escapes with the help of the gods.* ◼RL 3

• Recall with students the beginning of Book Ten and what occurred when Odysseus and his men sailed for nine days and nights. Ask: *What happened to make returning home quickly impossible? In lines 35–61, Odysseus falls asleep, and his men open the bag of winds. This sends them back to where they started. What does this suggest about Odysseus's "twists and turns"? Sample answer: Some of the trials Odysseus endures are self-inflicted.* ◼RL 2

Independent/Self-Selected Reading

Have students reread Books Five through Ten of *The Odyssey* independently to practice analyzing the text on their own or have them practice the skills using another book, such as:

• *The Odyssey* by Homer (Books 11 through 24)

• *The Iliad* by Homer ◼RL 10

Performance Task

WRITE & PRESENT

1. Have small groups discuss the plot events and themes of each segment of the story. Ask groups to analyze how the character of Odysseus—a "man of twists and turns"—reflects conflicting motivations through his interactions with other characters in the epic poem. ◼RL 3

2. Ask each student to write an essay analyzing the character of Odysseus and articulating how his conflicting loyalties during his long and complicated journey home both advance the plot of Homer's epic and develop themes. Encourage students to cite text evidence to defend their ideas. ◼W 2

3. Have students work with partners to revise and edit their essays. ◼W 5

4. Have students present their final analyses to the class. ◼SL 4

See Copying Masters, pp. 212–215.

STUDENT CHECKLIST

Writing

☑ Identify Odysseus's interactions with other characters in the poem.

☑ Compare his interactions with other characters to find evidence of conflicting motivations in Odysseus.

☑ Use complete sentences and developed paragraphs to structure writing.

Speaking & Listening

☑ Read writing aloud with a clear, audible voice.

☑ Present ideas in a meaningful way.

OBJECTIVES

- Examine how characters respond to major events
- Identify the theme of a story
- Analyze text using text evidence

This excerpt from *Metamorphoses* is broken into three instructional segments.

SEGMENTS

Options for Reading

Independent Students read the book independently or with a partner and then answer questions posed by the teacher.

Supported Students read a segment and answer questions with teacher support.

from Metamorphoses
by Ovid

SUMMARY Weaving together tales from Greek and Roman mythology, *Metamorphoses* describes the world from the moment when order first emerged from chaos up until the rise of Rome, the time when its author, Ovid, lived. Though written in epic form, this poem is a mock epic that does not star a single protagonist hero; instead, it finds unity by focusing on the subject of how the world is in constant change.

ABOUT THE AUTHOR Ovid was born in 43 B.C. and lived during the time of the Augustan Empire. Adapting and making fun at times of the epic form used by such previous poets as Homer and Virgil, Ovid inspired in turn such later epic poets as Dante and John Milton.

Discuss Genre and Set Purpose

EPIC POEM Point out characteristics of epic poetry in this work, such as beginning by stating the poem's theme, asking divine beings for help and inspiration, and relationships between gods and humans.

SET PURPOSE Help students set a purpose for reading, such as to figure out how and why the people, places, and things in this poem change from form to form.

COMMON CORE Connection

RL 1 cite textual evidence to support analysis of what the text says explicitly as well as inferences drawn; **RL 2** determine a theme or central idea of a text and analyze its development; **RL 3** analyze how characters develop and interact with others

TEXT COMPLEXITY RUBRIC

Overall Text Complexity		from *Metamorphoses* EPIC POEM MORE COMPLEX
Quantitative Measure	Lexile	N/A
Qualitative Measures	Text Structure	complex story concepts, unconventional story structure
	Language Conventionality and Clarity	archaic and unfamiliar words
	Knowledge Demands	cultural knowledge essential
	Purpose/Levels of Meaning	multiple levels of meaning

SEGMENT 1 pp. 1–34

Academic Vocabulary

Read each word with students and discuss its meaning.

soul (p. 3) • the spiritual part of a human being

metamorphoses (p. 3) • life-altering changes in form

chaos (p. 3) • a group of formless matter

sacrilegious (p. 7) • being disrespectful of something sacred

aspect (p. 12) • how something looks or appears

ELL **ENGLISH LANGUAGE
LEARNERS**

Use Visuals

Help students follow the
story line at the beginning
of the poem with a sequence
chain. Either make a class
chain or have pairs make
their own series of sketches
to show what changes occur
to people and the world
during this part of the story.
Have students use words
and phrases to tell about
the major events in the
sequence chain.

FIRST READ ## Think Through the Text

Have students use text evidence and draw inferences to answer questions.

p. 3 • *How can you tell from the text what Ovid's main topic is? He says
on page 3 that his soul wants to sing about the changes that have
happened in the world from its beginning until his time.* RL 2

pp. 10–15 • *What changes have led to Jove's decision to flood the earth?
The people of the world have become evil. Jove claims on page 10 that
he must destroy mortals to keep half-gods and rustic deities safe.
To prove his point that humans are dangerous, Jove describes on
pages 11–12 how Lycaon tried to murder him.* RL 1

pp. 15–19 • *Why does Themis tell Deucalion and Pyrrha to throw the
bones of the great mother behind them as they go? They are the only
humans left after the flood. Page 18 explains that they originally came
from Earth, and stones are Earth's bones, so Themis is telling them to
throw rocks behind them. When they do this, the stones change into
new men and women.* RL 1

RESPOND TO SEGMENT 1
**Classroom
Collaboration**

Have partners work together
to review and discuss their
summary. Encourage
students to ask questions
about things they still don't
understand.

SECOND READ ## Analyze the Text

• Remind students of the stories of Daphne and Io. Ask: *Are the
half-gods and rustic deities safer after Jove tries to destroy mankind?
no Explain. Phoebus and Jove chase Daphne and Io against their
wishes.* RL 3

• Tell students to think about the theme of change. Then ask: *Were
Daphne's and Io's lives changed for the better or for the worse by
their experiences? What examples from the text support your ideas?
Sample answer: On page 22, Daphne's beauty made her father and
Apollo expect her to take a man. Changing forms into a tree on page
24 allowed her deepest wish—avoiding marriage—to come true. Io
has her life changed for the worse when on page 27 she is turned into
a cow; however, in the end, on page 33, Io changes for the better to
become the goddess Isis.* RL 2

ENGLISH LANGUAGE LEARNERS

Use Comprehensible Input

Restate story events in simpler language. For example, say: *Arcas' mother Callisto was turned into a bear. Arcas was hunting and he almost killed her. Jove stopped Arcas in time and turned them both into constellations in the sky.* Ask: *Where did the Great and Little Bear constellations come from? Jove put Callisto and Arcas in the sky.* Follow a similar procedure for other story events.

RESPOND TO SEGMENT 2

 Classroom Collaboration

Have small groups work together to summarize what they have read. Then have them predict what might happen next in the poem.

COMMON CORE **Common Core Connection**

RL 1 cite textual evidence to support analysis of what the text says explicitly as well as inferences drawn; **RL 2** determine a theme or central idea of a text and analyze its development; **RL 3** analyze how characters develop and interact with others; **RL 10** read and comprehend literature; **W 2** write informative/explanatory texts; **W 5** develop and strengthen writing by planning, revising, editing, rewriting, or trying a new approach; **SL 4** present information, findings, and supporting evidence clearly, concisely, and logically

---

Academic Vocabulary

Read each word with students and discuss its meaning.

pledged (p. 38) • promised

fate (p. 39) • the force that pushes people toward certain events

mortal (p. 39) • a living thing that will die one day

fame (p. 40) • the state of being very well known

immortality (p. 63) • the state of living forever

FIRST READ **Think Through the Text**

Have students use text evidence and draw inferences to answer questions.

pp. 37–49 • *What happens when Phaethon tries to drive his father's chariot across the sky?* He cannot control its horses and he lets the hot sun's rays come too close to Earth, where they destroy people and places. ▬ **RL 1**

pp. 52–55 • *How do Diana and Juno know for certain that Jove had been close with Callisto?* Callisto bore Jove a son, Arcas. ▬ **RL 1**

pp. 68–70 • *What does Minerva ask Envy to do?* Minerva wants Envy to touch Agluaros so she will become jealous of her sister Herse and keep her from seeing Mercury. ▬ **RL 1**

SECOND READ **Analyze the Text**

• Guide students to think about how Ovid structures his poem. Say: *Use examples from the text to explain some ways Ovid connects one story to the next.* Sample answer: On pages 52–53, Ovid follows a character's actions—Jove's—to connect the story of Phaethon to the story of Callisto. On pages 62–63, Ovid goes from telling a story about a father (Apollo) to telling a story about his son (Aesculapius). *How does the way Ovid tells his stories connect to a theme of change?* Just as the things in the stories are always changing from one form to another, the stories themselves are changing into each other, too. ▬ **RL 2**

• Discuss the behavior of Jove. Ask: *How would you describe the character of Jove and his treatment of the women in his life? Support your ideas with examples from the text.* Sample answer: He does not respect his wife Juno, and on page 53 he is willing to risk her anger to please himself. He is sneaky and thinks he has the right to take whatever he wants; for instance, instead of wooing Callisto and Europa openly, he disguises himself as Diana (page 53) and a bull (page 72) to trick and catch them. ▬ **RL 3**

Academic Vocabulary

Read each word with students and discuss its meaning.

semblance (p. 77) • the outward appearance of something

founded (p. 81) • built or first set up

oath (p. 88) • a solemn promise that must be kept

penalty (p. 90) • a punishment that must be paid

deceptive (p. 94) • something that misleads or tricks the eye

FIRST READ ## Think Through the Text

Have students use text evidence and draw inferences to answer questions.

pp. 81–86 • *How does Juno feel about Actaeon's death and why does she feel this way?* Juno is happy to hear that something bad has happened to Actaeon's family. She hates his family because her husband, Jove, was in love with Actaeon's great aunt, Europa (page 86). ◾ RL 3

pp. 87–89 • *How does the text describe how Juno punishes Semele for being Jove's lover?* On page 87, Juno disguises herself as Semele's old nurse and convinces Semele to ask Jove to appear to her in his true form to prove he is a really a god. On page 89, Semele is burned to death because no mortal can survive seeing Jove's true form. ◾ RL 1

pp. 93–97 • *How did Narcissus die?* He fell in love with his own image reflected in a pool and could not leave. ◾ RL 1

SECOND READ ## Analyze the Text

• Guide students to review pages 81–86 and 97–106 and compare and contrast the fates of Actaeon and Pentheus. Ask: *How are their deaths alike?* Both men see something they should not have and both are torn to pieces as punishment. *How are their deaths different?* Actaeon is actually turned into a deer and killed by his dogs, while Pentheus' relatives think they see a wild boar when they see him and rip him apart. ◾ RL 1

• Have students think about everything the poem has said about the changes people undergo during life. Guide them to use text evidence to explain what Ovid might mean on page 81 when he says that until a man has died, one cannot call him blessed. *A man is blessed when he has children and grandchildren who honor the family.* ◾ RL 2

Independent/Self-Selected Reading

Have students reread *Metamorphoses* independently to practice analyzing the text on their own, or have them practice the skills using another book, such as:

• *Theogony* by Hesiod

• *The Aeneid* by Virgil   ◾ RL 10

Performance Task

WRITE & PRESENT

1. Have students analyze and discuss the opening lines of the poem and how they relate to the theme developed over the course of the poem. Suggest that students focus in particular on different kinds of changes that happen to the people and places mentioned in the poem. ◾ RL 2

2. Have each student write a short essay explaining Ovid's thoughts about the theme of change. Encourage students to cite examples from the text to defend their ideas. ◾ W 2

3. Have students share their work with partners. Ask them to revise and edit their writing based on their suggestions. ◾ W 5

4. Have students present their final writing to their classmates. Ask students to respond to the themes and ideas from each student's writing. ◾ SL 4

See Copying Masters, pp. 212–215.

STUDENT CHECKLIST

Writing

☑ Explain how a theme is developed, using text evidence and quotes from the poem.

☑ Use complete sentences and developed paragraphs to structure writing.

☑ Use correct language conventions.

Speaking & Listening

☑ Read writing aloud with a clear, audible voice.

☑ Present ideas in a meaningful way.

OBJECTIVES

- Describe how characters respond to major events
- Identify the theme of a story
- Interpret symbols and figurative language in fiction
- Analyze text using text evidence

"The Nose" is broken into three instructional segments.

SEGMENTS

Options for Reading

Independent Students read the story independently and then answer questions posed by the teacher.

Supported Students read a segment and answer questions with teacher support.

Common Core Connection

RL 1 cite textual evidence to support analysis of what the text says explicitly as well as inferences drawn; **RL 2** determine a theme or central idea of a text and analyze its development; **RL 3** analyze how characters interact with others and advance the plot; **RL 5** analyze how author's choices create surprise

"The Nose"
by Nikolai Gogol

SUMMARY One morning, barber Ivan Yakovlevich discovers a nose in his breakfast roll. Horrified, he sets about to dispose of the nose before anyone finds out. Meanwhile, Major Kovalyov discovers his nose is missing, replaced by a flat expanse of skin. Later that day, Kovalyov sees his nose walking about town on its own. Even worse, the nose is a higher-ranking official than Kovalyov. Eventually Kovalyov is reunited with his nose, though it's an uneasy alliance.

ABOUT THE AUTHOR **Nikolai Gogol** was born in 1809 in what is now Ukraine. His father was a minor poet and playwright, and Gogol followed in his footsteps, publishing his first volume of short stories when he was 23 years old. He is best known for his novel and play, *The Inspector General*.

Discuss Genre and Set Purpose

FICTION Remind students that a work of fiction includes characters, a setting, and events. Explain that while events in this story might be impossible, the reactions of the characters are still believable.

SET PURPOSE Help students set a purpose for reading, such as to identify ways Gogol uses absurd situations to comment on human behavior.

▲ TEXT COMPLEXITY RUBRIC

Overall Text Complexity		"The Nose" FICTION
		COMPLEX
Quantitative Measure	Lexile	1070L
Qualitative Measures	Text Structure	occasional shifts in point of view
	Language Conventionality and Clarity	some unfamiliar language
	Knowledge Demands	somewhat unfamiliar experience and situation
	Purpose/Levels of Meaning	multiple levels of meaning

Academic Vocabulary

Read each word with students and discuss its meaning.

indignation (p. 43) • anger caused by something improper

invective (p. 43) • insulting words

retaliation (p. 44) • revenge

averse (p. 47) • opposed

preposterous (p. 47) • ridiculous

 ENGLISH LANGUAGE LEARNERS

Use Comprehensible Input

Help students understand the plot and characters by connecting the Russian references to people and places with which they may be familiar.

FIRST READ ## Think Through the Text

Have students use text evidence and draw inferences to answer questions.

pp. 42–44 • *Where does Yakovlevich find the nose?* in his breakfast roll *To whom does the nose belong?* one of his customers *What keeps him from getting rid of the nose?* He keeps running into friends; when he drops the nose, a policeman makes him pick it up. 🔊 **RL 1**

p. 46 • *Why does Kovalyov look at his nose?* He thinks he has a pimple on it. *What does he do when he realizes his nose is missing?* He tries to wake himself up. 🔊 **RL 1, RL 3**

p. 48 • *What does Kovalyov see when he leaves the coffee shop?* He sees his nose get out of a carriage. 🔊 **RL 1**

pp. 49–50 • *Why does Kovalyov hesitate before speaking to his nose at the cathedral?* His nose has a higher rank than he does. *How does the nose respond to Kovalyov?* The nose says it doesn't know what he's talking about; it says they have nothing in common. 🔊 **RL 1**

SECOND READ ## Analyze the Text

• Ask: *What is the narrator's tone?* It is very matter of fact. *What does that tell the reader about the story?* The reader should accept the events as the narrator tells them, even though they are very strange. 🔊 **RL 5**

• Ask: *Why is Kovalyov most upset that he has lost his nose?* He feels it is inappropriate for a person in his position. 🔊 **RL 3**

• Ask: *What do you know about Kovalyov's character? Give examples from the text to support your ideas.* Sample answers: He's concerned about status; on page 46, Gogol says he likes to be called Major. He cares about money; on page 47, he says he's willing to get married if his wife has 200,000 roubles. He's interested in women; on page 50, he's distracted by the girl in the cathedral. *What do you think is a major theme of this segment?* Sample answer: self-importance, pomposity 🔊 **RL 1, RL 2, RL 3**

 RESPOND TO SEGMENT 1

Classroom Collaboration

Have partners create a summary of the plot events in this segment. Then have students predict what might happen next in the story.

Domain Specific Vocabulary

Collegiate Assessor (p. 43) • a midgrade rank for a person in civil service, according to the Table of Ranks in Imperial Russia

Caucasus (p. 46) • mountain range that separates Russia from the Middle East

 ENGLISH LANGUAGE LEARNERS

Use Peer Supported Learning

Have students work in pairs or small groups to summarize what happens at each place that Kovalyov visits during the story.

RESPOND TO SEGMENT 2

 Classroom Collaboration

Have small groups work together to summarize what they have read. Have them ask questions about what they don't understand.

 Common Core Connection

RL 1 cite textual evidence to support analysis of what the text says explicitly as well as inferences drawn; **RL 2** determine a theme or central idea of a text and analyze its development; **RL 3** analyze how characters interact with others and advance the plot; **RL 10** read and comprehend literature; **W 2** write informative/explanatory texts; **W 5** develop and strengthen writing by planning, revising, editing, rewriting, or trying a new approach; **SL 4** present information, findings, and supporting evidence clearly, concisely, and logically

Academic Vocabulary

Read each word with students and discuss its meaning.

futile (p. 52) • completely ineffective

blackguard (p. 54) • rude or dishonest person

conspicuous (p. 55) • very noticeable

disreputable (p. 58) • not trustworthy

incomprehensible (p. 59) • impossible to understand

FIRST READ **Think Through the Text**

Have students use text evidence and draw inferences to answer questions.

pp. 52–56 • *Why does Kovalyov go to the newspaper office?* He wants to place an advertisement asking people to return his nose. *What is the clerk doing when Kovalyov keeps trying to get his attention?* He's counting words to see what to charge for an ad. *What does the newspaper clerk do that offends Kovalyov?* He offers him some snuff. **RL 3**

pp. 57–58 • *What does the Inspector of Police love best?* government banknotes *What does this imply about him?* He takes bribes. *Why is Kovalyov offended by the Inspector?* The Inspector implies that Kovalyov isn't respectable. **RL 3**

pp. 58–59 • *Why does Kovalyov say it would have been better to have lost an arm or a leg?* Losing a limb is more acceptable; a lost arm or leg is easier to hide. **RL 1**

SECOND READ **Analyze the Text**

• Review pages 53–56 with students. Ask: *Why won't the clerk accept Kovalyov's advertisement?* He says the paper has to be concerned about its reputation. *How do the clerk's concerns relate to the story?* The clerk says an advertisement about a poodle was meant as a satire on the government, and much of the story may be read as a satire on government employees. **RL 2**

• Have students revisit page 58. Ask: *What is Kovalyov's footman doing when Kovalyov comes home?* He is lying on a couch and spitting at the ceiling. *What does this say about Kovalyov?* He is not as socially advanced as he would like to think. **RL 2**

Academic Vocabulary

Read each word with students and discuss its meaning.

prosaic (p. 62) • dull or ordinary

mercenary (p. 63) • caring only about making money

instigator (p. 64) • someone who starts trouble

edifying (p. 66) • morally educational

olfactory (p. 68) • related to the sense of smell

FIRST READ ## Think Through the Text

Have students use text evidence and draw inferences to answer questions.

p. 60 • *How does Kovalyov get his nose back?* A policeman returns it to him. *Where has the policeman appeared earlier in the story?* He's the same policeman who saw Yakovlevich drop the nose off the bridge. *What was the nose doing when it was caught?* It was leaving town. **RL 1**

pp. 67–69 • *How is Kovalyov's nose finally reattached?* Kovalyov wakes up one morning and it's back in place. *How do people treat Kovalyov after he gets his nose back?* They act as if nothing has happened. *How does Kovalyov act after he gets his nose back?* He has more confidence and applies for a higher position. **RL 3**

SECOND READ ## Analyze the Text

- Ask: *What rumors spread about the nose?* It went for a walk every afternoon. *What are some examples of how people responded to the rumors?* Crowds gathered to see the nose; one man set up seating; a store said it had the nose on display; a woman asked to have a private showing for her children. **RL 2**

- Ask: *What do you think is the theme of the whole story? Why?* Sample answer: Social class is nonsense. Kovalyov is more concerned with what people think of him than anything else; the nose passes as a high-ranking civil servant and no one notices. **RL 2**

Independent/Self-Selected Reading

Have students reread "The Nose" independently to practice analyzing the text on their own, or have them practice the skills using another story, such as:

- "Diary of a Madman" by Nikolai Gogol

- *The Master and Margarita* by Mikhail Bulgakov **RL 10**

Performance Task

WRITE & PRESENT

1. Have small groups discuss the plot events and themes of the story. **RL 2**

2. Ask students to think about the main themes of the entire story. Have them write about how Gogol uses humor and satire to communicate a theme. Encourage students to cite text evidence to defend their ideas. **RL 1, RL 2, W 2**

3. Have students share their work with partners and offer suggestions for revising and editing. Students edit their writing based on these suggestions. **W 5**

4. Have students present their final writing to their classmates. Ask students to respond to the themes and ideas from each student's writing. **SL 4**

See Copying Masters, pp. 212–215.

STUDENT CHECKLIST

Writing

☑ Identify at least one theme from the story.

☑ Examine how the author uses satire to communicate this theme, using text evidence and words and phrases from the story.

☑ Use complete sentences and developed paragraphs to structure writing.

Speaking & Listening

☑ Read writing aloud with a clear, audible voice.

☑ Present ideas in a meaningful way.

▶ OBJECTIVES

- Describe how characters respond to major events
- Identify the theme of a story
- Interpret symbols and figurative language in fiction
- Analyze text using text evidence

Candide is broken into three instructional segments.

SEGMENTS

SEGMENT 1 . . . . pp. 5–42
SEGMENT 2 . . . . pp. 43–84
SEGMENT 3 . . . . . . pp. 85–114

Options for Reading

Independent Students read the book independently or with a partner and then answer questions posed by the teacher.

Supported Students read a segment and answer questions with teacher support.

COMMON CORE **Common Core Connection**

RL 1 cite textual evidence to support analysis of what the text says explicitly as well as inferences drawn; RL 2 determine a theme or central idea of a text and analyze its development; RL 3 analyze how characters develop and interact with others; RL 5 analyze how author's choices create mystery, tension, or surprise

Candide
by F. A. M. de Voltaire

SUMMARY In the very first chapter, Candide is expelled from the castle of the Baron Thunder-ten-tronckh, where he was raised. Candide was taught by the scholar Pangloss that all is for the best in this best of all possible worlds. As Candide sets out on his adventures, endless horrors challenge his optimistic view. Along the way, Candide meets a wild assortment of characters, many of whom present worldviews of their own. Through it all, Candide remains his cheerful self.

ABOUT THE AUTHOR Voltaire is the pen name of François-Marie Arouet. He was born in France in 1694 and was one of the major writers of the Enlightenment. Voltaire wrote many different literary forms, including novels, plays, essays, and histories.

Discuss Genre and Set Purpose

FICTION Remind students that a work of fiction includes characters, a setting, and events. Discuss how events in this novel may be difficult to believe, but that the author's goal is not to write a realistic story.

SET PURPOSE Help students set a purpose for reading, such as to compare and contrast the different points of view of the characters.

◢ **TEXT COMPLEXITY RUBRIC**

Overall Text Complexity		*Candide* FICTION — COMPLEX
Quantitative Measure	Lexile	1110L
Qualitative Measures	Text Structure	some unconventional story elements
	Language Conventionality and Clarity	increased unfamiliar language, more complex sentence structure
	Knowledge Demands	increased amount of cultural knowledge useful
	Purpose/Levels of Meaning	multiple levels of meaning

Academic Vocabulary

Read each word with students and discuss its meaning.

countenance (p. 5) • facial expression

farthing (p. 16) • a coin without much value

mercantile (p. 16) • related to buying and selling

ingenuous (p. 24) • showing childlike simplicity

traverse (p. 38) • travel across

shrewdly (p. 41) • cleverly

ELL ENGLISH LANGUAGE LEARNERS

Use Peer Supported Learning

Have students read aloud through dialogue passages in the book. Encourage them to help each other with difficult words or ideas. Have students note things they do not understand for further questions or investigation.

FIRST READ ## Think Through the Text

Have students use text evidence and draw inferences to answer questions.

pp. 14 • *How does Candide meet Pangloss again?* Pangloss is begging on the street. *According to Pangloss, what happened to Cunegonde and the rest of the Baron's family?* They were all killed in the war. RL 1, RL 3

pp. 22–23 • *Who is the veiled woman?* Cunegonde *Why is this a surprise to Candide?* He thought she was dead. *What might this tell us about the book?* Other characters we think are dead will return; the story is not realistic. ⬛ RL 5

pp. 33–39 • *How are the Old Woman's experiences similar to those of Cunegonde?* Sample answers: They were both born wealthy; they both saw their mothers killed; they were both ravaged by men; they were both sold. *What does the Old Woman say about the other passengers onboard ship?* They have all been miserable at one time or another. ⬛ RL 1

SECOND READ ## Analyze the Text

• Review Chapter I. Ask: *What is Pangloss's philosophy?* This is the best of all possible worlds, and all is for the best. *According to Pangloss, why do we have spectacles and stockings?* because a nose was designed to bear spectacles and legs were designed to wear stockings *What is wrong with Pangloss's philosophy?* He reverses cause and effect. ⬛ RL 1

• Review Chapter IX with students. Ask: *What reasons does Candide give for killing the Grand Inquisitor?* He is defending himself and Cunegonde; the Grand Inquisitor had him whipped; since Candide has already killed one man, he might as well kill another. *What does this demonstrate about Candide's character?* He can be practical; he makes excuses for doing what he wants to do. ⬛ RL 3

• Ask: *How does Voltaire treat religious characters in the book?* They are two-faced. *What examples from the text support this view?* Sample answers: The Grand Inquisitor has a mistress; a friar steals their jewels; the Old Woman is the daughter of a pope. ⬛ RL 2

RESPOND TO SEGMENT 1

💬 **Classroom Collaboration**

Have partners create a summary of the plot events in this segment. Then have students predict what might happen next in the novel.

Domain Specific Vocabulary

Anabaptist (p. 12) • a member of a Protestant sect that believed in the separation of church and state

Jesuit (p. 15) • a Catholic order devoted to missionary and educational work

 ENGLISH LANGUAGE LEARNERS

Use Comprehensible Input

Ensure students understand the plot events and the theme by asking questions such as: *Why is Candide forced to leave the castle?* and *How do Candide and Cacambo get to El Dorado?*

 RESPOND TO SEGMENT 2

Classroom Collaboration

Have small groups work together to summarize what they have read. Have them ask questions about what they don't understand.

 Common Core Connection

RL 1 cite textual evidence to support analysis of what the text says explicitly as well as inferences drawn; **RL 2** determine a theme or central idea of a text and analyze its development; **RL 3** analyze how characters develop and interact with others; **RL 5** analyze how author's choices create mystery, tension, or surprise; **RL 10** read and comprehend literature; **W 2** write informative/explanatory texts; **W 5** develop and strengthen writing by planning, revising, editing, rewriting, or trying a new approach; **SL 4** present information, findings, and supporting evidence clearly, concisely, and logically

Academic Vocabulary

Read each word with students and discuss its meaning.

valet (p. 43) • personal servant

wary (p. 50) • cautious

provisions (p. 54) • stock of food and other supplies

circumspection (p. 56) • consideration of the feelings of others

obeisance (p. 60) • recognition of the superiority of another

moiety (p. 64) • half

convalescence (p. 75) • recovery from an illness

FIRST READ ## Think Through the Text

Have students use text evidence and draw inferences to answer questions.

pp. 43–48 • *Who is the Commandant?* Cunegonde's brother *How does their meeting relate to earlier events in the book?* It is similar to Chapter VII, when Candide is reunited with Cunegonde. *Why does Candide kill the Commandant?* He slaps Candide with his sword. *Based on your reading so far, what do you suspect about the death of the Commandant?* He's not really dead. ◗ **RL 5**

pp. 67–71 • *Why does Candide hire Martin to travel with him?* because Martin is the unhappiest man in Surinam *How does Martin's philosophy differ from Pangloss's philosophy?* Martin always sees the worst side of things. ◗ **RL 3**

pp. 82–84 • *Why are Candide and Martin arrested in France?* They are foreigners. *How do they avoid going before a judge?* They bribe the officer who arrested them. ◗ **RL 1**

SECOND READ ## Analyze the Text

- Review pages 43–53 with students. Ask: *What makes Cacambo a good companion for Candide?* He's very practical—he does what needs to be done, rather than following any philosophy. *What are examples of Cacambo's resourcefulness?* On page 43, he suggests Candide fight for the Jesuits; on page 52, he saves Candide from the Oreillon by telling them he killed a Jesuit. ◗ **RL 3**

- Review Chapters XVII to XIX. Ask: *Why does Candide begin to believe that Pangloss was wrong about some things?* He realizes that El Dorado is the best of all possible worlds. On page 55, he says that El Dorado is better than Westphalia, and on page 57, he says that things often went badly in Westphalia. *What makes Candide abandon optimism?* He meets a slave who has had his hand and leg cut off. ◗ **RL 1, RL 2**

Academic Vocabulary

Read each word with students and discuss its meaning.

mongrel (p. 87) • of mixed race

corsair (p. 102) • pirate

lackey (p. 106) • a weak servant

impertinence (p. 110) • disrespect

Dervish (p. 112) • a Muslim sect known for their vows of poverty

FIRST READ Think Through the Text

Have students use text evidence and draw inferences to answer questions.

pp. 87–92 • *Which character from the first chapter does Candide meet in Venice?* Paquette *What does Candide learn about Paquette and the Friar?* Though they look happy, they are both miserable. RL 1

pp. 108–110 • *In what condition does Candide find Cunegonde?* She is ugly and withered. *Why does he agree to marry her?* Cunegonde reminds him that he promised to marry her. *Who objects to the marriage?* Cunegonde's brother *What happens to him?* They sell him back to the captain of the galley where they found him. RL 3

p. 112 • *What does the Dervish tell Pangloss and Candide when they ask him about the meaning of life?* It's none of their business. *To what does the dervish compare mankind?* to mice on a ship RL 1

SECOND READ Analyze the Text

• Have students review Chapter XX. Then ask: *Why are the characters still unhappy?* Sample answers: They are bored; some, like Pangloss, focus on what they don't have instead of that they do have; they miss their exciting adventures. RL 2

• Ask: *At the end of the book, which philosophy proves most useful?* Hard work is the only thing that makes life worthwhile. RL 2

Independent/Self-Selected Reading

Have students reread *Candide* independently to practice analyzing the text on their own, or have them practice the skills using another book, such as:

• *The History of Tom Jones* by Henry Fielding

• *Gulliver's Travels* by Jonathan Swift RL 10

Performance Task

WRITE & PRESENT

1. Have small groups discuss the plot events and themes of each segment of the story. RL 2

2. Ask students to think about the main themes of the entire story. Have students write about how one of these themes relates to the philosophy of optimism. Encourage students to cite text evidence to defend their ideas. RL 1, RL 2, W 2

3. Have students share their work with partners and offer suggestions for revising and editing. Students edit their writing based on these suggestions. W 5

4. Have students present their final writing to their classmates. Ask students to respond to the themes and ideas from each student's writing. SL 4

See *Copying Masters*, pp. 212–215.

STUDENT CHECKLIST

Writing

☑ Identify at least one theme from the novel.

☑ Use text evidence and words and phrases from the novel to support ideas.

☑ Use complete sentences and developed paragraphs to structure writing.

Speaking & Listening

☑ Read writing aloud with a clear, audible voice.

☑ Present ideas in a meaningful way.

OBJECTIVES

- Describe how characters develop over the course of a story
- Identify the theme of a story
- Interpret a point of view determined by another culture
- Analyze text using text evidence

Fathers and Sons is broken into three instructional segments.

SEGMENTS

SEGMENT 1 . . . . pp. 5–69
SEGMENT 2 . . . . . . pp. 69–134
SEGMENT 3 . . . . . pp. 135–200

Options for Reading

Independent Students read the book independently or with a partner and then answer questions posed by the teacher.

Supported Students read a segment and answer questions with teacher support.

Common Core Connection

RL 1 cite textual evidence to support analysis of what the text says explicitly as well as inferences drawn; **RL 2** determine a theme or central idea of a text and analyze its development; **RL 3** analyze how characters develop and interact with others; **RL 6** analyze a point of view or experience reflected in literature outside the United States

Fathers and Sons
by Ivan Turgenev

SUMMARY *Fathers and Sons* tells a story of conflict between generations during a period of drastic social change. The Kirsanov family is part of the old Russian aristocracy. Arkady Kirsanov has brought a radical friend, Basarov, home from the university. Basarov's arrival sets off a series of changes in the household that reflect the conflict between the Russian ruling class and the revolutionaries who will change the nation's society.

ABOUT THE AUTHOR Ivan Turgenev was born into a land-owning family in the Russian empire of 1818. He was deeply opposed to serfdom in Russia and hoped to help bring about reforms in the country through his writing. However, the political climate of the mid-1800s was stifling for writers, and he did much of his work abroad. *Fathers and Sons* appeared in 1862 and has endured as a masterpiece of Russian realism.

Discuss Genre and Set Purpose

FICTION Point out that *Fathers and Sons* is a realistic novel about an earlier era in a different culture. Discuss how some story elements, such as setting, will be unfamiliar, but the themes and conflicts are timeless.

SET PURPOSE Help students set a purpose for reading, such as to find out how conflicts between family members can reflect conflicts in society.

TEXT COMPLEXITY RUBRIC

Overall Text Complexity		*Fathers and Sons* FICTION
		COMPLEX
Quantitative Measure	Lexile	980L
Qualitative Measures	Text Structure	less familiar story concepts
	Language Conventionality and Clarity	some unfamiliar words
	Knowledge Demands	increased amount of cultural knowledge useful
	Purpose/Levels of Meaning	multiple levels of meaning

Academic Vocabulary

Read each word with students and discuss its meaning.

propriety (p. 7) • properness or decorum

archaic (p. 18) • antiquated, out of date

magnanimous (p. 21) • generous of spirit

disabuse (p. 34) • free from an error or misunderstanding

adjudicate (p. 59) • settle an issue judicially

FIRST READ ## Think Through the Text

Have students use text evidence and draw inferences to answer questions.

pp. 7–12 • *How do Pyotr and Nikolay feel about their farm laborers?* On pages 10–11, it is clear that Pyotr has contempt for the peasants and Nikolay finds them difficult to work with. **RL 1**

pp. 13–14 • *How does the text describe Arkady's reaction as he returns to his home?* At the bottom of page 13, we see that his heart is sinking. *What does he conclude as a result?* On page 14, he feels that the lack of prosperity cannot be maintained and that something must be done. **RL 1**

pp. 23–39 • *How is Bazarov's philosophy described?* On page 23, we learn that Bazarov is a nihilist—someone who respects no tradition or authority. Uncle Pavel says this means he respects nothing, whereas Arkady says Bazarov is skeptical in his approach. **RL 2**

SECOND READ ## Analyze the Text

• Review pages 26–27 with students. Ask: *How are Bazarov's beliefs disturbing to Arkady's uncle? What does that suggest about the characters and how they will interact in the book?* Sample answer: Pavel Petrovich finds Bazarov's nihilism threatening. This may foreshadow a central conflict between Bazarov and Uncle Pavel. **RL 3**

• Review pages 45–56 with students. Then ask: *What purpose do you think the author has in showing the growing conflict between Bazarov's and Pavel's views of the world?* Sample answer: Turgenev is using the conflict between the two characters to address the larger conflict between tradition and modernism. **RL 6**

• Ask: *What does Pavel feel is ultimately threatened by nihilism?* civilization *What examples from the text support your idea?* On page 52, Pavel explicitly argues against calling the fruits of civilization worthless. On page 53, he suggests that the nihilists would heap scorn on even great painters to declare their independence from convention. **RL 1**

Use Peer Supported Learning

Have student pairs work together to outline the conflicts that are developing in this section of the novel. Have them pick two characters and speculate about what might develop, using frames such as the following:

*Conflict might develop between Arkady and Nikolay because _____ ....
between Nikolay and Pavel because _____ ....
between Arkady and Bazarov because _____.*

RESPOND TO SEGMENT 1

 Classroom Collaboration

Have partners create a character map for the main characters in this segment. Have them include in the map the relationships between the characters, both in literal terms (friends, brothers, father and son) and in emotional terms. Then have students predict how they think the relationships might change over the course of the novel.

DOMAIN SPECIFIC VOCABULARY

serfs (p. 12) • people in bondage who were attached to the land they worked

muzhiks (p. 107) • Russian peasants who had been serfs

 ENGLISH LANGUAGE LEARNERS

Use Visuals

Ensure students understand the plot events and the developing conflict by showing them a map of the Russian empire in the late 1800s along with statistics from the era—that out of a total Russian population of almost 61 million in 1857, nearly 41 million people were peasants.

RESPOND TO SEGMENT 2

 Classroom Collaboration

Have small groups work together to summarize what they have read. Have them ask questions about what they don't understand.

 Common Core Connection

RL 1 cite textual evidence to support analysis of what the text says explicitly as well as inferences drawn; **RL 2** determine a theme or central idea of a text and analyze its development; **RL 3** analyze how characters develop and interact with others; **RL 10** read and comprehend literature; **W 1** write arguments to support claims; **W 5** develop and strengthen writing by revising and editing; **SL 4** present information, findings, and supporting evidence clearly, concisely, and logically

Academic Vocabulary

Read each word with students and discuss its meaning.

cynicism (p. 73) • distrusting the honesty or motives of others

liveried (p. 78) • dressed in a servant's uniform

obtuse (p. 84) • slow, or not observant

timorously (p. 111) • timidly and in a way full of fear

surreptitiously (p. 117) • stealthily or secretly

FIRST READ ## Think Through the Text

Have students use text evidence and draw inferences to answer questions.

pp. 69–85 • *Why does Anna Sergeyevna invite Arkady and Bazarov to the country?* On page 75, we learn that she is bored in the country; she may have invited them for a diversion. *What is the initial reaction of the men when they arrive?* On pages 78–79, the men are initially uncomfortable. **RL 1**

pp. 100–105 • *What happens to make Anna Sergeyevna frightened by Bazarov?* On pages 101–102, Bazarov declares his love for her, but she is overwhelmed by his intensity. **RL 3**

pp. 110–122 • *How do you know from the text that Bazarov's father is very proud of his son?* On page 121, Bazarov's father listens to Arkady praising his son with such intense joy that he kisses Arkady's shoulder and tells the young man that he worships his son. **RL 1**

SECOND READ ## Analyze the Text

• Review pages 126–127 with students. Ask: *What is symbolized by Bazarov's negativity and Arkady's reaction in this scene?* Sample answer: Bazarov is striking a pose and may not be sincere in his nihilism; the author is exploring excesses of nihilism. **RL 3**

• Have students revisit pages 110–122. Ask: *How do Bazarov's and Arkady's homes compare?* Bazarov's family lives more humbly than Arkady's, to the point that Bazarov's father thinks Arkady must live luxuriously. **RL 3**

• Ask: *How do societal conflicts develop in this segment? What examples from the text support your opinions?* On pages 101–103, Bazarov's bold rejection of tradition leads to awkwardness with Anna Sergeyevna. Then, on pages 108–109, Bazarov asks a muzhik mocking questions. In addition, the contrast between Bazarov's and Arkady's homes underscores the conflict between the past and the future, which is strongly symbolized on pp. 124–125, when Bazarov equates self-destruction with love for a woman. **RL 2**

Academic Vocabulary

Read each word with students and discuss its meaning.

languor (p. 123) • sluggishness

averred (p. 137) • declared as truth

deferentially (p. 155) • with respectful submission

subaltern (p. 162) • someone lower in rank

sallies (p. 183) • clever or witty barbed remarks

FIRST READ ## Think Through the Text

Have students use text evidence and draw inferences to answer questions.

pp. 137–140 • *What text evidence suggests that Arkady is in love with Katya? On page 139, his excitement at traveling to town is compared to the thrilled fearfulness of an officer going into battle.* **RL 1**

pp. 146–157 • *Why does Pavel say he wants to fight Bazarov in a duel? On page 148, Pavel says he despises Bazarov. What is Pavel's real reason for wanting the duel? On page 157, it is confirmed that Pavel was offended when Bazarov kissed Fenechka on page 146.* **RL 3**

SECOND READ ## Analyze the Text

• Review pages 150–158. Then ask: *How would you describe the duel in this scene? Does it seem tense, or does it have an unreal air? There is a sense of unreality about the event, as if Bazarov does not take it seriously and wounds Pavel by accident.* **How might this represent the conflict between Pavel and Bazarov?** *Sample answer: The conflict between modernism and tradition is represented by Bazarov's casual indifference to Pavel's offended desire to duel.* **RL 2**

• Have students review pages 180–195. Ask: *How does Bazarov's point of view change in this scene? He becomes romantic in many ways, which is contrary to his claims about his own philosophy.* **RL 3**

• Ask: *How does the book's title relate to its theme? Sample answer: Arkady and Bazarov both adhere more closely to their fathers' values than they at first insisted they would, and the value of tradition is maintained, even though modernism is unstoppable.* **RL 2**

Independent/Self-Selected Reading

Have students reread *Fathers and Sons* independently to practice analyzing the text on their own, or have them practice the skills using another book, such as:

• *Doctor Zhivago* by Boris Pasternak

• *A Sportsman's Sketches* by Ivan Turgenev **RL 10**

Performance Task

WRITE & PRESENT

1. Have small groups identify and discuss the three major philosophical themes in the story, citing text examples that help them understand each point of view—Bazarov's, Pavel's, and Nikolay's. **RL 2**

2. Individual students write an opinion paragraph in favor of one of the points of view. Encourage students to cite text evidence to defend their arguments. **W 1**

3. Students work with partners to revise and edit their work. **W 5**

4. Have students present their work to the class. **SL 4**

See Copying Masters pp. 212–215.

STUDENT CHECKLIST

Writing

☑ Identify at least one thematic perspective from the novel.

☑ Relate this point of view to a specific character, using text evidence and quotes from the novel.

☑ Use complete sentences and developed paragraphs to structure writing.

Speaking & Listening

☑ Present opinions and ideas with a clear, audible voice.

☑ Present ideas in a meaningful way.

OBJECTIVES

- Analyze text using text evidence
- Identify figurative language
- Identify major themes
- Analyze how the author creates surprise

"The Gift of the Magi"

by O. Henry

SUMMARY This short story takes place in New York in the early 1900s. It is about a devoted husband and wife who give up their most prized possessions so that they can buy Christmas gifts for each other. The irony of their actions becomes evident when the gifts are revealed.

ABOUT THE AUTHOR O. Henry (1862–1910) was born William Sydney Porter in Greensboro, North Carolina. He changed his name in 1901 and moved to New York City in 1902. From 1903 to January 1906, he wrote a weekly story for the *New York World*. Henry often wrote about the lives of ordinary people in New York City. He was a master of irony, and his stories are known for their surprise endings. He published ten collections and over six hundred short stories.

"The Gift of the Magi" is broken into three instructional segments.

SEGMENTS

SEGMENT 1 . . . . .pp. 2–13
SEGMENT 2 . . . . . . .pp. 14–23
SEGMENT 3 . . . . . . .pp. 24–37

Discuss Genre and Set Purpose

FICTION Have students briefly page through the story and note the illustrations. Discuss with students that they can tell that this book is a work of fiction because it includes characters, a setting, and events.

SET PURPOSE Help students set a purpose for reading, such as to find out what the gift really is.

Options for Reading

Independent Students read the book independently or with a partner and then answer questions posed by the teacher.

Supported Students read with a partner and then answer questions with teacher support.

Common Core Connection

RL 1 cite textual evidence to support analysis of what the text says explicitly as well as inferences drawn; **RL 2** determine a theme or central idea of a text/analyze its development/ provide summary; **RL 4** determine the meaning of words and phrases, including figurative and connotative meanings/analyze impact of word choices; **RL 5** analyze how author's choices create mystery, tension, or surprise

TEXT COMPLEXITY RUBRIC

Overall Text Complexity		"The Gift of the Magi" FICTION
		ACCESSIBLE
Quantitative Measure	Lexile	870L
Qualitative Measures	Text Structure	simple familiar story structure
	Language Conventionality and Clarity	some figurative language; old-fashioned language usage
	Knowledge Demands	moderately complex themes
	Purpose/Levels of Meaning	single level of meaning

 ENGLISH LANGUAGE LEARNERS

Academic Vocabulary

Read each word with students and discuss its meaning.

parsimony (p. 4) • thriftiness

mendicancy (p. 7) • the practice of begging, as for money

vestibule (p. 8) • entrance hall

appertaining (p. 8) • belonging

depreciate (p. 13) • decrease in value

Use Visuals

Review the illustrations with students. Provide sentence frames to help students use the illustrations to describe how Della feels: *When Della counts her money, she feels _____. When Della sells her hair, she feels _____. When Della buys the gift for Jim, she feels _____.*

FIRST READ **Think Through the Text**

Have students use text evidence and draw inferences to answer questions.

p. 9 • *What problem does Della have? She only has $1.87. It is not enough to buy a nice Christmas gift for her husband.* **RL 1**

p. 13 • *What is special about Della's hair and Jim's watch? They are both prized possessions. What text evidence shows this? The text says that they took a lot of pride in these things. The author describes what the characters would do if they met two important and wealthy people from ancient history, the Queen of Sheba and King Solomon.* **RL 1**

p. 13 • *Find a simile that O. Henry uses to describe Della's hair. The author compares Della's hair to a cascade, or waterfall. Why is this simile effective? The reader gets the idea that her hair is very long and flowing.* **RL 4**

RESPOND TO SEGMENT 1

 Classroom Collaboration

Have small groups work together to create a summary of what has happened in this segment. Then have students predict what Della might do next.

SECOND READ **Analyze the Text**

- Have students reread page 9. Ask: *Why does the author repeat the word gray? By saying that everything is gray, he is also describing Della's depressed feelings about her finances.* **RL 4**

- Review pages 3, 4, 9, and 10. Ask: *Why does the author repeat the number $1.87 several times? By emphasizing the small amount, he creates tension around Della's feeling of hopelessness at not having enough money to buy a present.* **RL 5**

- Review pages 2–13. Ask: *What is the theme of the story in this segment? Giving a Christmas gift to a loved one is a good thing to do.* **RL 2**

Domain Specific Vocabulary

flat (p. 7) • an apartment

pier-glass (p. 10) • a tall, narrow mirror

fob (p. 21) • a chain for a pocket watch

ENGLISH LANGUAGE LEARNERS

Use Comprehensible Input

Ensure students understand the events and theme by having them answer questions such as *What does Della do with her hair? What does she want to get for Jim? What does Jim get for her?*

RESPOND TO SEGMENT 2

Classroom Collaboration

Have small groups work together to summarize what they have read. Have them ask questions about what they don't understand.

Common Core Connection

RL 1 cite textual evidence to support analysis of what the text says explicitly as well as inferences drawn; **RL 2** determine a theme or central idea of a text/analyze its development/ provide summary; **RL 5** analyze how author's choices create mystery, tension, or surprise; **RL 10** read and comprehend literature; **W 2** write informative/explanatory texts; **W 5** develop and strengthen writing by planning, revising, editing, rewriting, or trying a new approach; **SL 4** adapt speech to a variety of contexts and tasks, demonstrating command of formal English.

Academic Vocabulary

Read each word with students and discuss its meaning.

ransacking (p. 18) • scouring or rummaging

chaste (p. 21) • pure

meretricious (p. 21) • showy or vulgar

prudence (p. 22) • caution

ravages (p. 23) • damaging effects

FIRST READ Think Through the Text

Have students use text evidence and draw inferences to answer questions.

pp. 15–19 • *What does Della do to her hair?* She cuts it off and sells it. *Why does Della do to this?* She sells her hair to get enough money to buy Jim a Christmas gift. ◖RL 1

p. 21 • *What gift does Della select for Jim?* She picks a watch fob. *Why does she think this is the perfect gift?* Jim has a special gold pocket watch that was handed down two generations, but he does not have a chain for it. Also, this particular chain reminded Della of Jim. ◖RL 1

p. 22 • *What does Della do when she gets home?* She fixes her hair. ◖RL 1

SECOND READ Analyze the Text

• Review pages 15–16 with students. Ask: *How does the author's statement about Madame not looking the "Sofronie" create tension?* It seems clear that the woman's name is made up; she is not French. The reader is not sure what might happen to Della. ◖RL 5

• Review pages 22–23. Ask: *How does the author create mystery and tension on these pages?* He has Della wonder what her husband will say, and has her justify her decision to get her hair cut. ◖RL 5

• Review pages 14–23. Ask: *What is the theme of this segment?* Della sold her prized possession, her hair, out of a desire to do something for her husband. ◖RL 2

Academic Vocabulary

Read each word with students and discuss its meaning.

discreet (p. 28) • tactful or modest

ecstatic (p. 30) • overjoyed

hysterical (p. 30) • uncontrollable

coveted (p. 31) • much desired

FIRST READ · Think Through the Text

Have students use text evidence and draw inferences to answer questions.

p. 24 • *How does Della feel?* She is nervous. *What evidence from the text supports your conclusion?* She turns white and says a little prayer, hoping that Jim will still think she is pretty without her beautiful hair. **RL 1**

pp. 25–30 • *How does Jim respond when he sees Della?* He is unable to speak. *What is Jim's gift for Della?* a set of combs for her hair **RL 1**

p. 34 • *Why does Jim want to put the presents away?* He realizes that neither of them can use their gifts. He has sold his watch to buy the combs. **RL 1**

SECOND READ · Analyze the Text

• Remind students of the definition of irony as a contrast between what is expected or hoped for and what actually happens. Then review the segment with students. Ask: *What is the irony of this story?* The irony is that both Della and Jim in their desire to get the best gifts possible for each other, sacrifice their most precious possessions and thereby render their gifts useless. *What feelings does the irony create?* The irony creates a feeling of tension during the first part of the story, and then surprise at the end. **RL 5**

• Review the selection. Ask: *What is a theme of this story?* Sacrifice—Della and Jim give up prized possessions to give the other a gift. **RL 2**

• Reread page 36. *Why are Della and Jim compared to the Magi?* The Magi gave wise gifts as did Della and Jim. They gave the gift of love. **RL 2**

Independent/Self-Selected Reading

Have students reread *The Gift of the Magi* independently to practice analyzing the text on their own, or have them practice the skills using another story, such as:

• "The Necklace" by Guy de Maupassant

• "The Story of an Hour" by Kate Chopin **RL 10**

Performance Task

WRITE & PRESENT

1. Have students think about and discuss the main theme of the story. **RL 2**

2. Have each student write a short essay explaining how the theme relates to the title of the story and the symbol of the Magi. Encourage students to cite text evidence to defend their ideas. **W 2**

3. Have small groups share their work and suggest revisions. Students edit their writing based on these suggestions. **W 5**

4. Have students present their final writing to their classmates. Ask student to respond to the themes and ideas from each student's writing. **SL 4**

5. Individual students turn in their final drafts to the teacher.

See Copying Masters, pp. 212–215.

STUDENT CHECKLIST

Writing

☑ Write an essay that explains how the theme relates to the title of the story.

☑ Cite text evidence that supports your ideas.

☑ Use complete sentences and developed paragraphs to structure writing.

Speaking & Listening

☑ Read writing aloud with a clear, audible voice.

☑ Ask and answer questions to clarify what a speaker says.

▶ **OBJECTIVES**

- Describe how characters change over the course of a story
- Identify the theme of a story
- Analyze text using text evidence

The Metamorphosis
by Franz Kafka

The Metamorphosis is broken into three instructional segments.

SUMMARY *The Metamorphosis* tells the story of Gregor Samsa, a traveling salesman who awakens one morning to discover he has changed from man to insect. Gregor's condition brings about several dramatic changes in his family. Eventually, Gregor's transformation is the catalyst for much change in the Samsa household.

ABOUT THE AUTHOR **Franz Kafka** was born in Czechoslovakia but wrote his novels and short stories in German. He trained as a lawyer and was only able to write in his spare time. Kafka was Jewish and often wrote about conflict between parents and children, brutality, and terrifying transformations. His work heavily influenced the existentialism movement.

Options for Reading

Independent Students read the book independently or with a partner and then answer questions posed by the teacher.

Supported Students read a segment and answer questions with teacher support.

Discuss Genre and Set Purpose

FICTION *The Metamorphosis* requires the reader to suspend disbelief, and the account of Gregor's transformation seems magically real. The theme of parent-child conflict and feeling alienated by modern society are universal, which has made this story one of the most read pieces of literature since it was published in 1915.

SET PURPOSE Help students set a purpose for reading, such as to find out how conflicts between family members can reflect conflicts in society at large.

COMMON CORE **Common Core Connection**

RL 1 cite textual evidence to support analysis of what the text says explicitly as well as inferences drawn; **RL 2** determine a theme or central idea of a text and analyze its development; **RL 3** analyze how characters develop and interact with others

▲ TEXT COMPLEXITY RUBRIC

Overall Text Complexity		*The Metamorphosis* FICTION
		COMPLEX
Quantitative Measure	Lexile	1340L
Qualitative Measures	Text Structure	no major shifts in chronology
	Language Conventionality and Clarity	stream-of-consciousness perspective
	Knowledge Demands	unfamiliar experience and situation
	Purpose/Levels of Meaning	multiple levels of meaning

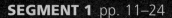

Academic Vocabulary

Read each word with students and discuss its meaning.

harbinger (p. 13) • a signal of something to come

lucid (p. 17) • clear

propulsion (p. 22) • the act of moving forward quickly

implacably (p. 23) • unbending, unappeasable

abraded (p. 23) • rubbed away

ELL **ENGLISH LANGUAGE LEARNERS**

Use Sentence Frames

Guide students to generate adjectives that could describe Gregor and his family. Then have students orally complete sentence frames such as the following:

Gregor is _____. *frightened*
Grete is _____. *crying*
Mrs. Samsa is _____.
unconscious

FIRST READ ## Think Through the Text

Have students use text evidence and draw inferences to answer questions.

pp. 11–13 • *How does Gregor first know that something is different? On page 11, Gregor wakes to see his segmented body and many legs. What is Gregor's most pressing concern as he tries to get out of bed? Gregor cannot move as he is accustomed to moving.* RL 1

pp. 16–18 • *For what two reasons does the chief clerk appear at the Samsa residence? He was to pick up Gregor from the train station, and on page 16, he comes to find out why Gregor missed the train. On page 18, he also wants to talk to Gregor about his poor performance at work.* RL 1

pp. 20–23 • *How do Gregor's parents react when they see his transformation? Mrs. Samsa tries to go to Gregor but faints at the sight of him. Mr. Samsa clenches his fist in anger but then breaks into sobs. On page 23, he chases Gregor with a cane.* **How does the chief clerk react?** *On page 20, he howls like the wind, and on page 21, he fearfully backs out of the apartment.* RL 3

SECOND READ ## Analyze the Text

• Review pages 11–18 with students. Ask: *Why are Gregor and his family so concerned about his not showing up for the early train to work? What does this tell you about their relationships? Gregor is never late for work and has not been sick in the five years he has been at his job. His parents and sister are confused and upset that he is still in his room. The family depends on Gregor to support them.* RL 3

• Ask: *What might be two interrelated themes of the story? transformation and conflict* **What conflicts does Gregor experience? Give examples from the text to support your ideas.** *Sample answers: Gregor struggles with his body after his dramatic transformation. His parents want him to get up and go to work, even though he might be sick. On page 16, Gregor wonders why his company has to send someone to check on him, and on page 21, he pleads with the chief clerk to put in a good word for him as a faithful employee, even though he has a poor performance.* RL 2

RESPOND TO SEGMENT 1
Classroom Collaboration

Have partners create a character map for the main characters in this segment. Have students include the relationships between the characters in the map, both in literal terms (son, father, mother, sister) and in emotional terms. Then have students predict how they think the relationships might change over the course of the story.

Domain Specific Vocabulary

conservatory (p. 29) • school of music or performing arts

gulden (p. 30) • golden coins from the Austrian empire

Academic Vocabulary

Read each word with students and discuss its meaning.

swoonlike (p. 24) • as if in a fainting spell

pallidly (p. 24) • palely; dimly

hearsay (p. 27) • unverified information, gossip

relinquish (p. 36) • to give up

RESPOND TO SEGMENT 2

Classroom Collaboration

Have small groups work together to summarize what they have read. Have them ask questions about what they do not understand.

FIRST READ **Think Through the Text**

Have students use text evidence and draw inferences to answer questions.

pp. 24–28 • *Why is it significant that Gregor does not like the food that his sister leaves for him? On page 25, we learn that Grete left milk and bread for Gregor (his favorite food), but when he tries to eat it, he does not like it. This shows that even his tastes have changed. What shows that his sister understands he does not like the food? On pages 27–28, Grete takes away the uneaten food and replaces it with rotting food, something an insect would probably like to eat.* ⬤RL 1

pp. 32–34 • *What does Gregor begin to do for fun at night when he is alone in his room? On page 32, Gregor begins to enjoy crawling on the walls and hanging on the ceiling in his room at night, like any good bug would.* ⬤RL 3

SECOND READ **Analyze the Text**

• Review pages 29–30 with students. Ask: *What is your impression of the lifestyle of Gregor's family prior to his change? Sample answers: Gregor's father has not worked in five years and has gotten fat from inactivity; his mother is old and suffering from asthma, so she spends time sitting near the window gasping for breath; Grete sleeps late, does few chores around the house, and plays the violin. The family seems spoiled because Gregor takes care of them financially.* ⬤RL 3

• Have students revisit pages 28–33. Ask: *How has Gregor's relationship with his sister changed? Gregor's sister now takes care of him by feeding him and cleaning his room. In the past, he earned money to support the family and was going to send her to the music conservatory.* ⬤RL 3

• Ask: *How do Gregor's mother and sister differ in their reactions to his transformation? On pages 34–35, Gregor's mother wants his room to remain the same, while his sister wants to remove the furniture so that it fits his new insect life better. One is stuck in the past, and the other is taking on a new role. How has Gregor's father changed? He has a new job, probably as a bank messenger, but he has not changed in his reaction to Gregor.* ⬤RL 2

Common Core Connection

RL 1 cite textual evidence to support analysis of what the text says explicitly as well as inferences drawn; **RL 2** determine a theme or central idea of a text and analyze its development; **RL 3** analyze how characters develop and interact with others; **RL 10** read and comprehend literature; **W 2** write informative/explanatory texts; **W 5** develop and strengthen writing by planning, revising, editing, rewriting, or trying a new approach; **SL 3** evaluate speaker's point of view, reasoning, use of evidence and rhetoric

Academic Vocabulary

Read each word with students and discuss its meaning.

stenography (p. 39) • art of writing in shorthand

retrenchments (p. 40) • reductions in expenses

multifarious (p. 44) • numerous and varied

FIRST READ   Think Through the Text

Have students use text evidence and draw inferences to answer questions.

pp. 38–39 • *How does Gregor's injury change the relationship with his father? Gregor has a rotten apple embedded in his back from when his father threw fruit at him. Now his father realizes he is a member of the family and should not be treated as an enemy.* ⬤ RL 3

pp. 46–47 • *How does Grete playing the violin change the course of the story? The boarders don't appreciate Grete's playing; Gregor wants to show her he likes her playing, but when the boarders see him they raise a fuss. Now the family admits they can't take care of him anymore.* ⬤ RL 1

SECOND READ   Analyze the Text

• Review pages 38–44. Then ask: *What transformation has taken place in the family since Segment 1? Give examples from the text to support your ideas. The father and sister have jobs, and the mother takes in sewing. They have begun to support themselves and take care of Gregor. On page 43, they take in boarders.* **How does their behavior change toward Gregor?** *They don't pay much attention to him.* ⬤ RL 2

• Have students review pages 44–52. Ask: *Do you agree that the only thing left for the family is to rid themselves of the burden of Gregor's condition? Why or why not? Sample answer: No, they are responsible for him because he is a member of the family and cannot help his condition. Even though he is a financial and social burden, they should take care of him.* ⬤ RL 3

• Ask: *Do you think Mr. and Mrs. Samsa and Grete are happier at the end of the story or at the beginning? Why? Sample answer: At the beginning, they were spoiled and lazy and thought they were happy. But they might be happier at the end because now they know that they can take care of themselves.* ⬤ RL 2

Independent/Self-Selected Reading

Have students reread *The Metamorphosis* independently to practice analyzing the text on their own, or have them practice the skills using another story, such as:

• *The Trial* by Franz Kafka

• *Love in the Time of Cholera* by Gabriel Garcia-Marquez ⬤ RL 10

Performance Task

WRITE & PRESENT

1. Have students form groups to discuss the theme of the story and suggest different ways for the story to end. ⬤ RL 2

2. Ask students to write a different ending to the story, related to the theme and based on the ideas they discussed in their groups. ⬤ W 2

3. Have students share their work and offer suggestions for revising and editing. Students edit their alternate endings based on these suggestions. ⬤ W 5

4. Have students present their alternate endings to the class. Ask students to respond to the new endings. ⬤ SL 3

See Copying Masters, pp. 212–215.

STUDENT CHECKLIST

Writing

☑ Identify at least one thematic element in the alternate ending.

☑ Thematically connect the alternate ending with other parts of the story, such as setting, characterization, or point of view.

☑ Use complete sentences and developed paragraphs to structure writing.

Speaking & Listening

☑ Present new story endings with a clear, expressive voice.

☑ Present ideas in a meaningful way.

▶ OBJECTIVES

- Make inferences based on text evidence
- Describe character relationships as they relate to the plot
- Understand major themes

The Grapes of Wrath

by John Steinbeck

SUMMARY The Joad family are sharecroppers from Oklahoma. In the 1930s, during the Great Depression and the Dust Bowl era, they are pushed off the land they have worked for generations. So they make their way across the country toward California in search of work. Tom Joad and his family experience hunger, hardship, injustice, and even violence as they seek a chance to work toward for a better life.

ABOUT THE AUTHOR John Steinbeck was born in California in 1902 and is best known for his Pulitzer Prize–winning novel *The Grapes of Wrath*, which also gained acclaim as a film. Steinbeck also wrote *Tortilla Flat*, *East of Eden*, and the novella *Of Mice and Men*. Outside of writing, he had worked many odd jobs, including farm work in California, and as a war correspondent during World War II.

The Grapes of Wrath is broken into three instructional segments.

SEGMENTS

Options for Reading

Independent Students read the book independently or with a partner and then answer questions posed by the teacher.

Supported Students read a segment and answer questions with teacher support.

Discuss Genre and Set Purpose

FICTION Point out that this novel is a work of narrative fiction that includes characters, a setting, and events. Explain that the novel is based upon the author's research and observation, but the story is invented.

SET PURPOSE Help students set a purpose for reading, such as to find out how people coped with the impact of the Great Depression.

COMMON CORE Connection

RL 1 cite textual evidence to support analysis of what the text says explicitly as well as inferences drawn; **RL 3** analyze how characters develop, interact with others, and advance the plot

▲ TEXT COMPLEXITY RUBRIC

Overall Text Complexity		The Grapes of Wrath FICTION
		COMPLEX
Quantitative Measure	Lexile	680L
Qualitative Measures	Text Structure	conventional story structure
	Language Conventionality and Clarity	some unfamiliar words
	Knowledge Demands	increased historical knowledge useful
	Purpose/Levels of Meaning	multiple themes

Academic Vocabulary

Read each word with students and discuss its meaning.

rivulet (p. 1) • a small stream

dissipated (p. 1) • broken up and scattered

truculent (p. 45) • fiercely opposed

cantankerous (p. 77) • quarrelsome

demure (p. 95) • reserved and modest

paralytic (p. 96) • unable to move

FIRST READ Think Through the Text

Have students use text evidence and draw inferences to answer questions.

pp. 12–13 • *Why was Tom in prison? He was found guilty of killing a man. Why does he have cheap new clothes? Tom is wearing the new clothes that he was given as he left prison.* ◖RL 1

pp. 31–39 • *What do the landowners tell the sharecroppers about the bankers? Why are they making the sharecroppers leave their homes? The landowners tell the sharecroppers that the banks are calling in their loans. They are making the sharecroppers leave so they can mechanize the farming business and save money on labor. They also talk about selling the depleted land to unsuspecting Easterners.* ◖RL 3

SECOND READ Analyze the Text

- Have students look back on Chapter 4. Ask: *Why is Casy no longer a pastor? Casy has come to believe that the human spirit may be the Holy Spirit, and that all men are perhaps part of one great soul. He knows that he can't hold successful church meetings with ideas like that.* ◖RL 3

- Review Chapter 13. Ask: *When the Joads stop for gas, what does the gas station owner tell them? He tells them that many other families have already passed through and that many of them could not even pay for gas. What does this foreshadow? The journey might be difficult and even desperate. Business people will not be particularly helpful, though some individuals might be fair.* RL 3

Domain Specific Vocabulary

Dust Bowl • the region in the south central U.S. that had dust storms in the 1930s

sharecropper • a tenant farmer who pays a share of the crop as rent

ELL ENGLISH LANGUAGE LEARNERS

Use Sentence Frames

Guide students to generate adjectives that could describe Tom, Ma, Pa, and Granma. Then have them orally complete sentence frames such as:

Tom is _____. loyal
Ma is _____. stable
Pa is _____. tired
Granma is _____. cranky

RESPOND TO SEGMENT 1

Classroom Collaboration

Have small groups work together to create a summary of what has happened to Tom in this segment. Then have students place events in order and attribute the events to the effects of poverty or the effects of change. Point out that some events are an effect of the interplay between poverty and change.

Domain Specific Vocabulary

Hooverville • a group of tents and shacks during the Depression years in the U.S.

typhoid • a serious, often fatal, waterborne intestinal infection

 ENGLISH LANGUAGE LEARNERS

Use Peer Supported Learning

Pair ELL students with classmates. Have each pair rewrite a page of dialogue in vernacular. Allow them to use contemporary slang, as long as the meaning is accurate. Ask pairs to share their work. ▬ **W 5**

RESPOND TO SEGMENT 2

 Classroom Collaboration

Have small groups work together to summarize what has happened to each of the main characters and identify how important events have affected them. Encourage students to ask questions about what they do not understand.

 Common Core Connection

RL 2 determine a theme or central idea of a text; **RL 3** analyze how characters develop, interact with others, and advance the plot; **W 3b** use narrative techniques to develop experiences, events, or characters; **W 4** produce writing in which development, organization, and style are appropriate to task, purpose, and audience; **W 5** develop and strengthen writing by planning, revising, editing, rewriting, or trying a new approach; **SL 4** present information, findings, and supporting evidence clearly, concisely, and logically

Academic Vocabulary

Read each word with students and discuss its meaning.

corrugated (p. 177) • bent into folds or wrinkles

vagrant (p. 186) • an idle person who wanders aimlessly

greasewood (p. 221) • a shrub common in western states containing an oil that can be used as fuel

flailing (p. 223) • thrashing about

FIRST READ **Think Through the Text**

Have students use text evidence and draw inferences to answer questions.

pp. 193–197 • *What are some of the unspoken rules of roadside camping among the poor families moving west? The families camp together. They do not intrude on others' privacy and do not ask about the past; they feed people who are hungry and do everything they can for the sick and pregnant. There is no theft, murder, or rape. The people all help each other with chores at night but stay to themselves during the day.* ▬ **RL 2, RL 3**

pp. 243–246 • *Why do those people who are hiring workers advertise for more workers than they really need? They know that the more workers there are to compete for jobs, the less the landowners have to pay them. The 300,000 people crowding the itinerant workers camps are all looking for the same work the Joads seek.* ▬ **RL 2, RL 3, RL 10**

SECOND READ **Analyze the Text**

• Review Chapters 18–20 with students. Ask: *What characters have abandoned or left the Joad family group? Granpa, the Wilsons, Casy, Noah, Connie, Granma How does this relate to the theme of change in the novel? Each character that leaves the scene affects the mental, emotional, and physical well-being of the group.* ▬ **RL 3**

• Review Chapters 21 and 22. Ask: *How does the Farmer's Association react to the influx of farm workers in California? They work together to set wages low so that the farmers can make more profit on their crops. When they begin to worry about growing resentment from the starving workers, they hire rabble rousers to cause trouble and provide a rationale for crackdowns.* ▬ **RL 2**

Academic Vocabulary

Read each word with students and discuss its meaning.

reedy (p. 328) • sounding thin and high like a reed instrument

gauged (p. 330) • evaluated

skirling (p. 341) • making a shrill sound

pellagra (p. 349) • dietary deficiency with symptoms such as burning skin, inflamed mouth, and mental impairment

wrath (p. 349) • intense anger

FIRST READ ▶ **Think Through the Text**

Have students use text evidence and draw inferences to answer questions.

pp. 346–349 • *Why are workers in California starving while food rots?* *The workers cannot get work so they have no money with which to buy food; townspeople in California are wary of the workers and refuse to help them; the price of food has gone so low that small-scale farmers simply let food rot rather than harvest it; large landowners spray excess crops with kerosene so they will not be stolen.* ▬RL 2

pp. 444–445 • Ask: *What does Ma mean when she tells Pa not to take the blame and that there are changes all over?* *She is saying that he is not at fault for the baby being stillborn and that they cannot control the changes they are facing.* ▬RL 1

SECOND READ ▶ **Analyze the Text**

• Review pages 375–376 with students. Then ask: *Why does Ma say that if a person is in trouble, it's best to get help from a poor person?* *After the man in the company store at the peach farm gives her a dime to get some sugar, she observes that she has experienced more compassion from poor people than from the wealthy banks and landowners.* ▬RL 3

• Ask: *How do Ma and Rose of Sharon show resilience in the face of change and loss?* *Sample answer: Even though her baby died, Rose of Sharon gives what she has so that another person can live.* ▬RL 2

Independent/Self-Selected Reading

Have students reread *The Grapes of Wrath* independently to practice analyzing the text on their own, or have them practice the skills using realistic novels, such as the following:

• *Of Mice and Men* by John Steinbeck

• *For Whom the Bell Tolls* by Ernest Hemingway ▬RL 10

WRITE & PRESENT

1. Ask students to think about how family relationships play a role in each character's development. ▬RL 2, RL 3

2. Individual students select a different main character and write about how each character fits into the family in the novel. Students should detail the character's function in the novel, the character's benefit to the family, and the causes for concern the character generates. Encourage students to cite text evidence to support their analysis. ▬W 3b

3. Small groups meet to share their work and suggest revisions. Students edit their writing and add details based on these suggestions. ▬W 5

4. Students present their final character analyses to classmates. ▬SL 4

5. Individual students turn in their final drafts to the teacher. ▬W 4

See Copying Masters, pp. 212–215.

STUDENT CHECKLIST

Writing

☑ Write about one main character's development.

☑ Analyze how poverty and family influenced this character, using text evidence and quotes from the novel.

☑ Use complete sentences and developed paragraphs to structure writing.

Speaking & Listening

☑ Participate effectively in collaborative discussions.

☑ Speak clearly at an understandable pace.

OBJECTIVES

- Describe how characters respond to major events
- Compare and contrast different points of view
- Identify the theme of a story
- Interpret symbols and figurative language in fiction
- Analyze text using text evidence

Fahrenheit 451 is broken into three instructional segments.

SEGMENTS

Options for Reading

Independent Students read the book independently or with a partner and then answer questions posed by the teacher.

Supported Students read a segment with a partner and answer questions with teacher support. Encourage students to read at least a portion of each segment on their own.

COMMON CORE **Common Core Connection**

RL 1 cite textual evidence to support analysis of what the text says explicitly as well as inferences drawn; **RL 2** determine a theme or central idea of a text and analyze its development; **RL 3** analyze how characters develop and interact with others

Fahrenheit 451
by Ray Bradbury

SUMMARY Guy Montag is a fireman in a futuristic city who loves his job—burning books and the places that house them. He meets a young girl who suggests that at one time firemen put *out* fires, people read books for ideas, and families had long, meaningful conversations. Later, during a burning, Montag grabs a book and hides it close to his chest. Once he becomes curious about why books are so valuable to some people that they would risk their lives to keep them, he begins to search for a way to change his life.

ABOUT THE AUTHOR Ray Bradbury published some 500 short stories, novels, poems, plays, musicals, TV scripts, and screenplays, challenging readers to dream, think, and create. He received the 2000 National Book Foundation's Medal for Distinguished Contribution to American Letters.

Discuss Genre and Set Purpose

SCIENCE FICTION Remind students that science fiction includes characters, settings, and events set in a future time or place. Discuss with students how they can tell that this story is not set in the present.

SET PURPOSE Help students set a purpose for reading, such as to find out how Montag's feelings about his job become conflicted.

TEXT COMPLEXITY RUBRIC

Overall Text Complexity		*Fahrenheit 451* SCIENCE FICTION
		COMPLEX
Quantitative Measure	Lexile	890L
Qualitative Measures	Text Structure	some unconventional story elements
	Language Conventionality and Clarity	some unfamiliar words
	Knowledge Demands	fairly complex theme
	Purpose/Levels of Meaning	multiple levels of meaning

Academic Vocabulary

Read each word with students and discuss its meaning.

illumination (p. 5) • the act of making bright with light

incinerator (p. 22) • a furnace or container for burning trash and waste

abstract (p. 28) • not representing anything specific

centrifuge (p. 42) • a machine that spins in order to separate things

Domain Specific Vocabulary

salamander (p. 4) • in mythology, a lizard capable of living in fire

phoenix (p. 4) • a mythological bird that consumed itself by fire and later rose from its ashes

FIRST READ ## Think Through the Text

Have students use text evidence and draw inferences to answer questions.

pp. 1–7 • *What is Guy Montag's job, and how does he feel about it?* Montag is a fireman who burns books and loves his job. *When did you first realize this story does not take place in the present? Cite evidence.* Sample answer: A fireman burning books is an immediate clue because that doesn't happen now. On page 5, Montag tells Clarisse that reading books is against the law. RL 1

pp. 8–21 • *How do the conversations with Clarisse affect Montag?* Sample answer: After she asks if he's happy, he realizes on page 9 that his life is empty and that happiness is a mask the girl has ripped off. The more they talk, the more conflicted he feels, and on page 21, he feels as if two parts of himself are fighting each other. RL 3

pp. 32–38 • *How does the fire at 11 No. Elm change Montag?* Montag realizes they aren't just burning things but also people. On page 34, his hand reaches out on its own and grabs a book to save. RL 3

pp. 51–59 • *How does Beatty explain why books are banned?* The people, not the government, banned books first. People wanted condensed books, more sports, and movies; they didn't want to offend minorities or be more intellectual than others; people were made equal by book banning because they sought pleasures and had no worries. RL 1

SECOND READ ## Analyze the Text

• Have students contrast the way Clarisse and Montag view the world. *Sample answer: Clarisse enjoys nature, and she doesn't participate in the activities of other teens and is considered antisocial. Montag loves his job and does what others tell him to do. Clarisse has long conversations with her family, while Montag can't talk to his wife because she constantly watches TV programs.* RL 3

• Ask: *What do you think is a major theme of this segment?* censorship *What are some text examples that support your idea?* Sample answer: When Clarisse asks Montag on page 5 if he's read any of the books, he says that reading books is against the law. On pages 51–59, Beatty explains that the government banned books to make people equal. RL 2

ELL ENGLISH LANGUAGE LEARNERS

Use Sentence Frames

Remind students that the author uses names of animals or things in nature to describe certain objects in the story. Have students orally complete sentence frames such as the following:

The fire truck is called a _____. salamander *The fire hose is like a _____.* python or snake *The firehouse has a pet mechanical _____.* hound or dog *Mildred's earphones are called _____.* seashells

RESPOND TO SEGMENT 1

Classroom Collaboration

Have partners create a summary of the way Montag changes in this segment. Then have students predict what might happen next in the novel.

ENGLISH LANGUAGE LEARNERS

Use Comprehensible Input

Ensure students understand the plot events and the theme by asking questions such as *Why does Montag want to change things?* and *Are people really as happy as they think they are?*

RESPOND TO SEGMENT 2

Classroom Collaboration

Have small groups work together to summarize what they have read. Have them ask questions about what they don't understand.

 Common Core Connection

RL 1 cite textual evidence to support analysis of what the text says explicitly as well as inferences drawn; **RL 2** determine a theme or central idea of a text and analyze its development; **RL 3** analyze how characters develop and interact with others; **RL 4** determine the meaning of words and phrases, including figurative and connotative meanings; **RL 10** read and comprehend literature; **W 2** write informative/explanatory texts; **W 5** develop and strengthen writing by planning, revising, editing, rewriting, or trying a new approach; **SL 4** present information, findings, and supporting evidence clearly, concisely, and logically

Academic Vocabulary

Read each word with students and discuss its meaning.

sieve (p. 67) • a wire mesh utensil used for sifting

infinite (p. 79) • having no limits

profusion (p. 79) • a state of abundance

insidious (p. 82) • sneakily and gradually becoming harmful

phosphorescent (p. 106) • glowing without giving off heat

FIRST READ # Think Through the Text

Have students use text evidence and draw inferences to answer questions.

pp. 67–68 • *Why are Montag and Mildred now reading books? In the last section, Montag brought a book home from a fire. On page 62, he shows Mildred a bunch of books he has been hiding. Now they are trying to figure out what the books mean.* ● RL 3

pp. 70–71 • *Why does Montag think Faber might help him? Montag remembers meeting an English professor, Faber, who talked about the meaning of things.* ● RL 1

pp. 79–81 • *According to Faber, what three things are necessary to appreciate the importance of books? One, quality of information; two, leisure to digest it; three, the right to carry out actions based on what we learn.* ● RL 1

pp. 82–84 • *What is Montag's plan? He wants to print books and plant them in firemen's houses, turn in an alarm, and watch firemen's houses burn. What does Faber think of the plan? He says it's an insidious plan but not enough. He thinks the coming war will change civilization completely.* ● RL 3

SECOND READ # Analyze the Text

• Explain that *irony* is when what you see or say is different from what is actually real. Discuss with students why it is ironic that Montag had hidden books even though he was a fireman. Review pages 102–103 where Beatty talks to Montag. Ask: *What is ironic about Beatty's words? Sample answer: Beatty is quoting from books, so he has obviously read a lot. However, he is trying to confuse Montag in order to prove that books don't make sense.* ● RL 4

• Ask: What is a major theme of this segment? *revolution What examples from the text support your idea? Sample answer: Montag has a plan to get rid of the firemen. Faber knows a retired printer who might print more books once the war destroys civilization and needs to begin again. Faber thinks of himself as both a coward and a revolutionary.* ● RL 2

COMMON CORE

Academic Vocabulary

Read each word with students and discuss its meaning.

incomprehensible (p. 108) • not able to be understood

nuzzling (p. 110) • rubbing gently

gout (p. 110) • a large blob

bewilderment (p. 112) • a state of confusion

scapegoat (p. 141) • a person chosen to take the blame for something

FIRST READ ## Think Through the Text

Have students use text evidence and draw inferences to answer questions.

pp. 110–113 • *Why does Beatty have Montag torch Montag's own house? Beatty thinks Montag brought it on himself when he started reading books and quoting poetry, thinking he was better than others and wouldn't get caught. How does Montag respond? Montag burns his house and then burns Beatty.* ⊂RL 3

pp. 143–145 • *In what way does Montag meet Jonathan Swift, Charles Darwin, and other great authors? Montag meets other book burners who have memorized books. What does Montag have to offer them? Montag says he can remember Ecclesiastes from the Bible.* ⊂RL 1

SECOND READ ## Analyze the Text

• Review pages 141–142 with students. Ask: *Why was it more important for the helicopters to kill a fake Montag than find the real one? Sample answer: It was more important that people believe the government was successful in catching Montag. They couldn't admit failure.* ⊂RL 1

• Reread Granger's description of the phoenix on page 156. Ask: *How does Granger compare his group to the phoenix? Like the phoenix, people have to start over again. How are they different from the phoenix? This time they will remember what they did in their lives and what people have done for a thousand years and pass it on.* ⊂RL 1

• Ask: *What do you think is the theme of the whole book? Why? Sample answer: Censorship—Getting rid of books led to people focusing only on the pleasures of the present, without regard for new ideas or lessons of the past.* ⊂RL 2

Independent/Self-Selected Reading

Have students reread *Fahrenheit 451* independently to practice analyzing the text on their own, or have them practice the skills using another book, such as:

• *Dandelion Wine* by Ray Bradbury

• *Something Wicked This Way Comes* by Ray Bradbury ⊂RL 10

Performance Task

WRITE & PRESENT

1. Have small groups compare and contrast the way firemen use the symbol of the phoenix with how Granger uses the lesson of the phoenix. ⊂RL 2

2. Ask students to think about the main theme of the entire story. Have students write an explanation of how firemen use the symbol of the phoenix to justify their work and then contrast those ideas with what Granger thinks is the lesson of the phoenix, explaining what he plans to do. Encourage students to cite text evidence. ⊂W 2

3. Have students share their work with partners and then edit it. ⊂W 5

4. Have students present and discuss their final work. ⊂SL 4

See Copying Masters, pp. 212–215

STUDENT CHECKLIST

Writing

☑ Identify at least one way the firemen and Granger agree and one way they disagree.

☑ Relate the theme of the novel to the symbol of the phoenix, using text evidence and quotes.

☑ Use a topic sentence and developed paragraphs to structure each explanation.

Speaking & Listening

☑ Read writing aloud with a clear, audible voice.

☑ Present ideas in a meaningful way.

"I Stand Here Ironing"

by Tillie Olsen

SUMMARY This story, or narrative, is told from the first person point of view. The narrator has received a request to come to school to discuss her daughter, Emily. As she irons, she contemplates Emily's upbringing and her own experience as a young, poor mother. She expresses her regrets about the past and her hope that her daughter may be able to rise above it.

ABOUT THE AUTHOR **Tillie Olsen** is an American Book Award winner best known for her stories about working people during the Great Depression. She was born in Nebraska in 1912 and left school at the age of fifteen to go to work. She had four children and worked in low-income jobs to support them from the 1930s through the 1950s. Once her children grew up, she began writing in her spare time.

Discuss Genre and Set Purpose

FICTION Students should recall that short stories are a genre of fiction. This realistic story is fictional but has many elements of real life.

SET PURPOSE Help students set a purpose for reading such as analyzing why the writer chose to depict the narrator ironing.

▶ OBJECTIVES

- Analyze text using text evidence
- Identify the theme of a story
- Identify the characters and plot of a story
- Describe how stories can reflect history

"I Stand here Ironing" is broken into three instructional segments.

Options for Reading

Independent Students read the story independently and then answer questions posed by the teacher.

Supported Students read a segment and answer questions with teacher support.

 Common Core Connection

RL 1 cite textual evidence to support analysis of what the text says explicitly as well as inferences drawn; **RL 2** determine a theme or central idea of a text/analyze its development/ provide summary; **RL 3** analyze how characters develop/interact with others/advance the plot; **RL 4** determine the meaning of words and phrases, including figurative and connotative meanings/analyze the impact of word choices

TEXT COMPLEXITY RUBRIC

Overall Text Complexity		"I Stand Here Ironing" FICTION
		COMPLEX
Quantitative Measure	Lexile	940L
Qualitative Measures	Text Structure	use of flashback
	Language Conventionality and Clarity	more complex sentence structure and descriptions
	Knowledge Demands	increased amount of cultural knowledge useful
	Purpose/Levels of Meaning	multiple levels of meaning

Academic Vocabulary

Read each word with students and discuss its meaning.

tormented (p. 3) • tortured

engulfed (p. 3) • overwhelmed

WPA (p. 4) • Work Projects Administration, a federal agency that put unemployed people to work during the Great Depression

hashing (p. 5) • chopping, dicing, and preparing ingredients in a diner

denunciations (p. 5) • public condemnations

somber (p. 6) • extremely serious

FIRST READ ## Think Through the Text

Have students use text evidence and draw inferences to answer questions.

p. 3 • *Who might be speaking in the second paragraph? The person might be someone from Emily's school, calling to talk to the mother about her daughter.* RL 3

p. 4 • *How old was the narrator when her daughter was born? Emily was born when the narrator was 19.* RL 1

p. 5 • *How did the narrator cope with Emily's chicken pox? She brought Emily to her ex-husband's family and left her there. What was the result of her action? It took her a long time to get Emily back, and when she did, Emily was thin, pockmarked, and unhealthy looking.* RL 3

SECOND READ ## Analyze the Text

- Review pages 4–6. *What does the narrator mean when she says that her daughter is uneasy in her newfound attractiveness? She means her daughter has felt ugly and unattractive most of her life.* RL 2

- Review pages 4–6. Ask: *Why did the narrator have to leave Emily at a nursery school? The father of her baby left, so the narrator had to get a job to support herself and her baby. How did she know Emily hated the school? Though she never rebelled, Emily used to invent reasons why she couldn't go to school.* RL 3

- Review pages 4–6. *Using evidence from the text, evaluate the ways in which the narrator feels she failed Emily. The narrator feels guilty that she nursed Emily on a rigid schedule in opposition to her instincts and Emily's needs. She left Emily with her ex-husband's family and then with an "evil" nursery school teacher. She rarely smiled at her daughter and sometimes left her alone at night for hours at a time.* RL 1

ELL **ENGLISH LANGUAGE LEARNERS**

Use Sentence Frames

Guide students to copy from the text quotes spoken by Emily as a young child. Then have students collaborate on writing replies for the character of the mother. Interested students might read their created dialogue aloud. RL 3, RL 4

RESPOND TO SEGMENT 1

Classroom Collaboration

Have small groups of students create a live reading of the first scenes in the story by having one student read while others provide background pantomime to summarize the events in this segment.

ENGLISH LANGUAGE LEARNERS

Use Comprehensible Input

Ensure students understand the plot and theme by asking questions such as the following: *Why did the narrator make that choice? What was Emily's response to that event?*

RESPOND TO SEGMENT 2

Classroom Collaboration

Have small groups of students write a one-paragraph summary of what was covered in this segment. Ask one student per group to read their summary to the class.

Common Core Connection

RL 1 cite textual evidence to support analysis of what the text says explicitly as well as inferences drawn; **RL 2** determine a theme or central idea of a text/analyze its development/ provide summary; **RL 3** analyze how characters develop/interact with others/advance the plot; **RL 10** read and comprehend literature; **W 2** write informative/explanatory texts; **W 5** develop and strengthen writing by planning, revising, editing, rewriting, or trying a new approach; **SL 1** initiate/participate in a range of collaborative discussions; **SL 1a** come to discussions prepared/draw on preparation to stimulate exchange of ideas; **SL 4** present information, findings, and supporting evidence clearly, concisely, and logically

Academic Vocabulary

Read each word with students and discuss its meaning.

sterner (p. 7) • stricter, firmer
convalescent (p. 7) • related to rest and recovery
ravaged (p. 7) • badly damaged
fluted (p. 7) • ruffled
frailer (p. 8) • more delicate and fragile
fretted (p. 9) • worried

FIRST READ ## Think Through the Text

Have students use text evidence and draw inferences to answer questions.

p. 7 • *Why did Emily get sent away to a convalescent home?* Emily had red measles and did not recover quickly. She was sent to a convalescent home to recuperate over several months. ▬ RL 3, RL 10

pp. 7–8 • *How did the narrator and Emily communicate when Emily was at the home?* The mother visited when allowed. Emily and her mother also wrote letters to each other. Emily was allowed to listen to but not keep the letters. ▬ RL 3, RL 10

pp. 8–9 • *How long did Emily remain in the home?* Emily was at the home for eight months. *Why was she allowed to leave?* Emily wasn't eating or regaining her lost weight. ▬ RL 1, RL 10

SECOND READ ## Analyze the Text

• Review page 7 with students. Ask: *Why does the mother say it is too late for her to offer her daughter comfort?* She used to send her sick daughter back to bed when Emily was young, and now Emily refuses comfort. ▬ RL 1, RL 3

• Review pages 7–8 with students. Ask: *How does the narrator communicate the cruelty of the convalescent home?* She describes the restrictions on visitation, the rules that prohibited Emily from keeping a few personal things, and the runny eggs and lumpy mush. She also notes the discrepancy between the clothing appearance of the society people who raised funds for the home and the children who stayed there. ▬ RL 3, RL 10

• Have students examine page 9. Ask: *Why did Emily's mother sometimes allow her to stay home from school?* Emily's mother sometimes let Emily stay home because Emily's asthma flared up or because she wanted to be with Emily and the other children together at the same time at home. ▬ RL 2, RL 3

Academic Vocabulary

Read each word with students and discuss its meaning.

corroding (p. 10) • wearing away

articulate (p. 10) • express clearly

anonymity (p. 12) • state of being unknown

convulsing (p. 12) • shaking uncontrollably

dredging (p. 13) • bringing up something buried

FIRST READ ## Think Through the Text

Have students use text evidence and draw inferences to answer questions.

p. 10 • *What kind of relationship did Emily have with her sister Susan?* Emily resented Susan. **Why?** *Susan was healthy, beautiful, quick, and confident, while Emily was none of those things. She broke Emily's things and stole Emily's riddles, gaining applause for herself.* ▬ RL 3

p. 11 • *As Emily was growing up, how did she help her mother at home? Emily helped by doing housework, shopping, and minding her siblings.* ▬ RL 3

pp. 12–13 • *How did Emily discover her talent for comedy? She was entertaining her mother at home, and her mother encouraged her to perform at an amateur talent show, which she won.* ▬ RL 1

SECOND READ ## Analyze the Text

• Review page 10. Ask: *What is a major theme of this section?* limitations and regret *What examples from the text support your answers? On page 11, the narrator describes the way in which the daily routine imposed itself upon her and Emily. On page 12, the narrator describes the way in which Emily's talent imprisons her in another kind of social role. On page 13, she recalls Emily's certainty that her future is limited by the invention of the atom bomb.* ▬ RL 2

Independent/Self-Selected Reading

Have students reread "I Stand Here Ironing" independently to practice analyzing the text on their own, or have them practice the skills using other stories, such as:

• "The Yellow Wallpaper" by Charlotte Perkins Gilman

• "The Awakening," in *The Awakening and Selected Short Stories* by Kate Chopin ▬ RL 10

Performance Task

WRITE & PRESENT

1. Have small groups discuss the theme of regret as it applies to the story's setting. ▬ RL 2, SL 1a

2. Have students research and write an essay about Depression-era life for the working poor. How does historical fact mirror the lives of the characters in this story? What regrets do historical figures report? ▬ W 2

3. Have students share their essays in groups of three and offer suggestions for revising and editing. Students edit their writing based on these suggestions. ▬ W 5

4. Have students present their final writing to their classmates. Ask individual students to respond to the themes and ideas from each student's writing. ▬ SL 4

See Copying Masters, pp. 212–215.

STUDENT CHECKLIST

Writing

☑ Identify at least one theme from the story.

☑ Relate this theme to the activity of ironing, using text evidence and quotes from the story.

☑ Use complete sentences and developed paragraphs to structure writing.

Speaking & Listening

☑ Read writing aloud with a clear, audible voice.

☑ Present ideas in a meaningful way.

OBJECTIVES

- Describe how characters become tragic figures
- Identify the themes of a story
- Analyze text using text evidence

Things Fall Apart
by Chinua Achebe

Things Fall Apart is broken into three instructional segments.

SEGMENTS

SEGMENT 1. . . . . . . .pp. 3–125
SEGMENT 2. . . . . .pp. 129–167
SEGMENT 3. . . . . .pp. 171–209

Options for Reading

Independent Students read the book independently or with a partner and then answer questions posed by the teacher.

Supported Students read a segment and answer questions with teacher support.

SUMMARY Okonkwo, a tragic figure in an African tribal clan, experiences conflicts within his own tribe as well as cultural clashes with the White British missionary and colonial powers.

ABOUT THE AUTHOR **Chinua Achebe** was born in 1930 in Nigeria, which had been subject to colonization in the late 1800s and early 1900s. Achebe presents literary and political situations with a unique voice that speaks to the common and ongoing human condition of cultural misunderstandings and conflicts.

Discuss Genre and Set Purpose

FICTION Discuss literary styles and prepare students for the unique style of an African author who writes in English but includes the rhythms and characteristics of African languages plus the use of proverbs as figurative musical notes in a sad but jarring piece of modern music.

SET PURPOSE Help students set a purpose for reading, such as to find out what happens in the story.

Common Core Connection

RL 1 cite textual evidence to support analysis of what the text says explicitly as well as inferences drawn; **RL 2** determine a theme or central idea of a text/analyze its development/provide summary; **RL 3** analyze how characters develop/interact with others/advance the plot

TEXT COMPLEXITY RUBRIC

Overall Text Complexity		*Things Fall Apart* FICTION
		COMPLEX
Quantitative Measure	Lexile	890L
Qualitative Measures	Text Structure	some unconventional story elements, use of flashback
	Language Conventionality and Clarity	more complex sentence structure and descriptions
	Knowledge Demands	somewhat unfamiliar experience and situation, increased amount of cultural knowledge useful
	Purpose/Levels of Meaning	multiple levels of meaning

SEGMENT 1 pp. 3–125

Academic Vocabulary

Read each word with students and discuss its meaning.

improvident (p. 4) • irresponsible

kites (p. 5) • birds

proverb (p. 7) • wise saying

oracle (p. 16) • prophesy; vision

abomination (p. 18) • disgusting disgrace

suitor (p. 65) • admirer

ELL **ENGLISH LANGUAGE LEARNERS**

Use Graphic Organizer

Guide students to create a T-chart and use it to generate adjectives comparing Okonkwo and Unoka. Provide sentence frames to help students state comparisons:

Okonkwo is _____. ambitious but Unoka is _____. lazy

FIRST READ ## Think Through the Text

Have students use text evidence and draw inferences to answer questions.

pp. 3–7 • *Why does Okonkwo despise his father, Unoka?* Okonkwo is afraid that he might have some of his father's weaknesses. *What drives Okonkwo to such extreme actions?* He wants to be the village leader. *What are Okonkwo's main characteristics?* strength, pride, bad temper, arrogance RL 1

pp. 26 • *What conflicts does Okonkwo have with members of his tribe?* He called a fellow tribe member a woman and caused people to take sides. RL 3

pp. 57–61 • *How does Okonkwo's pride get him banished from this tribe?* He beat his wife during Peace Week. He killed the Mbaino boy, Ikemefuna, when warned by a wise man not to; his desire to look strong was more important than his love for the boy. RL 3

pp. 124–125 • *How does Okonkwo's combative nature cause trouble?* He takes a gun to a funeral and accidentally shoots the son of the dead man. RL 3

RESPOND TO SEGMENT 1

Classroom Collaboration

Have small groups create a summary of the main plot events in this segment and discuss why the chapters are so detailed.

SECOND READ ## Analyze the Text

• Review pages 95–109. Ask: *Why does the author take time to tell the fable of how the tortoise got its shell?* The fable is about pride, one of Okonkwo's tragic flaws; it also builds suspense by delaying the outcome of the story. RL 2

• Ask: *What do you think is the theme of this segment?* Sample answer: Igbo life has a long cultural history. *What examples from the text support your idea?* The rich customs, traditions, and belief systems are all described. RL 2

Domain Specific Vocabulary

ochu (p. 129) • a murderer

chi (p. 131) • personal god

umuada (p. 132) • girls' gathering

iron horse (p.139) • bicycle

isa-ifi (p. 131) • ceremony

efulefu (p. 154) • undesirable one

 ENGLISH LANGUAGE LEARNERS

Use Comprehensible Input

Ensure students understand the plot events and the theme by asking questions such as: *Why does Okonkwo struggle so hard?* and *Why will Okonkwo never get what he wants?*

RESPOND TO SEGMENT 2

 Classroom Collaboration

Have small groups work together to summarize what they have read. Have them ask questions about what they don't understand.

 Common Core Connection

RL 1 cite textual evidence to support analysis of what the text says explicitly as well as inferences drawn; **RL 2** determine a theme or central idea of a text/analyze its development/ provide summary; **RL 3** analyze how characters develop/interact with others/advance the plot; **RL 6** analyze a point of view or experience reflected in literature outside the United States; **RL 10** read and comprehend literature; **W 2** write informative/explanatory texts **W 5** develop and strengthen writing by planning, revising, editing, rewriting, or trying a new approach; **SL 4** present information, findings, and supporting evidence clearly, concisely, and logically

Academic Vocabulary

Read each word with students and discuss its meaning.

scorched (p. 130) • burned

destiny (p. 131) • fate

despair (p. 131) • hopelessness

exile (p. 133) • banishment

missionary (p. 143) • disciple, messenger

FIRST READ ## Think Through the Text

Have students use text evidence and draw inferences to answer questions.

pp. 130–135 • *What does Okonkwo learn from his exile? He learns that the mother figure is one of protector, refuge, and comfort. He learns that his role in exile is to find his soft side and protect his wives and children.* ◗RL 3

pp. 136–147 • *Why does Obierika come to visit Okonkwo? Obierika comes to give him some comfort and to warn him (and the reader) of the arrival of the white missionaries, who have wiped out the Abame village.* ◗RL 3

pp. 151–153 • *What does Nwoye do when Okonkwo hits him with a stick? He leaves the hut and tells the white missionary he wants to go to Umuofia to learn to read and write.* **How does Okonkwo respond to this news?** *He frets that he has been cursed with an unmanly son. He compares himself to a fire and his son to the ashes.* ◗RL 1

SECOND READ ## Analyze the Text

- Review pages 162–167. Ask: *What are the main reasons Okonkwo gives such a large feast? He wants to thank his relatives for their generosity during his exile. He also wants to show the younger generation the importance of kinship. He fears the white man's religion will separate more families, as it did to his own family.* ◗RL 1

- Review pages 129–167. Ask: *What is the theme of this segment? Exile is a consequence of disobeying the law.* ◗RL 2

- Review pages 129–167. *Why is this segment so short compared with the first segment? Sample answer: Seven years is nothing compared to the length of time that the Igbo culture had lived and thrived in Africa.* ◗RL 6

Academic Vocabulary

Read each word with students and discuss its meaning.

high-handed (p. 174) • overbearing

dispensation (p. 178) • relaxation of the rules

zeal (p. 178) • passion, eagerness

FIRST READ **Think Through the Text**

Have students use text evidence and draw inferences to answer questions.

pp. 182–183 • *How does Okonkwo feel about his return to his village?* *He is disappointed because he is not especially noticed. He is also concerned about the changes he sees, as he feels his clan falling apart because of the changes brought by the white men.* **RL 1**

pp. 198–205 • *How does Okonkwo respond to the church and the District Commissioner?* *He only thinks about obliterating them through war; he still believes that his physical courage is enough to solve the problem.* *Why doesn't the Umuofia tribe rise up against the colonizers?* *They know it is hopeless.* **RL 3**

SECOND READ **Analyze the Text**

• Review pages 206–209. Ask: *Why does the author have Okonkwo kill himself when tribal rules forbid his clansmen to touch his body or bury it?* *Sample answer: Okonkwo chooses to hang himself rather than be captured, to symbolize the death of the Umuofia culture.* **RL 3**

• Review pages 171–209. Ask: *What is the theme of this segment?* *the effects of domination by one culture over another; the destruction of the Umuofia culture by the British colonization traditions* **RL 3**

• Ask: *What does the Nigerian author think about traditions? Support your ideas with examples from the text.* *Sample answers: The author shows the impact of cultural traditions through the speech and actions of the characters. Traditions can be positive and negative. Igbo negotiation traditions can avoid war. Traditions of colonizing can destroy cultures.* **RL 6**

Independent/Self-Selected Reading

Have students reread *Things Fall Apart* independently to practice analyzing the text on their own, or have them practice the skills using another book, such as:

• *Kaffir Boy: An Autobiography* by Mark Mathabane

• *The Power of One* by Bryce Courtenay **RL 10**

WRITE & PRESENT

1. Have small groups refer to the text to discuss the ways the author presents and elaborates on the main themes of the novel. **RL 2**

2. Have students select one theme they discussed and write a short essay explaining how the author presents and elaborates on the theme. Encourage students to cite text evidence to defend their ideas. **W 2**

3. Have students share their work with partners and offer suggestions for revising and editing. Students edit their writing based on these suggestions. **W 5**

4. Have students present their final writing to their classmates. Ask students to respond to the themes and ideas from each student's writing. **SL 4**

See Copying Masters, pp. 212–215.

STUDENT CHECKLIST

Writing

☑ Identify at least one theme from the novel.

☑ Explain how the author presents and elaborates on the theme.

☑ Use complete sentences and developed paragraphs to structure writing.

Speaking & Listening

☑ Read writing aloud with a clear, audible voice.

☑ Present ideas in a meaningful way.

OBJECTIVES

- Describe how characters respond to major events
- Identify the theme of a story
- Interpret symbols and figurative language in fiction
- Analyze text using text evidence

To Kill a Mockingbird

by Harper Lee

To Kill a Mockingbird is broken into three instructional segments.

SEGMENTS

SEGMENT 1........pp. 1–149
SEGMENT 2......pp. 151–266
SEGMENT 3......pp. 267–376

Options for Reading

Independent Students read the book independently or with a partner and then answer questions posed by the teacher.

Supported Students read a segment and answer questions with teacher support.

SUMMARY Scout Finch and her brother Jem spend their childhood playing games and making up stories about their reclusive neighbor Boo Radley. When their lawyer father defends an African-American man unjustly accused of rape, the children learn about racism from the actions of the townspeople. After being unexpectedly helped by Boo, however, Scout begins to see the good as well as the bad in everyone.

ABOUT THE AUTHOR Harper Lee grew up in a small Alabama town, surrounded by people similar to the characters who populate her only novel. Though she worked as a writer before the publication of *To Kill a Mockingbird,* she retired from public view after it became popular, leaving her work, which won the Pulitzer Prize in 1961, to speak for itself.

Discuss Genre and Set Purpose

FICTION Remind students that a work of fiction includes characters, a setting, and events. Discuss how parts of this novel might be based upon the author's own experiences, but also how the story itself is made up.

SET PURPOSE Help students set a purpose for reading, such as to find out how Scout's feelings about the people in her life change over time.

COMMON CORE Common Core Connection

RL 1 cite textual evidence to support analysis of what the text says explicitly as well as inferences drawn; **RL 2** determine a theme or central idea of a text and analyze its development; **RL 3** analyze how characters develop and interact with others; **RL 4** determine the meaning of words and phrases, including figurative and connotative meanings

TEXT COMPLEXITY RUBRIC

Overall Text Complexity		To Kill a Mockingbird FICTION COMPLEX
Quantitative Measure	Lexile	870L
Qualitative Measures	Text Structure	somewhat complex story concepts
	Language Conventionality and Clarity	increased figurative language and unfamiliar words
	Knowledge Demands	fairly complex theme
	Purpose/Levels of Meaning	multiple levels of meaning

Academic Vocabulary

Read each word with students and discuss its meaning.

malevolent (p. 10) • evil

intimidation (p. 14) • the act of frightening someone to control them

condescension (p. 36) • the act of treating someone as inferior

defend (p. 99) • to represent in a court of law

compassion (p. 139) • sympathy for someone else

ELL **ENGLISH LANGUAGE LEARNERS**

Use Sentence Frames

Guide students to generate adjectives that could describe Scout, Atticus, and the other characters. Then have students orally complete sentence frames such as the following:

Atticus is _____. *caring*
Scout is _____. *spirited*
Jem is _____. *imaginative*

FIRST READ **Think Through the Text**

Have students use text evidence and draw inferences to answer questions.

pp. 10–19 • *Who is Boo Radley?* He is a neighbor who never comes out of his house. *What are some things Jem imagines about Boo?* He thinks Boo is kept chained up, looks like a monster, and eats raw animals. RL 3

pp. 99–102 • *What does Atticus think about defending Tom Robinson?* He does not expect to win, but he thinks he must try to help Tom no matter what other people think. RL 3

p. 119 • *Why does Miss Maudie agree that it is a sin to kill a mockingbird?* Mockingbirds do not do anything to hurt anyone; they just sing. RL 1

pp. 147–149 • *How do you know from the text what Atticus considers to be true bravery?* Using Mrs. Dubose as an example, Atticus says on page 149 that true courage is when you know you're licked before you begin but you begin anyway and see it through. RL 1

RESPOND TO SEGMENT 1

Classroom Collaboration

Have partners create a summary of the plot events in this segment. Then have students predict what might happen next in the novel.

SECOND READ **Analyze the Text**

• Review pages 39–40. Ask: *What does Atticus mean by suggesting that Scout climb into someone else's skin and walk around in it?* Atticus is saying that Scout can get along better with other people by imagining what it would be like to be them. *When is a time when Scout tries to do this during this segment?* She tries to understand Jem's behavior after going to the Radley Place late at night by imagining how she would feel doing the same thing. RL 4

• Review pages 77–84 with students. Then ask: *Why does Jem cry at the end of this chapter?* Sample answer: He has figured out that Boo Radley was the one leaving them presents, and it makes him sad that Nathan is stopping Boo from trying to be their friend. RL 3

• Ask: *What do you think is a major theme of this segment?* bravery *What examples from the text support your ideas?* Scout obeys her father and lets herself be called a coward for refusing to fight. Atticus stresses to Jem how brave Mrs. Dubose was so that Jem won't use the memory of Atticus shooting the dog as his model for bravery. RL 2

Domain Specific Vocabulary

trial (p. 194) • court meeting to decide if someone is innocent or guilty of a crime

jury (p. 214) • group of people who decide a court case

 ENGLISH LANGUAGE LEARNERS

Use Comprehensible Input

Ensure students understand the plot events and the theme by asking questions such as *Of what is Tom Robinson accused?* and *Why do some people have a problem with Atticus defending Tom?*

 RESPOND TO SEGMENT 2

Classroom Collaboration

Have small groups work together to summarize what they have read. Have them ask questions about what they don't understand.

 Common Core Connection

RL 1 cite textual evidence to support analysis of what the text says explicitly as well as inferences drawn; **RL 2** determine a theme or central idea of a text and analyze its development; **RL 3** analyze how characters develop and interact with others; **RL 10** read and comprehend literature; **WS 2** write informative/explanatory texts; **WS 5** develop and strengthen writing by planning, revising, editing, rewriting, or trying a new approach; **SL 4** present information, findings, and supporting evidence clearly, concisely, and logically

Academic Vocabulary

Read each word with students and discuss its meaning.

values (p. 153) • beliefs and morals by which a person lives

mob (p. 210) • group of aggressive people

testify (p. 213) • give information in court

appoint (p. 218) • pick for an important position

humiliation (p. 236) • embarrassment

FIRST READ ## Think Through the Text

Have students use text evidence and draw inferences to answer questions.

pp. 185–189 • *How does Jem break the code of childhood?* *When Dill turns up, instead of continuing to hide him, Jem goes to tell Atticus so they can let Dill's mother know that he is okay.* **RL 3**

p. 218 • *What confuses Scout about the town's attitude toward Atticus for defending Tom?* *Atticus was appointed to defend Tom, but the people are mad at him for trying to give Tom a fair trial.* **RL 3**

pp. 222–249 • *How do you know from the text that Tom did not attack Mayella?* *On pages 224–225, Mr. Tate says the right side of her face was bruised. On pages 248–249, Scout notices that Tom's left hand is crippled. Tom could not have hit the right side of her face.* **RL 1**

SECOND READ ## Analyze the Text

• Review pages 193–207 with students. Ask: *Why does the group of people come to the jail?* *They have come to hurt Tom Robinson, who is inside the jail.* **Why do they leave?** *Scout speaking politely to Mr. Cunningham makes him ashamed of his actions.* **RL 3**

• Have students revisit pages 208–211. Ask: *What does Atticus mean when he says that a mob is always made up of people?* *Even though the mob was behaving like a group of animals, the people in the mob had goodness in them that made them human and stopped them before they hurt Tom or Atticus.* **RL 3**

• Ask: *What is a major theme of this segment?* *compassion* *What examples from the text support your ideas?* *On pages 201–206, Atticus puts himself in harm's way to protect Tom Robinson. On page 206, Mr. Cunningham calls off the mob when he sees how wrong their actions are. On pages 206–207, Mr. Underwood protects Atticus and therefore helps Tom even though (as the children learn on page 209) he doesn't like Negroes.* **RL 2**

Academic Vocabulary

Read each word with students and discuss its meaning.

evidence (p. 270) • proof

pity (p. 271) • feel sadness and sympathy for

cynical (p. 273) • assumption that other people are selfish

despise (p. 304) • hate

grudge (p. 335) • feeling of anger toward someone else

FIRST READ ## Think Through the Text

Have students use text evidence and draw inferences to answer questions.

pp. 314–318 • *What happens to Tom Robinson?* *After losing the trial, he tries to escape during an exercise period and is shot.* ◼RL 1

pp. 347–370 • *What does Atticus think happened when Bob Ewell attacked Jem and Scout?* *Jem stabbed Mr. Ewell.* **Why does Atticus think Mr. Tate is claiming that Bob Ewell fell on his knife?** *He thinks Mr. Tate is trying to protect Jem from being tried for murder.* **How do you know?** *Atticus says on page 366 that he wants to clear the air and he does not want anyone saying that Atticus paid to get Jem out of trouble.* **What really happened?** *Boo stabbed Mr. Ewell.* **How do you know?** *Atticus thanks Boo for his children on page 370.* ◼RL 1

SECOND READ ## Analyze the Text

• Remind students of the previous mention of mockingbirds in the novel. Then ask: *What does Scout mean when she says that Mr. Tate is right?* *He is right to protect Boo by saying Mr. Ewell fell on his knife.* **What does she compare to shooting a mockingbird?** *letting Boo be arrested for the crime of stabbing Mr. Ewell* **Why?** *Sample answer: Like a mockingbird, Boo does not mean anyone any harm.* ◼RL 2

• Ask: *What do you think is the theme of the whole book? Why?* *Sample answer: Empathy—Scout learns from her father to put herself in the shoes of other people to better understand them and the things that they do.* ◼RL 2

Independent/Self-Selected Reading

Have students reread *To Kill a Mockingbird* independently to practice analyzing the text on their own, or have them practice the skills using another book, such as:

• *Roll of Thunder, Hear My Cry* by Mildred D. Taylor

• *A Tree Grows in Brooklyn* by Betty Smith ◼RL 10

Performance Task

WRITE & PRESENT

1. Have students think about and discuss the main themes of the entire novel. ◼RL 2

2. Have each student write a short essay explaining how any of these themes relates to the title of the novel and the symbol of the mockingbird. Encourage students to cite text evidence to defend their ideas. ◼WS 2

3. Have students share their work with partners and offer suggestions for revising and editing. Students edit their writing based on these suggestions. ◼WS 5

4. Have students present their final writing to their classmates. Ask students to respond to the themes and ideas from each student's writing. ◼SL 4

See Copying Masters, pp. 110–114.

STUDENT CHECKLIST

Writing

☑ Identify at least one theme from the novel.

☑ Relate this theme to the symbol of the mockingbird, using text evidence and quotes from the novel.

☑ Use complete sentences and developed paragraphs to structure writing.

Speaking & Listening

☑ Read writing aloud with a clear, audible voice.

☑ Present all ideas in a meaningful way.

OBJECTIVES

- Describe how characters develop over the course of a story
- Identify the theme of a story
- Analyze word choices and structure in a story
- Analyze text using text evidence

The Killer Angels is broken into three instructional segments.

Options for Reading

Independent Students read the book independently or with a partner and then answer questions posed by the teacher.

Supported Students read a segment and answer questions with teacher support.

Common Core Connection

RL 1 cite textual evidence to support analysis of what the text says explicitly as well as inferences drawn; **RL 2** determine a theme or central idea of a text and analyze its development; **RL 3** analyze how characters develop, interact with others, and advance the plot; **RL 5** analyze how author's choices create mystery, tension, or surprise

The Killer Angels
by Michael Shaara

SUMMARY A work of historical fiction, this book recounts the Battle of Gettysburg in 1863, which was the decisive engagement of the American Civil War that sealed the fate of the Confederacy. It is told through the eyes of key participants in the battle to provide both the factual details of the conflict as well as some of the reasons behind the Civil War and the emotional elements of warfare.

ABOUT THE AUTHOR Michael Shaara (1929–1988) wrote science fiction, sports stories, and historical fiction—most famously, *The Killer Angels,* for which he was awarded the Pulitzer Prize in 1975. He sold short stories to magazines throughout the 1950s and taught literature at Florida State University.

Discuss Genre and Set Purpose

FICTION Point out that *The Killer Angels* is a historical novel about a real battle in the American Civil War. Discuss how some text elements, such as the maps and the characters, are historically accurate, but the characters' thoughts and interactions are fictionalized.

SET PURPOSE Help students set a purpose for reading, such as to examine how the author creates a sense of tension and surprise surrounding an event whose outcome is already known to the reader.

TEXT COMPLEXITY RUBRIC

Overall Text Complexity		*The Killer Angels* FICTION
		COMPLEX
Quantitative Measure	Lexile	610L
Qualitative Measures	Text Structure	many shifts in point of view
	Language Conventionality and Clarity	some unfamiliar language
	Knowledge Demands	fairly complex theme, somewhat unfamiliar experience and situation
	Purpose/Levels of Meaning	multiple levels of meaning

Academic Vocabulary

Read each word with students and discuss its meaning.

polyglot (p. *xv*) • able to speak several languages

mutineers (p. 17) • people who have rebelled against authority

doctrine (p. 44) • something that is taught

ineradicable (p. 79) • impossible to completely remove

repulsed (p. 91) • driven back, repelled

FIRST READ ## Think Through the Text

Have students use text evidence and draw inferences to answer questions.

pp. 5–16 • *How do the Confederate officers react to the spy, Harrison?* They treat him with distrust and scorn for being a spy and for being an actor. *What does this suggest about their attitudes about war?* Sample answer: It suggests that they view war aristocratically, as if it is a matter of honor and a source of glory. ⬤RL 2

pp. 17–32 • *What does Chamberlain tell the mutinous troops that he is supposed to guard?* On pages 29–31, he tries to explain why he and the 300 men who remain of the thousand men who enlisted in his regiment are still fighting. ⬤RL 1

pp. 33–48 • *How do the maps on pages 35 and 39 establish the scene for the rest of the book?* The maps show where the battle will be fought. *Between the maps and Buford's thought about the terrain, what tension about the battle is created?* They foreshadow the outcome of the battle; that the victor will be the army that holds the high ground. ⬤RL 5

SECOND READ ## Analyze the Text

• Review pages 49–69 with students. Ask: *What words would describe the attitudes of the Confederate officers on the first day?* Sample answer: The general attitude is happy, confident, and excited, as if the battle was a sporting event. Some of the officers, like Longstreet, are concerned with practical matters; others are hoping for glory from combat. ⬤RL 3

• Ask: *What about the view of the Confederate officers is most different from Chamberlain's view?* Sample answer: On page 66, the officers argue that the war is not about slavery or freedom but states' rights, while Chamberlain thinks on page 27 and argues on page 30 that the war is about individual freedom. ⬤RL 2

• Have students review pages 73–77. Ask: *How does General Lee seem in this scene, and how does this build up tension?* Sample answer: He seems weary and in poor health, which puts the whole enterprise in doubt. *What examples from the text support your ideas?* On page 73, Lee feels a pain and on page 76 a weakness in his chest; on page 74, he feels a rush of frailty. ⬤RL 5

Domain Specific Vocabulary

guidons (p. 3) • small flags identifying military units

dragoon (p. 41) • heavily armed mounted soldier

 ENGLISH LANGUAGE LEARNERS

Use Visuals

Have student pairs work together to examine the maps that establish the scene for the battle. Have them answer questions such as:

The main Confederate forces will approach from the _____. north *The Union cavalry commander gets ready to fight because _____.* he hopes to defend the high ground and have an advantage in the battle

RESPOND TO SEGMENT 1

💬 **Classroom Collaboration**

Have small groups of students outline the events they know so far as they lead up to the battle and list the primary characters they have met so far on each side. Then have groups write predictions about what they think will happen to each of these main characters on the next day of the battle.

Domain Specific Vocabulary

flank (p. 143) • the right or left side of a group of soldiers in formation

caissons (p. 146) • wagons that carry artillery ammunition

 ENGLISH LANGUAGE LEARNERS

Use Peer Supported Learning

Have pairs of students review what occurred in the first part of the battle. Encourage them to concentrate on the tactics of specific individuals and their interactions with other characters, such as Buford's joy at seeing General Reynolds and his reaction when Reynolds died. Invite them to use their review of the first segment to help them understand the second.

RESPOND TO SEGMENT 2

 Classroom Collaboration

Have small groups work together to summarize the events of the battle. Have them ask questions about what they don't understand.

 Common Core Connection

RL 2 determine a theme or central idea of a text and analyze its development; **RL 3** analyze how characters develop, interact with others, and advance the plot; **RL 5** analyze how author's choices create mystery, tension, or surprise; **RL 10** read and comprehend literature; **W 2** write informative/ explanatory texts; **W 5** develop and strengthen writing by planning, revising, editing, rewriting, or trying a new approach; **SL 4** present information, findings, and supporting evidence clearly, concisely, and logically

Academic Vocabulary

Read each word with students and discuss its meaning.

abide (p. 127) • continue in a particular attitude

interpose (p. 139) • to get in the way or between things

glowered (p. 157) • stared with sudden dislike or anger

inscrutable (p. 168) • difficult to read or understand, mysterious

foraging (p. 175) • gathering food; searching for food

pontifically (p. 185) • pompously or pretentiously

FIRST READ ## Think Through the Text

Have students use text evidence and draw inferences to answer questions.

pp. 114–124 • *What is Chamberlain's hope at the end of another very long march?* On page 124, he hopes that General McClellan is leading the troops. *How do his men react?* They share his hope. ▬ RL 1

pp. 155–165 • *Which character has the greatest doubts about the battle?* Longstreet *Why does the author reveal those doubts in such detail?* Sample answer: The author is creating a contrast between the practical officers and those who believe warfare is glorious. ▬ RL 2

SECOND READ ## Analyze the Text

• Review pages 114–135 with students. Ask: *How does Chamberlain's hope to serve under McClellan compare to the way the Confederate troops feel about Lee?* Sample answer: It is the same impulse—both armies want to follow a leader they trust. ▬ RL 3

• Have students revisit pages 155–159. Ask: *Why do you think the author presents the views of an Englishman, Fremantle, at this point?* Sample answer: He uses the viewpoint of an outside observer to emphasize the aristocratic tendencies of the Confederate officers as well as a way to show that the death and destruction of battle were not being taken seriously by those aristocrats. ▬ RL 2

• Ask: *What incidents could be used in a report of this day in the battle to show its excitement and intensity?* Sample answers: On page 205, even Longstreet takes off his hat and cheers as soldiers from Mississippi attack the Union lines; the intensity of Chamberlain's fight on pages 216–228 is savage and compelling. ▬ RL 5

Academic Vocabulary

Read each word with students and discuss its meaning.

languid (p. 244) • lacking in energy

secession (p. 263) • withdrawal from the union of states

dapper (p. 301) • neat and trim

declaiming (p. 317) • reciting in a formal manner

FIRST READ ## Think Through the Text

Have students use text evidence and draw inferences to answer questions.

pp. 237–242 • *How does the author create a sense of foreboding at the beginning of this segment?* He opens with Longstreet visiting a wounded officer, showing that the failed attack was a blunder. **RL 5**

p. 245 • *What example on this page might be used in a report of the day's fight to show how things went wrong for the Southern troops?* Sample answer: Lee's physical weakness can represent the harm that had been done to his army. **RL 2**

pp. 294–300 • *How does Longstreet feel at the end of this chapter?* He is horrified and almost in despair. *What leads him to feel this way?* He has opposed the assault from the start, and on page 299, he begins to envision exactly what will happen to his men when they try to advance up the hill—he knows they will be slaughtered. **RL 3**

SECOND READ ## Analyze the Text

- Have students review pages 256–259. Ask: *How does Armistead's story reveal the tragedy of the Civil War?* Sample answer: His recollection of a dear friend against whom he must now fight poignantly illustrates the horror of countrymen fighting against one another. **RL 2**

- Have students reread the Afterword, pages 349–355. Ask: *How does the postwar information about the main characters intensify the tragedy of the Battle of Gettysburg and the Civil War?* Sample answer: The ordinariness of many of the outcomes is in stark contrast to the carnage of the battle; the bitterness of some of the characters underlines the waste of human life on the battlefield. **RL 2**

Independent/Self-Selected Reading

Have students reread *The Killer Angels* independently to practice analyzing the text on their own, or have them practice the skills using another book, such as:

- *Gods and Generals* by Jeff Shaara

- *Stars in Their Courses: The Gettysburg Campaign, June–July, 1863* by Shelby Foote **RL 10**

WRITE & PRESENT

1. Ask small groups to discuss and analyze how Michael Shaara creates a sense of tension and surprise regarding the outcome of events at the battle through pacing, ordering of events, and the overall structure of the novel. **RL 5**

2. Have individual students write essays that describe the means by which Michael Shaara creates tension and surprise in his book. Remind them to cite specific information from the text that supports their ideas. **W 2**

3. Have partners share their essays and edit their writing. **W 5**

4. Have students present their final writing to their classmates. **SL 4**

See Copying Masters, pp. 212–215.

STUDENT CHECKLIST

Writing

☑ Identify ways word choice and text structure can create tension and surprise in a novel.

☑ Cite text evidence and quotes from the novel to support ideas.

☑ Use complete sentences and developed paragraphs to structure writing.

Speaking & Listening

☑ Read aloud with a clear, audible voice.

☑ Present ideas in a meaningful way.

OBJECTIVES

- Describe how characters interact with one another
- Identify the theme of a story
- Interpret symbols and figurative language in fiction
- Analyze text using text evidence

The Joy Luck Club is broken into three instructional segments.

Options for Reading

Independent Students read the book independently or with a partner and then answer questions posed by the teacher.

Supported Students read a segment and answer questions with teacher support.

COMMON CORE   Common Core Connection

RL 1 cite textual evidence to support analysis of what the text says explicitly as well as inferences drawn; **RL 2** determine a theme or central idea of a text/analyze its development/provide summary; **RL 3** analyze how characters develop and interact with others; **RL 4** determine the meaning of words and phrases, including figurative and connotative meanings

The Joy Luck Club
by Amy Tan

SUMMARY Jing-mei "June" Woo joined the Joy Luck Club as a replacement for her mother, who had died. For forty years, four Chinese-born mothers had met to play mah jong, eat fine food, raise money, and share good stories even in difficult times. Sixteen interwoven stories describe the relationships between Chinese mothers and their American-born daughters trying to bridge the divide between old-world traditions and modern life.

ABOUT THE AUTHOR Amy Tan was born in 1952 in California. In 1987, Tan traveled with her mother to China to meet three half-sisters left behind when Tan's mother fled China just before the Communist takeover in 1949. Tan used her mother's story as the inspiration for her first book, *The Joy Luck Club*.

Discuss Genre and Set Purpose

FICTION Remind students that a work of fiction includes characters, setting, and events. Discuss with students how parts of this novel might be based upon the author's own experiences, but the story itself is made up.

SET PURPOSE Help students set a purpose for reading, such as to find out what the Joy Luck Club is and why it is important to the characters.

TEXT COMPLEXITY RUBRIC

Overall Text Complexity		The Joy Luck Club FICTION COMPLEX
Quantitative Measure	Lexile	930L
Qualitative Measures	Text Structure	somewhat complex story concepts
	Language Conventionality and Clarity	more complex sentence structure and descriptions
	Knowledge Demands	some cultural knowledge useful
	Purpose/Levels of Meaning	multiple levels of meaning

SEGMENT 1 pp. 17–83

Academic Vocabulary

Read each word with students and discuss its meaning.

meager (p. 23) • having little

consulate (p. 30) • the residence of a foreign government official

ritual (p. 32) • a series of actions followed regularly

dialect (p. 34) • the regional variety of a language

dowry (p. 44) • property from a bride's family given to the groom at marriage

Domain Specific Vocabulary

mah jong (p. 19) • a Chinese game played with tiles decorated with designs

cerebral (p. 19) • related to the brain and to knowing, to intelligence

FIRST READ ## Think Through the Text

Have students use text evidence and draw inferences to answer questions.

pp. 20–25 • *What is the Joy Luck Club? It is a gathering of four women to play mah jong. Why is it so important to the women? When they have their Joy Luck Club meetings, they remember good times and express hopes for the future.* RL 1

pp. 39–40 • *What do the "aunties" ask Jing-mei to do? The aunties want Jing-mei to go to China, find her twin half-sisters, and tell them about the mother they never knew.* RL 3

pp. 40–41 • *What does Jing-mei come to realize is the aunties' real fear? On page 40, Jing-mei realizes the aunties fear that their own daughters are also unaware of who their mothers are and don't appreciate the culture, hopes, and dreams of their mothers.* RL 1

pp. 67, 83 • *What is the wish Ying-ying St. Clair reveals on page 83? She wishes to be found. How does this wish relate to what Ying-ying says on page 67 about being unknown by her daughter? She wishes her daughter to see her and know her.* RL 1

SECOND READ ## Analyze the Text

• Review pages 46–47. Ask: *In what two ways did An-mei Hsu's wound heal? Once the burn scar healed, it didn't hurt so much. In the same way, An-mei didn't remember her mother and the pain it caused when she left.* RL 4

• Ask: *What is the major theme of this segment? relationships between mothers and daughters What examples from the text support your ideas? Sample answers: On pages 39–41, Jing-mei's mother hoped to reunite with the daughters she left in China, but now Jing-mei will take her place. On page 48, An-Mei Hsu visits her dying, estranged mother and makes a soup she hopes will cure her mother's illness. On pages 63–66, Lindo Jong describes how she managed to escape an unhappy arranged marriage, while keeping the promise she made to her mother about not shaming the family.* RL 1, RL 2

ELL ### ENGLISH LANGUAGE LEARNERS

Use Comprehensible Input

Ensure that students understand the changes in setting and point of view. On pp. 21, 42, 49, and 67, ask: *What is the setting, or time and place, here? Whose point of view are we reading?*

RESPOND TO SEGMENT 1

Classroom Collaboration

Have partners identify the mother and daughter pairs. Then partners write a summary of each mother's story.

ENGLISH LANGUAGE LEARNERS

Use Peer Supported Learning

Have partners orally summarize the mothers' and daughters' stories, connecting to the summaries they wrote in Section 1.

RESPOND TO SEGMENT 2

Classroom Collaboration

Have small groups work together to summarize what they have read. Have them ask questions about what they didn't understand.

 Common Core Connection

RL 1 cite textual evidence to support analysis of what the text says explicitly as well as inferences drawn; **RL 2** determine a theme or central idea of a text/analyze its development/ provide summary; **RL 3** analyze how characters develop/interact with others/advance the plot; **RL 4** determine the meaning of words and phrases, including figurative and connotative meanings/analyze impact of word choices; **RL 10** read and comprehend literature; **W 2** write informative/explanatory texts; **W 5** develop and strengthen writing by planning, revising, editing, rewriting, or trying a new approach; **SL 4** present information, findings, and supporting evidence clearly, concisely, and logically

---

Academic Vocabulary

Read each word with students and discuss its meaning.

circumstances (p. 89) • factors of life beyond one's control

adversary (p. 94) • enemy; opponent

benevolently (p. 95) • in a generous ways

concessions (p. 98) • what has been given up

malignant (p. 124) • harmful; threatening to life

FIRST READ **Think Through the Text**

Have students use text evidence and draw inferences to answer questions.

p. 96 • *How does Waverly Jong use the art of invisible strength?* Waverly wants to play in a chess tournament but knows her mother won't let her play with strangers. So instead of asking if she can play, Waverly says she doesn't want to play. ▬ RL 3

pp. 112; 126–131 • *Lena St. Clair and Rose Hsu Jordan describe their mothers' loss of a child. How does each mother react?* Lena's mother begins to fall apart piece by piece (page 112). When Rose's brother drowns, her mother seems determined not to believe he is dead. ▬ RL 1, RL 3

pp. 173–175 • *Why was Waverly Jong worried about her mother meeting Rich Fields?* She thought her mother would criticize him, giving Waverly doubts about him, which happened with her first husband. ▬ RL 3

SECOND READ **Analyze the Text**

• Review Waverly Jong's argument with her mother on page 99 and Jing-mei Woo's determination to put a stop to her mother's foolish pride on page 138. Ask: *Why were the daughters upset about their mothers' bragging?* Waverly was embarrassed that her mother bragged about her; her mother also seemed to take the credit for something that Waverly learned on her own. Jing-mei felt her mother was trying to make her someone she was not. ▬ RL 3

• Review the image of a chessboard and Waverly's opponent on the bottom of page 100. Ask: *What was the significance of the chess game on page 101?* Waverly sees her mother as an opponent who is beating her, and she's trying to figure out a strategy to win. ▬ RL 4

• Ask: *What is the major theme of this segment?* relationships between mothers and daughters *What examples from the text support this?* On page 116, Rose thinks her mother will insist that she find a way to save her marriage. On page 142, Jing-mei says her mother has been disappointed in her failings many times. On pages 160–162, Lena is worried about what her mother thinks of sharing expenses with her husband. On page 167, Waverly thinks her mother will be critical of her fiancé. ▬ RL 1, RL 2

Academic Vocabulary

Read each word with students and discuss its meaning.

kowtowed (p. 236) • bowed down showing great respect

character (p. 254) • the qualities that make up a person

intention (p. 264) • the action one plans to use

FIRST READ ▶ ## Think Through the Text

Have students use text evidence and draw inferences to answer questions.

pp. 215, 241 • *What is the cultural conflict An-mei describes? An-mei says she was raised the Chinese way to desire nothing, swallow other people's misery, and eat her own bitterness. She taught her daughter the opposite, but is afraid her daughter turned out the same way.* **▬ RL 3**

p. 254 • Lindo Jong feels her daughter has learned about American circumstances but not Chinese character. Ask: *What does she mean? She thinks her daughter has not learned the Chinese character of obeying your parents, hiding your feelings to take advantage of hidden opportunities, and knowing your own worth and polishing it.* **▬ RL 1, RL 4**

SECOND READ ## Analyze the Text

• Remind students that the mothers are telling stories about their childhoods in China they have never before revealed. Ask: *Why are the mothers telling these stories now? The mothers feel that their daughters don't know them and are slipping from them. The mothers want to have their daughters understand them, and so the mothers tell their daughters about themselves through the stories of their past.* **▬ RL 3**

• Ask: *What do you think is the theme of the whole book? Why? Sample answer: Relationships between mothers and daughters—each of the daughters learn things about their mothers' past that they never knew before, which helps the daughters better understand their mothers and brings them closer.* **▬ RL 1, RL 2**

Independent/Self-Selected Reading

Have students reread *The Joy Luck Club* independently to practice analyzing the text on their own, or have them practice the skills using another book, such as:

• *The Kite Runner* by Khaled Hosseini

• *Life of Pi* by Yann Martel **▬ RL 10**

WRITE & PRESENT

1. Have partners think about and discuss the theme of relationships between mothers and daughters developed in the novel. **▬ RL 2**

2. Have students write an essay describing the development of the theme using a mother-daughter pair of their choosing. Remind students to cite text evidence from the novel in their essays. **▬ W 2**

3. Have partners share their work, offering suggestions for revising and editing. Students should edit their writing based on these suggestions. **▬ W 5**

4. Have students present their final writing to their classmates. Ask students to respond to the themes and ideas from each student's writing. **▬ SL 4**

See Copying Masters, pp. 212–215.

STUDENT CHECKLIST

Writing

☑ Identify the characters, describe each childhood, and show how their adult relationship developed.

☑ Relate the theme of the novel to each mother and daughter, using text evidence and quotes from the novel.

☑ Use a topic sentence and developed paragraphs to structure each description.

Speaking & Listening

☑ Read writing aloud with a clear, audible voice.

☑ Present ideas in a meaningful way.

▶ OBJECTIVES

- Describe how an author develops characters
- Summarize the experiences of people involved in a resistance movement in the Dominican Republic
- Analyze text using text evidence

In the Time of the Butterfiles is broken into three instructional segments.

Options for Reading

Independent Students read the book independently and then answer questions posed by the teacher.

Supported Students read the sections aloud as a class and answer questions with teacher support.

COMMON CORE **Common Core Connection**

RL 1 cite textual evidence to support analysis of what the text says explicitly as well as inferences drawn; **RL 3** analyze how characters develop and interact with others; **RL 6** analyze a point of view or experience reflected in literature outside the United States

In the Time of the Butterflies
by Julia Alvarez

SUMMARY The four Mirabal sisters were leaders in the resistance movement against the dictatorship of Rafael Trujillo in the Dominican Republic. Three of the sisters were killed in the movement. The book is a fictional account of their lives told from the perspective of the surviving sister, Dedé.

ABOUT THE AUTHOR Julia Alvarez lived in the Dominican Republic until she was about ten years old. Her family fled the country in 1960 and moved to New York City. They left the Dominican Republic because Julia's father was involved in the resistance movement. Alvarez went on to become a teacher, college professor, and writer.

Discuss Genre and Set Purpose

HISTORICAL FICTION Explain that historical fiction is a specific type of fiction. While the story itself is fictional, it is about real people who lived during a specific time period in history. Some of the characters and events are real, but other parts are fictional, or made up.

SET PURPOSE Help students set a purpose for reading, such as to find out what happened to each of the Mirabal sisters.

▲ TEXT COMPLEXITY RUBRIC

Overall Text Complexity		*In the Time of the Butterflies* HISTORICAL FICTION
		COMPLEX
Quantitative Measure	Lexile	910L
Qualitative Measures	Text Structure	use of flashback
	Language Conventionality and Clarity	increased figurative language and unfamiliar words
	Knowledge Demands	increased amount of cultural knowledge useful
	Purpose/Levels of Meaning	multiple levels of meaning

Academic Vocabulary

Read each word with students and discuss its meaning.

commemorations (p. 3) • ceremonies in memory of important events or people

posthumous (p. 3) • after someone's death

impertinent (p. 4) • rude, disrespectful

volition (p. 45) • free will or choice

swarthy (p. 48) • dark skinned

FIRST READ **Think Through the Text**

Have students use text evidence and draw inferences to answer questions.

pp. 3–10 • *Why is the woman coming to visit Dedé?* She wants to hear Dedé's story and the story of her family. *What does Dedé worry about before the woman arrives?* She thinks the woman will ask her questions that are too personal. RL 3

pp. 16–17 • *What is Sinita's big secret?* Trujillo and his men killed all of the men in her family. She knows the bad things Trujillo did to come to power. ⬤ RL 6

p. 32 • *Why does María Teresa leave some of her i's undotted?* She does not want to win the penmanship award again because she also wants to have friends, and she is afraid the other girls won't like her for winning so often. ⬤ RL 3

p. 48 • *How did Patria meet Pedrito González?* She was washing his feet in a church service during Holy Week. ⬤ RL 1

SECOND READ **Analyze the Text**

• Review pages 24–28. Ask: *Why does Sinita tell Minerva she wants to do the play at the palace?* She wants to show what life was like before the dictator came. *What is the real reason that Sinita wants to perform at the palace?* She plans to kill Trujillo. ⬤ RL 3, RL 6

• Review pages 30 31 with students. Then ask: *Why do you think the writer presents María Teresa's story through her diary?* Sample answer: This is a way to show what she is thinking. It helps to give a better picture of how she matures and grows up. ⬤ RL 3

• Ask: *What word or phrase would you use to describe each of the Mirabal sisters up to this point in the story?* Sample answers: Dedé: strong, regretful; Minerva: strong-willed, a born leader, determined; María Teresa: young, trusting; Patria: religious, emotional ⬤ RL 3

ELL **ENGLISH LANGUAGE LEARNERS**

Use Visuals

Create a chart showing the four Mirabal sisters. As you discuss the book, point to the name of the person you are discussing and then add notes about that character based on the discussion. Notes should be simple phrases or words to help students keep track of the characters as they are acquiring language.

RESPOND TO SEGMENT 1

Classroom Collaboration

Have partners discuss each of the four Mirabal sisters and summarize what they learned about each character. Have students ask each other questions to clarify what they do not understand, seeking your input as needed.

Domain Specific Vocabulary

Read each word with students and discuss its meaning.

police state (p. 75) • a government that does not allow any freedoms or protect civil rights

cell (p. 143) • a small group of people within a larger resistance movement

 ENGLISH LANGUAGE LEARNERS

Comprehensible Input

Have students who understand the text well act out the scene with Minerva and El Jefe at the dinner party. Help students describe what happened, teaching the word *lie* and its different forms *(lied to, she lied)*.

RESPOND TO SEGMENT 2

Classroom Collaboration

Have small groups work together to summarize what they have read. Have them ask questions about what they don't understand.

 Common Core Connection

RL 1 cite textual evidence to support analysis of what the text says explicitly as well as inferences drawn; **RL 3** analyze how characters develop and interact with others; **RL 5** analyze how author's choices create mystery, tension, or surprise; **RL 6** analyze a point of view or experience reflected in literature outside the United States; **W 1** write arguments to support claims; **W 5** develop and strengthen writing by planning, revising, editing, rewriting, or trying a new approach; **SL 1** initiate/participate in a range of collaborative discussions

Academic Vocabulary

Read each word with students and discuss its meaning.

sanctioned (p. 63) • said or indicated that something was acceptable

mandatory (p. 64) • required

vehemence (p. 100) • hatred, disgust

admonishes (p. 109) • tells someone they have done wrong

gallant (p. 123) • a brave or noble person

FIRST READ ## Think Through the Text

Have students use text evidence and draw inferences to answer questions.

pp. 65–66 • *How does the visitor help show what is important in Dedé's story?* She asks questions that Dedé answers. On page 66, she asks why the friendship with Lío was important, and Dedé explains that he showed Minerva how to fight against Trujillo. **RL 5**

pp. 100–102 • *What does Minerva do at the dinner that creates a problem for her with El Jefe?* On page 99, she talks about Virgilio Morales. To protect herself, she says she does not know him. But then she forgets her purse (on page 101), which has letters from him to her. She also slaps the dictator before they leave. **RL 3**

p. 119 • *What is María Teresa's nightmare?* She is getting married and her wedding dress is in her father's coffin, which also contains his body. **RL 1**

SECOND READ ## Analyze the Text

• Have students review pages 82–83. Ask: *Why does Dedé burn the letter?* She is afraid that Minerva will say yes to Lío, and then she will get killed in the revolution. Direct students to page 87. *How does Minerva find out about the proposal after all?* She finds some letters addressed to her in her father's jacket pocket (page 87). **RL 3**

• Review pages 127–128. *How does the writer show that María Teresa is a typical girl?* She describes needing to send thank-you notes for things she didn't even like that much. She also describes deciding not to pursue two boys because of their mother. **RL 1**

• Review the description of what happens to Galindez on page 136. Ask: *What is the significance of the story of Galindez?* There was no way to escape from Trujillo. Even if they got out of the country, El Jefe could have them killed. **RL 6**

• Review pages 160–164. Ask: *How did the events at the retreat change Patria and the church?* They led Patria and the church to take an active role in the resistance. **RL 6**

SEGMENT 3 pp. 171–324

Academic Vocabulary

Read each word with students and discuss its meaning.

tenuous (p. 174) • weak

perforce (p. 182) • due to the events taking place

anguish (p. 194) • tremendous pain or heartache

empathetic (p. 205) • able to relate to someone else's feelings

desecrating (p. 207) • disrespecting a holy place

FIRST READ ## Think Through the Text

Have students use text evidence and draw inferences to answer questions.

pp. 180–183, 188–189 • *What did Dedé need to decide before she could join the resistance?* She needed to decide that she was going to leave her husband. *How do Minerva and Minalo show that they have different feelings about this decision?* Minalo encourages them to make up, but Minerva says that some people just don't belong together. **RL 3**

pp. 210–211 • *Why does Patria see Papá's other daughters as part of God's plan?* It is the other sisters who are able to send gifts to the girls in prison. *What is ironic about this?* When the women first learned of his other family, they were very angry and wanted nothing to do with them. But they had helped the women get an education, and now that education was helping them. **RL 1**

SECOND READ ## Analyze the Text

• Ask: *How did the different sisters feel about whether or not to accept the pardon? What does this suggest about their characters?* Minerva would not accept it on principle. María Teresa disagreed but followed Minerva's lead. It shows how much hold Minerva had over her own family. *What might this suggest about people involved in resistance movements?* The movements require people to do things that benefit the movement, even if it causes them great harm. **RL 3, RL 6**

• Ask: *Why do you think that Dedé continues to allow people to visit her home and ask her about the past?* It helps her to heal a little each time she tells the story. It is her way of being a part of what they did. She does not want to fully give up that part of her life. **RL 3**

Independent/Self-Selected Reading

Have students reread *In the Time of the Butterflies* independently to practice analyzing the text on their own, or have them practice the skills using another book, such as:

• *When I Was Puerto Rican* by Esmerelda Santiago

• *Other Voices, Other Vistas* by Barbara H. Solomon **RL 10**

WRITE & PRESENT

1. Have small groups discuss the characters and events of the book and relate them to the title of the book. **RL 2**

2. Ask students whether or not they think the title matches the story itself. Tell students to write an argument to support their view. Students should cite text evidence to defend their ideas. **W 1**

3. Have students share their work with partners and suggest revisions and edits. Students edit their writing based on these suggestions. **W 5**

4. Have students present their final writing to the class by giving an oral presentation. Ask students to respond to the ideas from each student's writing. **SL 1**

See Copying Masters, pp. 212–215.

STUDENT CHECKLIST

Writing

☑ Decide if the title of the book matches the events and ideas.

☑ Write an argument supporting the claims, using text evidence from the novel.

☑ Strengthen writing by revising it.

Speaking & Listening

☑ Read writing aloud with a clear, audible voice.

☑ Present ideas in a meaningful way.

OBJECTIVES

- Make inferences based on text evidence
- Describe characters' actions as they relate to the plot
- Understand major themes

The Book Thief

by Marcus Zusak

The Book Thief is broken into three instructional segments.

SEGMENTS

SEGMENT 1 . . . . pp. 1–170
SEGMENT 2 . . . . . pp. 171–350
SEGMENT 3 . . . . . pp. 351–550

Options for Reading

Independent Students read the book independently or with a partner and then answer questions posed by the teacher.

Supported Students read a segment and answer questions with teacher support.

SUMMARY Liesel is a German girl who is left with foster parents just before World War II. After her brother dies, Liesel steals a book, the first of a series of book thefts. Liesel learns to read, and her obsession with books grows as the war closes in and air raids begin. Hans, Liesel's stepfather, repays a debt by hiding Max, a Jewish man, in the basement. When Max is forced to leave and Hans is forced into the army, Liesel loses hope, but is encouraged to write a book about her life.

ABOUT THE AUTHOR Marcus Zusak was born in Australia to an Austrian father and a German mother, both of whom experienced World War II firsthand. Zusak has stated that *The Book Thief* was inspired by stories his parents told him as a child about wartime Munich and Vienna. *The Book Thief* is Zusak's fifth novel. It received a Printz Honor for literary excellence in young adult literature.

Discuss Genre and Set Purpose

FICTION Have students examine the book's format and note the stories and sketches. Discuss how this is a work of fiction because it includes characters, a setting, and events. Discuss how parts of this text might be based upon the author's own experiences, but that the story is made up.

SET PURPOSE Help students set a purpose for reading, such as to find out how Liesel survives living in Nazi Germany during World War II.

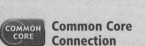

Common Core Connection

RL 1 cite textual evidence to support analysis of what the text says explicitly as well as inferences drawn; **RL 3** analyze how characters develop, interact with others, and advance the plot; **RL 10** read and comprehend literature

TEXT COMPLEXITY RUBRIC

Overall Text Complexity		*The Book Thief* FICTION COMPLEX
Quantitative Measure	Lexile	730L
Qualitative Measures	Text Structure	several shifts in chronology
	Language Conventionality and Clarity	more complex sentence structure
	Knowledge Demands	fairly complex theme
	Purpose/Levels of Meaning	multiple themes

Academic Vocabulary

Read each word with students and discuss its meaning.

illustrious (p. 29) • extremely distinguished and deservedly famous

hiatus (p. 30) • an unexpected gap

profanity (p. 32) • language that shows disrespect; abusive or vulgar language

prolific (p. 32) • present in large numbers

auspicious (p. 39) • promising well for the future

raucous (p. 41) • unpleasantly loud

Domain Specific Vocabulary

Communist (p. 31) • a member of the Communist political party, which believes in the idea of a classless society where wealth is owned by all members of society.

Mein Kampf (p. 125) • a book written by Adolf Hitler, the ruler of Germany during World War II

FIRST READ ## Think Through the Text

Have students use text evidence and draw inferences to answer questions.

pp. 19–39 • *Why does Liesel steal the first book? She takes the book from the burial ground as a reminder of her losses—of both her brother and her mother. What is ironic about her stealing this book? It is ironic because on page 39, it is revealed that Liesel has not yet learned how to read.* ⬤RL 1

pp. 83–122 • *Why does Liesel steal the second book? Liesel was upset at Hitler's birthday party book burning. She finally realized that the reason her mother left her in foster care was because she was a Communist. She understood that the Nazis hated and persecuted Communists and that she would never see her mother again. So when she saw that some of the books had not burned, she took another chance.* ⬤RL 3

SECOND READ ## Analyze the Text

• Have students look back on pages 133–134. *Why is Liesel surprised at the Mayor's house? Liesel is surprised because she knows that the Mayor's wife saw her steal the second book. She expects to be punished. Instead, the Mayor's wife, Ilsa, shows up with an armful of books and introduces Liesel to her library.* ⬤RL 10

• Review pages 138–141. *We are introduced to a new character. Who is Max? What is he doing and why? Why is he pleading with Hans Hubermann? Max is a Jew hiding in a basement in 1940 Nazi Germany. We know from history that it is very dangerous to be a Jew at this time in Germany. Max thinks that Hans can help him, but we do not know why. We will have to read further to find the connection between Max and Hans.* ⬤RL 3

ELL ## ENGLISH LANGUAGE LEARNERS

Use Sentence Frames

Guide students to generate adjectives that could describe Liesel, Hans, Rosa, and Rudy. Then have them orally complete sentence frames such as:

Liesel is _____. brave
Hans is _____. loving
Rosa is _____. loud
Rudy is _____. fast

RESPOND TO SEGMENT 1

 Classroom Collaboration

Have small groups work together to create a summary of what has happened to Liesel in this segment. Then have students predict what will happen to Max and how Hans might get involved with him.

Domain Specific Vocabulary

air-raid shelter
(p. 340) • a place to go (usually a basement) to take shelter from bombings

Auschwitz (p. 349) • a German concentration camp during World War II where millions of Jews were killed

Mauthausen
(p. 349) • another German concentration camp

 ENGLISH LANGUAGE LEARNERS

Use Visuals
Read aloud pages 224–236, "The Standover Man," point out the illustrations, and discuss the meaning with students.

 RESPOND TO SEGMENT 2

Classroom Collaboration

Have small groups work together to summarize what has happened to the main characters. Have students ask questions about what they don't understand.

 Common Core Connection

RL 2 determine a theme or central idea of a text; **RL 3** analyze how characters develop, interact with others, and advance the plot; **RL 10** read and comprehend literature; **W 3b** use narrative techniques to develop experiences, events, or characters; **W 5** develop and strengthen writing by planning, revising, editing, rewriting, or trying a new approach; **SL 1b** set rules for collegial discussion and decision-making, clear goals and deadlines, and individual roles; **SL 4** present information, findings, and supporting evidence clearly, concisely, and logically

Academic Vocabulary

Read each word with students and discuss its meaning.

appalled (p. 173) • shocked by something awful

malignant (p. 175) • harmful

ludicrous (p. 185) • absurdly ridiculous

morose (p. 198) • gloomy

caustic (p. 223) • sarcastic or biting

gratuitous (p. 246) • unjustifiable or unnecessary

FIRST READ ## Think Through the Text

Have students use text evidence and draw inferences to answer questions.

pp. 173–179 • *Why does Hans feel obligated to Max? How does Hans repay his obligation?* *Hans feels that Max's father saved his life during World War I. If Erik Vandenburg hadn't volunteered Hans for the writing assignment, he would have been killed with the rest of the men. Hans repays his friend Erik by taking in his son, Max, and hiding him in his basement.* **RL 3**

pp. 282–292 • *What is the third book Liesel steals?* *Liesel steals* The Whistler. *Why does she steal it?* *This is the book she was reading at the Mayor's house. It is the book the Mayor's wife offered her when she fired her mother's washing services. Liesel felt it was better to steal it than have it as a gift of pity.* *What does Rudy call Liesel at the end of the chapter?* *On page 292, Rudy calls Liesel a book thief.* **RL 3**

SECOND READ ## Analyze the Text

- Review pages 224–236 with students and note the illustrations. Ask: *What is the significance of* The Standover Man? *The Standover Man is the book Max writes and gives to Liesel for her birthday. It tells the story of Max's relationship with Liesel and reveals how close they have become.* *Who is the standover man?* *Liesel is the standover man, a source of comfort to a fellow lost soul.* **RL 3**

- Review this segment. Ask: *How does the author show the power of words in the lives of the main characters?* *Hans avoids death by writing letters. Hans helps to ease Liesel's grief by teaching her to read and by reading to her. Max writes Liesel a book that shows how they have helped each other grieve their losses. Liesel steals another book to read to Max to try to help him recover from his illness.* **RL 2**

- Read aloud the first sentence of the last paragraph on page 328. *How does this quote convey a major theme of the book?* *Sample answer: This is an example of how words can heal and shows the power of words.* **RL 2**

Read each word with students and discuss its meaning.

epitome (p. 360) • a typical example

immutable (p. 382) • unchanging or unchangeable

vindication (p. 402) • the act of justifying something

miscreants (p. 439) • evil doers

innocuous (p. 454) • harmless

FIRST READ ## Think Through the Text

Have students use text evidence and draw inferences to answer questions.

pp. 379–384 • *How did Liesel's words help others in the shelter? By reading to her neighbors in the shelter, Liesel calmed everyone down and distracted them.* ●RL 1

pp. 445–450 • *What does* The Word Shaker *say about the power of words? They can be used for both good and evil.* ●RL 2

pp. 497–499 • *How do words save Liesel again? Liesel is the only one to survive the bombing of Himmel Street because she was in the basement writing her book.* ●RL 1

SECOND READ ## Analyze the Text

• Review pages 445–450 with students. Then ask: *Why does Max write* The Word Shaker *for Liesel? Sample answers: He wrote it to show Liesel how powerful her words could be and how strong she is; to give Liesel comfort while he was gone; to show how important their friendship was; to give her hope that he would return.* ●RL 3

• Ask: *Why does the narrator, Death, save Liesel's book? Sample answer: Death was attracted to Liesel from the first time he met her when her brother died. As much as he tries to avoid her, he runs into her many other times. At the end of the book Death says that he is haunted by humans. He is haunted by Liesel. Liesel's life, as written in her book, shows the triumph of good over evil and the power of words to do good things.* ●RL 2

Independent/Self-Selected Reading

Have students reread *The Book Thief* independently to practice analyzing the text on their own, or have them practice the skills using another book, such as:

• *Milkweed* by Jerry Spinelli

• *The Boy in the Striped Pajamas* by John Boyne ●RL 10

WRITE & PRESENT

1. Have small groups analyze how the main characters develop to advance the plot. Ask students to think about how words and books play a role in each character's development. ●RL 2, RL 3

2. Individual students select a different main character and write about character development and the role of words for each. Encourage students to cite text evidence to support their analysis. ●W 3b, SL 1b

3. Small groups reconvene to share their work and suggest revisions. Students edit their writing based on these suggestions. ●W 5

4. Students present their final character analyses to classmates. ●SL 4

5. Individual students turn in their final drafts to the teacher. ●W 4

See Copying Masters, pp. 212–215

STUDENT CHECKLIST

Writing

☑ Write about one main character's development.

☑ Analyze how words/books influenced this character, using text evidence and quotes from the novel.

☑ Use complete sentences and developed paragraphs to structure writing.

Speaking & Listening

☑ Participate effectively in collaborative discussions.

☑ Speak clearly at an understandable pace.

OBJECTIVES

- Describe how characters respond to major events
- Identify the theme of a play
- Examine how the author's choices create mystery, tension, and surprise
- Analyze text using text evidence

Oedipus Rex is broken into three instructional segments.

Options for Reading

Independent Students read the play independently or with a partner and then answer questions posed by the teacher.

Supported Students read a segment and answer questions with teacher support.

Common Core Connection

RL 1 cite textual evidence to support analysis of what the text says explicitly as well as inferences drawn; **RL 3** analyze how characters interact with others and advance the plot; **RL 5** analyze how author's choices create mystery, tension, or surprise

Oedipus Rex
by Sophocles

SUMMARY *Oedipus Rex* is the original mystery story. A plague has descended on the ancient Greek city of Thebes, and the citizens have come to their king, Oedipus, to save them. Oedipus learns that in order to end the plague, the killer of Thebes's former king must be found and punished. This sets in motion a series of events destined to carry out a fate that has been waiting for Oedipus since before he was born.

ABOUT THE AUTHOR **Sophocles** was one of the three great tragedians from the golden age of Greece, along with Aeschylus and Euripides. He was born about 500 B.C.E. and lived to the age of 90. In that time, he wrote 123 plays, only seven of which have survived as complete texts.

Discuss Genre and Set Purpose

DRAMA Remind students that drama includes characters, a setting, and a plot that unfolds in a series of scenes. Explain to students that Greek audiences often knew the story of a play in advance, so their interest in a play depended on how the events played out.

SET PURPOSE Help students set a purpose for reading, such as to examine how Oedipus discovers information throughout the play and to decide whether or not Oedipus deserves his fate.

TEXT COMPLEXITY RUBRIC

Overall Text Complexity		*Oedipus Rex* DRAMA
		COMPLEX
Quantitative Measure	Lexile	N/A
Qualitative Measures	Text Structure	use of flashback
	Language Conventionality and Clarity	figurative, less accessible language
	Knowledge Demands	increased amount of cultural knowledge useful
	Purpose/Levels of Meaning	multiple levels of meaning

SEGMENT 1 pp. 3–26

Academic Vocabulary

Read each word with students and discuss its meaning.

sphinx (p. 5) • creature with a lion's body, a woman's head, and the claws and wings of an eagle

defilement (p. 7) • something that is impure or has been made morally foul

lustration (p. 13) • ritual purification

contagion (p. 17) • disease that can infect others

Domain Specific Vocabulary

parados (p. 10) • first song sung by the chorus in a Greek play, usually following the prologue

strophe (p. 10) • the first part of the ode in Greek tragedy

antistrophe (p. 11) • the second part of the ode

choragos (p. 15) • the leader of the chorus who sometimes speaks as a character

FIRST READ ## Think Through the Text

Have students use text evidence and draw inferences to answer questions.

pp. 6–8 • *What does the text say that Oedipus did to find the cause of the plague before the play started?* On page 6, he sent Creon to Delphi to ask Apollo for an answer. *What was Apollo's response?* Creon reports on page 8 that Apollo commands that the person who killed the previous king of Thebes must be killed or exiled. ◼ RL 1

pp. 13–14 • *What penalty does Oedipus lay upon the murderer of Laïos?* No one can speak to him, he can't join in any religious ceremony, and he will be driven from every house. ◼ RL 1

pp. 16–22 • *Why is Teiresias unwilling to tell Oedipus what he knows?* He knows Oedipus is guilty of killing Laïos. *Why is it ironic that Teiresias is blind?* He can't see but he knows the truth. *Why does Oedipus say that Teiresias accused him of killing Laïos?* Oedipus thinks Teiresias is conspiring with Creon to overthrow him. ◼ RL 3

SECOND READ ## Analyze the Text

• Review the segment with students. Say: *Summarize the information Oedipus learns.* Sample answer: He learns the cause of the plague; he learns that Laïos was murdered; he is told that he killed Laïos. ◼ RL 1

• Ask: *What do you discover about Oedipus's character in the first section? Support your ideas with examples from the text.* Oedipus is sympathetic: on page 5, he says he weeps for the city. He is stubborn: on pages 19–20, he won't believe what Teiresias tells him. He has a short temper: he gets angry with Teiresias and threatens him. ◼ RL 3

• Ask: *What is an example of one way Sophocles creates suspense, mystery, and tension in this segment? Cite text evidence.* Sample answer: On pages 22–23, Teiresias hints that it will be important to find out who Oedipus's parents are, says Oedipus does not know the things he has done wrong, and predicts a coming misfortune. ◼ RL 5

ELL ### ENGLISH LANGUAGE LEARNERS

Use Sentence Frames

Guide students to make a chart of the play's major characters and list their roles in the world of the play. Then have them complete descriptive sentences such as:

Oedipus is _____. King of Thebes

Creon is _____. his wife's brother

Teiresias is _____. a blind prophet

Have students continue to add characters to the list as they read the play.

RESPOND TO SEGMENT 1

 Classroom Collaboration

Have partners create a summary of the plot events in this segment. Then have students predict what might happen next in the play.

Oedipus Rex • **67**

Domain Specific Vocabulary

exodos (p. 67) • the final scene in a Greek play

 ENGLISH LANGUAGE LEARNERS

Use Visuals

Help students understand the plot by working with them to create a timeline listing the events described in the play in chronological order.

RESPOND TO SEGMENT 2

 Classroom Collaboration

Have students work in small groups to review the odes and explain how they relate to the action of the scenes.

 Common Core Connection

RL 1 cite textual evidence to support analysis of what the text says explicitly as well as inferences drawn; **RL 2** determine a theme or central idea of a text and analyze its development; **RL 3** analyze how characters interact with others and advance the plot; **RL 5** analyze how author's choices create tension or surprise; **RL 10** read and comprehend literature; **W 2** write explanatory texts; **W 5** develop and strengthen writing by planning, revising, editing, rewriting, or trying a new approach; **SL 4** present information, findings, and supporting evidence clearly, concisely, and logically

Academic Vocabulary

Read each word with students and discuss its meaning.

grave (p. 27) • serious and important

perquisites (p. 31) • benefits or privileges

goad (p. 43) • a pointed staff used for prodding and herding animals

malediction (p. 43) • curse

sepulchre (p. 49) • tomb

FIRST READ **Think Through the Text**

Have students use text evidence and draw inferences to answer questions.

pp. 38–40 • *Why does Iocaste tell Oedipus the story of the prophecy that Laïos would be killed by his son?* to tell him that prophecies don't always come true *What effect does it have on Oedipus?* It makes him think he may have killed Laïos. **RL 3**

pp. 42–43 • *Why did Oedipus leave Corinth?* The oracle told him he would kill his father and marry his mother. *Why is this oracle significant to the plot?* It is the same prediction that Laïos received. **RL 3**

pp. 51–57 • *Why is Oedipus happy to hear Polybos is dead?* He thinks Polybos was his father. Since he is dead, Oedipus can't kill him. *Why does Iocaste tell Oedipus to forget about the Shepherd?* She learns that Oedipus is her son. *Why does Oedipus think she wants him to forget the man?* He thinks she's ashamed of his real parents. **RL 3**

SECOND READ **Analyze the Text**

• Review pages 39–45. Ask: *Why does Oedipus think he killed Laïos?* The details of Laïos's death match the details of the death of the man Oedipus killed. **RL 1**

• Ask: *How does Iocaste come to realize that Oedipus is her son? Cite text evidence.* On page 38, Iocaste says that the oracle predicted Laïos would be killed by his son; on page 42, Oedipus repeats the same oracle. On page 53, the Messenger reveals that Polybos was not Oedipus's father. On page 38, Iocaste says that the king tied his son's ankles together and left him to die on a mountain. **RL 3**

• Ask: *How does Sophocles create suspense, mystery, and tension in this segment? Cite text evidence.* Sample answer: On page 39, Oedipus says a shadowy memory crossed his mind and chilled his heart while Iocaste was speaking. This tells the audience that this memory will be important and connected to the oracle. The vivid language helps the audience feel apprehensive. **RL 5**

Academic Vocabulary

Read each word with students and discuss its meaning.

wretched (p. 64) • extremely miserable and distressed

primal (p. 73) • original or very first

execrable (p. 74) • horrible and deserving to be denounced as evil

parricide (p. 76) • person who murders a parent

FIRST READ ## Think Through the Text

Have students use text evidence and draw inferences to answer questions.

pp. 59–63 • *How does the Shepherd show he is unwilling to tell what he knows about Oedipus?* He doesn't look at Oedipus; he says he doesn't know the Messenger; he tells the Messenger to be quiet. **RL 3**

pp. 67–69 • *What happens to Iocaste?* She hangs herself. *How does Oedipus blind himself?* with the brooches from her dress **RL 1**

pp. 72–73 • *Why does Oedipus blind himself?* He can't bear to see his children, knowing they're the result of incest; he doesn't want to see the faces of his parents in the afterlife. **RL 1**

pp. 76–80 • *Why doesn't Creon let Oedipus leave Thebes?* He wants to consult the gods first. *How does this relate to the previous action of the play?* The gods have foretold what would happen to Oedipus throughout the play. Creon thinks it is best to follow the counsel of the gods. **RL 1**

SECOND READ ## Analyze the Text

- Explain that tragic characters usually have a central flaw that is responsible for their fall. Ask: *What flaw is responsible for Oedipus's fall?* Sample answer: *His anger led him to kill Laïos; his pride makes him think he knows everything; he refuses to see the truth and attacks other people when they disagree with him.* **RL 3**

- Ask: *What are some themes in this play?* Sample answers: self-knowledge—Oedipus doesn't know who he is, and that leads him to commit horrible crimes; sight and blindness—Teiresias is blind but knows the truth, the truth leads Oedipus to blind himself. **RL 2**

Independent/Self-Selected Reading

Have students reread *Oedipus Rex* independently to practice analyzing the text on their own, or have them practice skills using another play, such as:

- *Antigone* by Sophocles

- *The Oresteia* by Aeschylus **RL 10**

Performance Task

WRITE & PRESENT

1. Have students explore how the truth of Oedipus's past is revealed throughout the play. **RL 3**

2. Have students write about how Sophocles constructed the plot to create mystery, tension, and surprise. Encourage students to cite text evidence to defend their ideas and interpretation. **W 2**

3. Have students share their work with partners and offer suggestions for revising and editing. Students edit their writing based on these suggestions. **W 5**

4. Have students present their final writing to their classmates. Ask students to respond to the ideas from each student's writing. **SL 4**

See Copying Masters, pp. 212–215.

STUDENT CHECKLIST

Writing

☑ Review the events of the play.

☑ Relate these events to the elements of mystery and tension, using text evidence and quotes from the play.

☑ Use complete sentences and developed paragraphs to structure writing.

Speaking & Listening

☑ Read writing aloud with a clear, audible voice.

☑ Present ideas in a meaningful way.

▶ OBJECTIVES

- Describe how characters respond to major events
- Identify the theme of a play
- Interpret symbols and figurative language in drama
- Analyze using text evidence

Macbeth **is broken into three instructional segments.**

SEGMENTS

SEGMENT 1 . . . . . . Acts I and II
SEGMENT 2 . . . . Acts III and IV
SEGMENT 3 . . . . Act V

Options for Reading

Independent Students read the play independently or with a partner and then answer questions posed by the teacher.

Supported Students read individual acts aloud with teacher support and answer questions.

Common Core Connection

RL 1 cite textual evidence to support analysis of what the text says explicitly as well as inferences drawn; **RL 2** determine a theme or central idea of a text/analyze its development/provide summary; **RL 3** analyze how characters develop and interact with others/advance the plot; **RL 4** determine the meanings of words and phrases, including figurative and connotative meanings; **RL 5** analyze how author's choices create tension or surprise

The Tragedy of Macbeth
by William Shakespeare

SUMMARY The *Tragedy of Macbeth* is the study of a man with a character defect so deep that he betrays and murders his king. From that unnatural act, he goes on to kill his countrymen, his friends, and their children, until he suffers a violent death at the hands of a Scot loyal to the crown. Ambitious and superstitious, Macbeth values power and acclaim above virtue, duty, friendship, and loyalty.

ABOUT THE AUTHOR **William Shakespeare** was England's master playwright during the late 1500s and early 1600s and is often characterized as the greatest of all English poets and playwrights. Like other plays of the time, his plays often contain references to omens, witchcraft, ghosts, and spirits.

Discuss Genre and Set Purpose

DRAMA Remind students that drama includes characters, a setting, and a plot with events that unfold in acts and scenes. Explain that this play includes historical elements but is not a historical reenactment. Shakespeare took poetic license to change events, settings, and characters and fulfill his own creative vision.

SET PURPOSE Help students set a purpose for reading, such as considering how character traits affect a character's actions.

TEXT COMPLEXITY RUBRIC

Overall Text Complexity		*The Tragedy of Macbeth* DRAMA COMPLEX
Quantitative Measure	Lexile	N/A
Qualitative Measures	Text Structure	many shifts in point of view
	Language Conventionality and Clarity	ambiguous language requiring inferences
	Knowledge Demands	complex, sophisticated theme
	Purpose/Levels of Meaning	multiple levels of meaning

Academic Vocabulary

Read each word with students and discuss its meaning.

hurlyburly (Act I, Scene 1) • commotion

broil (Act I, Scene 2) • battle

composition (Act I, Scene 2) • peace terms

corporal (Act I, Scene 3) • of the physical body

palpable (Act II, Scene 1) • feeling almost real enough to touch

knell (Act II, Scene 1) • the ring of a bell

filthy witness (Act II, Scene 2) • bloody evidence

FIRST READ ## Think Through the Text

Have students use text evidence and draw inferences to answer questions.

Act I, Scenes 1–7 • *How does Macbeth act on the battleground?* He fights courageously to defeat his king's enemies. *What could the witches represent?* temptation, evil, wicked thoughts, fate RL 1

Scenes 3–5 • *How do the witches interact with Macbeth and Banquo?* They tease Macbeth, saying he will be king and Banquo will be the father of kings. *To what theme do the deep desires of Macbeth apply?* ambition (Scene 4) ▬RL 1, RL 2, RL 3, RL 5

Scenes 6–7 • *How do you know from the text that Lady Macbeth has doubts about her husband's ability to be treacherous?* She says she fears his nature because it is too kind (Scene 5). *How does Macbeth interact with Lady Macbeth?* Macbeth tries to talk himself out of murder, but Lady Macbeth challenges him. ▬RL 1, RL 3, RL 4, RL 5

Act II, Scenes 1–4 • *How do Macbeth and Lady Macbeth collaborate to murder Duncan?* Lady Macbeth drugs the servants' drinks; Macbeth stabs Duncan and the men to death; Lady Macbeth takes the daggers and smears blood everywhere to implicate the servants. *What text shows that Lady Macbeth's character flaws are as deep as Macbeth's?* She comments that the murders were easy and that a little water washes away the deed. ▬RL 3, RL 4

SECOND READ ## Analyze the Text

• **Review Act I** • *Summarize the action in Act I.* Macbeth wins Duncan's forces a great battle, and three witches predict his future kingship and kingship for Banquo's sons. Duncan goes to Macbeth's castle to reward him. Macbeth and Lady Macbeth give themselves up to ambition and plot the murder of their king. ▬RL 3, RL 4

• **Review Act II** • *After the horror of Act I Scene 2, why does Shakespeare have the porter talk about drinking and carousing?* The scene creates comic relief and makes the finding of the dead Duncan more terrible by comparison. ▬RL 1, RL 4, RL 5

ELL **ENGLISH LANGUAGE LEARNERS**

Use Visuals

Display titles for each scene from Acts I and II. Help students articulate what the titles could mean and guide them to summarize each scene as they read.

Act I
Scene 1: Witches
Scene 2: Battleground
Scene 3: Witches, Macbeth, Banquo
Scene 4: Macbeth and King Duncan
Scene 5: Macbeth and Lady
Scene 6: King at Macbeth Castle
Scene 7: The Discussion

Act II
Scene 1: Macbeth and Banquo
Scene 2: The Murder
Scene 3: The Discovery
Scene 4: The Worriers

RESPOND TO SEGMENT 1

 Classroom Collaboration

Have partners read to identify the main idea in each scene. Have students devise their own titles for each scene and each act.

Domain Specific Vocabulary

drama • play; performance

soliloquy • a solo speech

comic relief • a section that relieves tension for a short time

 ENGLISH LANGUAGE LEARNERS

Use Comprehensible Input

Ensure students understand the key players in this drama by helping them describe each main character.

Use Visuals

Have English proficient and ELL students work together in pairs to draw a witches' cauldron with its contents labeled (toad, eye of newt, toe of frog, tongue of dog).

RESPOND TO SEGMENT 2

 Classroom Collaboration

Have groups of students read aloud scenes and help each other with comprehension and oral expression. ▬ SL 1

 Common Core Connection

RL 1 cite textual evidence to support analysis of what the text says explicitly as well as inferences drawn; **RL 2** determine a theme or central idea of a text and analyze its development; **RL 3** analyze how characters develop and interact with others; **RL 10** read and comprehend literature; **W 1** write arguments to support claims; **W 4** produce writing in which development, organization, and style are appropriate to task, purpose, and audience; **W 5** develop and strengthen writing by planning, revising, editing, rewriting, or trying a new approach; **SL 1** initiate/participate in a range of collaborative discussions; **SL 4** present information, findings, and supporting evidence clearly, concisely, and logically

Academic Vocabulary

Read each word with students and discuss its meaning.

gospl'd (Act III, Scene 1) • religious

eminence (Act III, Scene 2) • importance

'scap'd (Act III, Scene 4) • escaped

bedlams (Act III, Scene 5) • uproars, mayhems

contriver (Act III, Scene 5) • plotter; schemer

bodements (Act IV, Scene 1) • predictions; promises

perchance (Act IV, Scene 3) • by chance; maybe

FIRST READ ## Think Through the Text

Have students use text evidence and draw inferences to answer questions.

ACT III, Scenes 1–6 • *Why does Macbeth have Banquo killed?* so that Banquo won't have any further children (Scene 2) *What in the text shows how Lady Macbeth covers up Macbeth's horror when he sees Banquo's ghost?* She says he is having a fit (Scene 3). ▬ RL 1, RL 3

ACT IV, Scenes 1–4 • *The cauldron scene shows the witches brewing up a wicked charm for Macbeth. What three apparitions do they show him?* an armed head (Macduff's head in a helmet); a bloody child; a crowned child with a tree in his hand (Scene 1) *Find the text that gives seemingly conflicting information to Macbeth.* The witches' advice to watch out for Macduff seems to conflict with their claim that no one born of woman can harm him. *Why is Scene 2 horrific?* Macduff's wife and son are murdered on stage. This shows that Macbeth has become totally corrupt. ▬ RL 1, RL 3

SECOND READ ## Analyze the Text

- **Review Act III.** • Ask: *Why does Shakespeare let Fleance escape?* to retain tension; Fleance can come back and avenge his father. ▬ RL 1

- **Review Act IV.** • Ask: *Why is it that Malcolm and Macduff do not trust each other?* They are not sure about the other's loyalties to Scotland and to Macbeth. *What evidence from the text shows that Macduff despises Macbeth?* He says that Macbeth is the most evil devil to ever come from hell (Scene 3). *Describe orally and in writing Malcolm's and Macduff's interactions and plan of action.* Sample answer: Malcolm and Macduff cobble together an alliance and create a plan to lead troops to fight Macbeth. When the two learn that Macduff's family has been slain, Malcolm shores up Macduff's resolve (Scene 3). ▬ RL 3

Academic Vocabulary

Read each word with students and discuss its meaning.

perturbation (ACT V, Scene 1) • upset

accompt (ACT V, Scene 1) • account

FIRST READ ● **Think Through the Text**

Have students use text evidence and draw inferences to answer questions.

Scene 1 • *What evidence from the text shows that Lady Macbeth is going insane?* *The Doctor and Gentlewoman watch her sleepwalking and trying to wash imaginary "spots," or bloodstains, from her hands. These are symbolic of the murders she helped commit.* **RL 1**

Scenes 2–3 • *Armies assemble to attack Macbeth, but he remains confident. Which lines reveal how Macbeth's ambition leads him to misapply the witch's riddle?* *He assumes that Birnam wood simply cannot come to his castle at Dunsinane. He exults that there is no such thing as a man not born from a woman (Scene 3).* **RL 1**

Scenes 4–6 • *How does Scene 4 reveal the riddle's solution?* *Malcolm and his army cut down branches from Birnam wood as camouflage and move forward to Dunsinane.* **RL 1**

Scene 7 • *When Macbeth sees branches from Birnam Wood, he knows he will lose the battle. Why does he retain hope that the witches' charm will hold?* *He still thinks there is no such thing as a man not born of woman.* *When does Macbeth know he has lost his crown?* *When Macduff reveals that he was born early via caesarean birth.* **RL 2, RL 3**

SECOND READ ● **Analyze the Text**

Review Scenes 1–6. • Ask: *How does Shakespeare portray Macbeth and Lady Macbeth in these scenes? How does he portray Macduff and Malcolm?* *Macbeth and Lady Macbeth appear increasingly unhinged. Macduff and Malcolm are courageous and clever.* **RL 1, RL 3**

Review Scene 7. • Ask: *Discuss students' reactions to Macbeth's fate. What does the text reveal about Macbeth and Macduff at the climax?* *Macbeth says that he is tied to a stake like a bear who cannot escape. Macduff calls Macbeth a hound from hell and beheads him.* **RL 1**

Independent/Self-Selected Reading

Have students reread *The Tragedy of Macbeth* independently to practice analyzing the text on their own, or have them practice the skills using another drama, such as:

- *Romeo and Juliet* by William Shakespeare

- *West Side Story, A Novelization* by Irving Schulman **RL. 10**

WRITE & PRESENT

1. Have small groups identify transitions between events in Act V. **RL 2, SL 1**

2. Have each student write a summary of Act V, including descriptions of Macbeth's and Lady Macbeth's characters and their decline. Have them explain how the two paths are alike and different. Suggest that students use a Venn diagram to plan their characterizations. **RL 1, RL 3, W 4, SL 4**

3. Have students share their work with partners and offer suggestions for revising and editing. Students edit their writing based on these suggestions. **W 5**

4. Have students present their final writing to their classmates. Ask them to respond to each student's plot and character analysis. **SL 4**

See Copying Masters, pp. 212–215.

STUDENT CHECKLIST

Writing

☑ Identify and discuss at least one of the play's themes, such as ambition or betrayal, and one subtheme, such as fate or innocence and guilt.

☑ Discuss how ambition and betrayal mark the characters of Macbeth and Lady Macbeth.

☑ Use complete sentences and developed paragraphs to structure writing.

Speaking & Listening

☑ Read writing aloud with a clear, audible voice.

☑ Present ideas in a meaningful way.

OBJECTIVES

- Describe how characters respond to society's pressures
- Identify the themes of the play
- Interpret symbols and figurative language in drama
- Analyze text using text evidence

A Doll's House **is broken into three instructional segments.**

SEGMENTS

SEGMENT 1...ACT I...pp. 145–180
SEGMENT 2...ACT II..pp. 181–206
SEGMENT 3...ACT III..pp. 207–232

Options for Reading

Independent Students read the book independently or with a partner and then answer questions posed by the teacher.

Supported Students read a segment and answer questions with teacher support.

 Common Core Connection

RL 1 cite textual evidence to support analysis of what the text says explicitly as well as inferences drawn; **RL 2** determine a theme or central idea of a text and analyze its development; **RL 3** analyze how characters develop and interact with others; **RL 4** determine the meaning of words and phrases, including figurative and connotative meanings; **RL 5** analyze how author's choices create tension or surprise

A Doll's House
by Henrik Ibsen

SUMMARY The Helmers live a conventional life in which Torvald is the head and Nora the heart of the household. They seem content, but Nora is hiding a secret: she once unknowingly committed a crime to save Torvald's life. When her secret becomes known, Nora finds that she is relieved. She chooses to leave her family for a voyage of self-discovery.

ABOUT THE AUTHOR **Henrik Ibsen** lived and wrote in both Rome and his native Norway. His literary verse dramas launched his writing career and influenced experimental playwrights throughout the twentieth century. Ibsen's later realistic plays explored the tension between individualism and social expectations.

Discuss Genre and Set Purpose

DRAMA Remind students that plays are meant to be acted and thus are subject to interpretation regarding characters' motives, values, and goals. Point out that this play presents characters who must confront difficult choices and who express conflicting values. The conflicts within them and between them create dramatic tension.

SET PURPOSE Help students set a purpose for reading, such as analyzing why Nora lies to Torvald.

TEXT COMPLEXITY RUBRIC

Overall Text Complexity		A Doll's House DRAMA
		COMPLEX
Quantitative Measure	Lexile	N/A
Qualitative Measures	Text Structure	many shifts in point of view
	Language Conventionality and Clarity	ambiguous language requiring inferences
	Knowledge Demands	fairly complex theme
	Purpose/Levels of Meaning	multiple levels of meaning

SEGMENT 1 ACT I, pp. 147–180

Academic Vocabulary

Read each word with students and discuss its meaning.

constrained (p. 149) • unnatural

crestfallen (p. 149) • disappointed

prodigal (p. 150) • wasteful; extravagant

FIRST READ ## Think Through the Text

Have students use text evidence and draw inferences to answer questions.

pp. 148–149 • *What are Torvald's nicknames for Nora in the first two pages of Act I?* little skylark, little squirrel, little feather brain, little scatterbrain *What does this say about their relationship?* Torvald is kind but condescending, and Nora encourages his behavior. **Nora and Torvald seem obsessed with money. What does this suggest?** They are part of a struggling middle class; they have constant money pressures. ▬ **RL 3**

p. 153 • *What functions are served by the character of Kristina Linde?* She provides narrative function, because when Nora confides in Kristina, she confides in the audience. She also presents another side of women's lives at the time. ▬ **RL 1**

pp. 170–175 • *Why are Kristina, Krogstad, and Nora each desperate?* Kristina needs to support herself; Krogstad is terrified of losing his bank job; Nora is afraid her secret will be revealed. ▬ **RL 1**

SECOND READ ## Analyze the Text

• Review pages 145–180 with students. *This play takes place in the family home at Christmas time. What symbolism behind this setting increases dramatic tension?* The space, like their lives, is restricted. Christmas is a holiday of charity and redemption, concepts which are both tested. **How have social expectations shaped the conflicts presented in the play?** In general, strict social expectations make it difficult for the characters to avoid scandal (page 175). Women's roles are interpreted in a very narrow way, and laws reinforce women's dependency on their husbands (page 160). ▬ **RL 4, RL 5**

• Review pages 178–180 with students. *Why do Torvald's remarks about Krogstad devastate Nora?* Like Krogstad, Nora has committed forgery. Torvald's judgments about Krogstad also apply to her. ▬ **RL 3**

• *What evidence from the text shows how Ibsen maintains tension?* The characters express themselves by revealing secrets. Nora has to hide her macaroons from Torvald (page 151). Even before she is aware that she's committed forgery, she hides the life-saving actions she took in order to protect his pride (page 161). ▬ **RL 2, RL 5**

Use Visuals
Make a Chart •
Characterization

Guide students to make a chart of the play's major characters. In one column, have students list adjectives that could describe them. In another, have students list words that describe the conflicts they face.

Then have students state sentences such as:

Torvald is _____ critical **as he decides** _____. *how to treat Nora*

Nora is _____ nervous **as she decides** _____. *how to escape from tradition*

Have students continue the chart using adjectives and verbs that pertain to other characters and segments of the play.

RESPOND TO SEGMENT 1

 Classroom Collaboration

Have students begin writing character studies based on each character's motivations. Encourage them to continue to refine their studies throughout the play.

Have small groups summarize the plot events in this act. Invite students to predict what might happen in the next act.

Domain Specific Vocabulary

setting • place and time

character • play participant

coincidence • accidental turn of events

literary device • a technique to produce an effect upon readers or viewers

 ENGLISH LANGUAGE LEARNERS

Use Comprehensible Input

Ensure students understand the plot events and the themes by asking: *What fears motivate each character? What assumptions underlie their actions?*

RESPOND TO SEGMENT 2

 Classroom Collaboration

Have students read dialogue or scenes with expression and emotion.

 Common Core Connection

RL 1 cite textual evidence to support analysis of what the text says explicitly as well as inferences drawn; **RL 2** determine a theme or central idea of a text and analyze its development; **RL 3** analyze how characters develop and interact with others; **RL 4** determine the meaning of words and phrases, including figurative and connotative meanings; **RL 10** read and comprehend literature; **W 2** write informative/explanatory texts; **W 5** develop and strengthen writing by planning, revising, editing, rewriting, or trying a new approach; **SL 1** initiate/participate in a range of collaborative discussions; **SL 4** present information, findings, and supporting evidence clearly, concisely, and logically

Academic Vocabulary

Read each word with students and discuss its meaning.

obstinate (p. 188) • stubborn; willful

petty (p. 189) • small-minded; trivial

notice (n.) (p. 189) • warning

FIRST READ ## Think Through the Text

Have students use text evidence and draw inferences to answer questions.

pp. 190–195 • *What could Nora be thinking about when she flirts with Dr. Rank?* borrowing money *Why can't Nora ask Dr. Rank for money after he declares his love?* It would diminish her character; she would be a manipulator and unworthy of his affection. ●RL 3

pp. 189 and 199 • *Why do Torvald and Krogstad lose audience sympathy?* On page 189, Torvald has a tantrum. On page 199, Krogstad threatens blackmail. ●RL 3

p. 200 • *What action does Krogstad take in response to Torvald's dismissal notice?* On page 200, after a hostile exchange with Nora, he drops a letter that exposes Nora's secret in the letterbox. ●RL 3

p. 202 • *How do you know from the text that Kristina will try to save Nora?* On page 202, Kristina promises to help her. ●RL 1

SECOND READ ## Analyze the Text

• Review pp. 187–189 with students. *When Nora and Torvald argue about Krogstad, why can't Nora tell Torvald the truth?* On page 179, Torvald has already told her what he thinks: that forgery is corruption; lying, cheating, and being a hypocrite are evil and like poisons; and it is mostly mothers who are to blame. *What does Nora's inability to confide in Torvald say about their marriage?* Their marriage lacks true intimacy and features an uneven balance of power. ●RL 1, RL 3

• Have students revisit Act II. *Explain the pressures Nora undergoes.* Society dictates that Nora be a pleasant and entertaining wife and a prudent yet playful mother. At the same time, she has had to take on the responsibility of saving her husband and shielding her father without letting them know what she was doing. ●RL 3

• *Some writers use a literary device in which they assign names to characters that reflect their characters. What are some examples?* Nora has No and Rah in it; Torvald could mean Tore World; Dr. Rank stinks of death; Kristina is like a crystal; Krog is like frog and grog. ●RL 4

Academic Vocabulary

Read each word with students and discuss its meaning.

capricious (p. 213) • impulsive; unreliable

gruesome (p. 218) • ugly; hideous; repugnant

FIRST READ ## Think Through the Text

Have students use text evidence and draw inferences to answer questions.

pp. 207–211 • Invite students to explore the theme of love. *Why are Kristina and Krogstad willing to renew their love despite disappointments? They are both like shipwrecked people (pp. 208–209) clinging to life; love is what gives their lives meaning.* ◼ **RL 1, RL 3**

pp. 220–221 • *Why doesn't Torvald give Nora a chance to explain Krogstad's letter? Torvald assumes that he knows everything about the situation. He believes his wife is silly and shallow. He doesn't care about the reasons for the situation but only how they reflect upon him.* ◼ **RL 3**

pp. 221–225 • *What from the text shows that Torvald has no idea of Nora's strength? Torvald "forgives" Nora for being so "helpless" (pp. 223–224). What does Nora learn about herself? She has no idea how society works and no sense of her relationship to the world. She has until now adopted the values of her father and her husband (page 225).* ◼ **RL 1, RL 3**

SECOND READ ## Analyze the Text

• Review the title of the play. *In what way is the Helmer house like a doll's house? Both Nora and Torvald are playing roles, as if they are puppets or dolls that belong to children playing house.* **How does the text show Nora's development?** *On page 228, she explains that she is first a human being.* **Why does the drama end with a slam of the door and silence?** *On page 232, Nora and Torvald's relationship has ended; nothing has filled the void, but nothing has prevented change, either.* ◼ **RL 2, RL 3**

• Explore the themes in the play. *Why and how might audiences understand differently over time? Sample answers: Themes include social norms and pressures, the role of women, love, friendship, and redemption. As social expectations change, the characters' actions will continue to be interpreted differently.* ◼ **RL 2**

Independent/Self-Selected Reading

Have students reread *A Doll's House* independently to practice analyzing the text on their own, or have them practice the skills using another play with similar themes, such as the following:

• *A Raisin in the Sun* by Lorraine Hansbury

• *Hedda Gabbler* by Henrik Ibsen ◼ **RL 10**

Performance Task

WRITE & PRESENT

1. Have small groups discuss the play's themes and their relationship to the title. ◼ **RL 2, SL 1**

2. Ask students to choose one theme and write to explain how it applies to a particular character from the play. ◼ **W 2**

3. Have students share their work with partners and offer suggestions for revising and editing. Students edit their writing based on these suggestions. ◼ **W 5**

4. Have students present their final writing to their classmates. Ask students to respond to the themes and ideas from each student's writing. ◼ **SL 4**

See Copying Masters, pp. 212–215.

STUDENT CHECKLIST

Writing

☑ Identify at least one theme from the novel.

☑ Relate this theme to the symbol of a doll's house or cookie-cutter shapes, using text evidence and quotes from the play.

☑ Use complete sentences and developed paragraphs to structure writing.

Speaking & Listening

☑ Read play dialogue with expression.

☑ Present ideas in a meaningful way.

▶ **OBJECTIVES**

- Describe how characters respond to society's pressures
- Identify the themes of the play
- Interpret symbols and figurative language in drama
- Analyze text using text evidence

The Glass Menagerie **is broken into three instructional segments.**

SEGMENTS

Options for Reading

Independent Students read the play independently or with a partner and then answer questions posed by the teacher.

Supported Students read a segment and answer questions with teacher support.

COMMON CORE **Common Core Connection**

RL 1 cite textual evidence to support analysis of what the text says explicitly as well as inferences drawn; **RL 2** determine a theme or central idea of a text/analyze its development/provide summary; **RL 3** analyze how characters develop and interact with others; **RL 4** determine the meaning of words and phrases, including figurative and connotative meanings

The Glass Menagerie
by Tennessee Williams

SUMMARY Amanda, the matriarch of the Wingfield family, cannot let go of her past as a popular girl. She regrets choosing a husband who abandoned her and her son (Tom) and daughter (Laura). Laura's slight physical disability is insignificant compared to her crippling shyness. When Laura's first beau comes to call, he does not understand the weight his simple visit holds.

ABOUT THE AUTHOR **Tennessee Williams** was born in Mississippi and is considered one of the most important playwrights of the twentieth century. Much of his work is set in the South and explores family tensions, class issues, women's concerns, and the treatment of the mentally ill and infirm. Williams won almost every award a playwright can win, including the Pulitzer Prize for *Cat on a Hot Tin Roof*.

Discuss Genre and Set Purpose

DRAMA Drama often presents situations in which characters are confronted with difficult choices and challenged by their situations. No change happens without conflict, and drama is a strong venue for exploring how and why human beings respond to difficulty.

SET PURPOSE Help students set a purpose for reading, such as why Laura enjoys cleaning and polishing her collection of glass animals.

▲ TEXT COMPLEXITY RUBRIC

Overall Text Complexity		*The Glass Menagerie* DRAMA
		COMPLEX
Quantitative Measure	Lexile	N/A
Qualitative Measures	Text Structure	use of narrator breaks down fourth wall
	Language Conventionality and Clarity	some language requiring inferences
	Knowledge Demands	fairly complex theme
	Purpose/Levels of Meaning	multiple levels of meaning

Academic Vocabulary

Read each word with students and discuss its meaning.

expressionism (p. 23) • a dramatic style stressing emotion and abstractions of reality

immutable (p. 25) • not subject to changing

nostalgia (p. 26) • a longing for the past

automatism (p. 27) • condition of being automatic or mechanical

patronage (p. 43) • financial support by someone

Domain Specific Vocabulary

proscenium (p. 28) • the wall on the sides of a theater stage that separate the stage from the audience

scrim (p. 30) • thin fabric curtain that can be used as an opaque background or a translucent curtain for a scene on a stage

FIRST READ ## Think Through the Text

Have students use text evidence and draw inferences to answer questions.

pp. 26 • *Why does Williams want the lighting of the play to be dim?* The play is a memory play, so shadows and darkness will show that memories are often unclear and hard to see or recall. RL 2

pp. 30–36 • *What is Amanda anticipating for the afternoon?* Amanda is expecting gentlemen callers to come for her daughter, Laura. *What can you tell from the text about what Tom thinks of Amanda's expectations?* Tom thinks his mother is too focused on reliving her past. On page 32, he says he knows what's coming when she starts describing her days of receiving gentlemen callers, as if he has heard the same thing over and over. He groans and throws his paper down on page 35, when she still believes that callers will be coming. RL 3

pp. 48–51 • *Where does Tom go in the evenings?* Tom goes to the movies every night to try to escape his living situation. RL 1

SECOND READ ## Analyze the Text

• Review pages 23–26 with students. Ask: *Why are the extra elements Williams describes in his production notes important?* The use of projected titles and music can set a mood for the play that might be hard to explain in the script without describing the projections and music. Williams says on page 24 that he wants to make sure the audience understands the whole play, not just the individual scenes. RL 2

• Review pages 39–43 with students. Ask: *What is the "crust of humility" and how does it relate to Amanda and Laura's stories?* It is Amanda's term for what unwanted spinsters must eat because they have to rely on the generosity of others for their survival, since they have no way to support themselves. RL 4

• *What do you think is at the heart of Amanda's differences with Tom?* Amanda sees Tom as the same as her husband who left her to raise two children on her own. She is angry that he will not rise up to the responsibility of taking care of her and Laura. She is worried about what will happen to Laura if Tom leaves for adventure. RL 3

ELL ENGLISH LANGUAGE LEARNERS

Use Visuals to Create a Character Study

Guide students to make a collage of pictures of items that they associate with each member of the Wingfield family. Students can cut photos out of magazines, find images on the Internet, or draw pictures. Have students continue to add to their collages as they read the rest of the play.

RESPOND TO SEGMENT 1

Classroom Collaboration

Have small groups summarize the plot events of the scenes they have read so far. Then have students predict what might happen in the next scene of the play.

ENGLISH LANGUAGE LEARNERS

Use Comprehensible Input

Ensure students understand the plot events and the themes by asking questions such as: *Why does Laura dust and rearrange the glass animals so often?*

 RESPOND TO SEGMENT 2

Classroom Collaboration

Have students deepen their understanding of this section by reading dialogue between two characters with expression and emotion.

COMMON CORE **Common Core Connection**

RL 1 cite textual evidence to support analysis of what the text says explicitly as well as inferences drawn; **RL 2** determine a theme or central idea of a text/analyze its development/provide summary; **RL 3** analyze how characters develop and interact with others; **RL 4** determine the meaning of words and phrases, including figurative and connotative meanings and analyze the impact of word choices; **RL 10** read and comprehend literature; **W 2** write informative/explanatory texts; **W 5** develop and strengthen writing by planning, revising, editing, rewriting, or trying a new approach; **SL 4** present information, findings, and supporting evidence clearly, concisely, and logically

---

Academic Vocabulary

Read each word with students and discuss its meaning.

emulate (p. 69) • imitate someone to try to be as good as them

imminent (p. 71) • likely to occur at any moment

ominous (p. 80) • foreshadowing that something bad will happen

vivacity (p. 98) • the quality of being lively or animated

paragon (p. 98) • a model of excellence

FIRST READ **Think Through the Text**

Have students use text evidence and draw inferences to answer questions.

pp. 69–71 • *What is Tom's relationship like with Jim, the gentleman caller?* Tom knew Jim briefly in high school, where Jim was a star athlete and debater; now they work at the same place in almost the same job. *What is Tom's attitude toward Jim now?* Tom is disappointed that Jim has not had more success; he feels more similar to Jim than he did in high school. ◾RL 3

pp. 83–85 • *What does Tom's speech at the beginning of Scene 5 foreshadow?* From reading Tom's speech, it becomes clear that Jim is the boy Laura loved from afar in high school. ◾RL 1

pp. 87–102 • *How does Amanda react to the gentleman caller's visit?* Amanda dresses up in an outfit from her youth, and she cleans and puts new lamps and curtains up to impress their guest. *What is Laura's reaction to the gentleman caller?* Laura can barely bring herself to answer the door, and she is physically sick because she is so shy and anxious. ◾RL 3

SECOND READ **Analyze the Text**

• Have students revisit Scene 5. Ask: *Why do you think Tom agreed to ask his friend from the warehouse home for dinner?* Sample answer: *Even though he did not want to ask Jim for dinner, he did it because he wants to leave his job and get away from his mother. He knows that he should not leave his sister alone, so he tries to get a gentleman caller interested in her.* ◾RL 3

• *A subtheme of this play is responsibility. Explain what each character's attitude is about responsibility, providing textual evidence for all answers.* Sample answers: *Amanda's husband does not appear in the play, but he is mentioned often in the dialogue and stage directions. He was irresponsible about fulfilling his family duties. When Tom introduces him as the fifth character on page 30, Tom describes how he skipped out of town. He is also described as faithless on page 50.* ◾RL 2, RL 3

Academic Vocabulary

Read each word with students and discuss its meaning.

slackening (p. 103) • becoming less intense

intimated (p. 106) • made known or announced

novelty (p. 126) • quality of being a new experience

rejuvenated (p. 131) • made young again

jalopy (p. 133) • an old broken-down car

FIRST READ **Think Through the Text**

Have students use text evidence and draw inferences to answer questions.

pp. 103–109 • *What happens to the light at the beginning of Scene 7? The electricity goes out, so Jim and Laura must talk by candlelight. How does Laura's behavior change with the lighting? The lack of scrutiny gives Laura more courage to overcome her shyness and talk to Jim freely.* **RL 3**

pp. 118–124 • *When Jim talks to Laura about her self-confidence problem, who else might he be addressing? Sample answer: He could be giving himself a pep talk since he admits that he has not been as successful as he thought he would be. His own self-confidence has been shaken by his not meeting expectations. He could also be speaking to the audience, indirectly relaying Williams's message that we all must overcome differences in our lives to rise to our potential.* **RL 3**

SECOND READ **Analyze the Text**

• Review the title of the play. Ask: *How are all of the characters a part of a "glass menagerie"? Each one plays out a role.* **RL 4**

• *How is Mr. Wingfield a character in the play, even though he never appears in the drama? His photograph on the wall is frequently looked at by the other family members. Amanda and Tom, in particular, talk about his abandonment of the family. Tom says that he is following in his father's footsteps in the last speech of the play.* **RL 2, RL 3**

• Ask students to identify some possible themes of the play. *Sample answers: memory; responsibility; abandonment; one's place in society; class conflict; yearning for another life* **RL 2**

Independent/Self-Selected Reading

Have students reread *The Glass Menagerie* independently to practice analyzing the text on their own, or have them practice the skills using another play, such as:

• *Cat on a Hot Tin Roof* by Tennessee Williams

• *Young Man from Atlanta* by Horton Foote **RL 10**

WRITE & PRESENT

1. Have small groups discuss and record the possible themes and titles of this play. **RL 2**

2. Ask students to think about the main themes of the entire drama and choose one to explain by writing an explanatory essay including specific references to the play. **W 2**

3. Have students share their work with partners and offer suggestions for revising and editing. Students edit their writing based on these suggestions. **W 5**

4. Have students present their final writing to their classmates. Ask students to respond to the themes and ideas from each student's writing. **SL 4**

See Copying Master, pp. 212–215.

STUDENT CHECKLIST

Writing

☑ Identify at least one theme from the play

☑ Use text evidence and quotes from the play to analyze this theme.

☑ Use complete sentences and developed paragraphs to structure writing.

Speaking & Listening

☑ Logically present claims and findings.

☑ Speak clearly at an understandable pace.

OBJECTIVES

- Describe how characters respond to society's pressures
- Identify the themes of the play
- Interpret symbols and figurative language in drama
- Analyze text using text evidence

Rhinoceros is broken into three instructional segments.

SEGMENTS

SEGMENT 1...ACT I...pp. 3–37
SEGMENT 2...ACT II...pp. 38–71
SEGMENT 3...ACT III..pp. 71–107

Options for Reading

Independent Students read the play independently or with a partner and then answer questions posed by the teacher.

Supported Students read a segment and answer questions with teacher support.

Common Core Connection

RL 1 cite textual evidence to support analysis of what the text says explicitly as well as inferences drawn; **RL 2** determine a theme or central idea of a text/analyze its development/provide summary; **RL 3** analyze how characters develop and interact with others/advance the plot

Rhinoceros
by Eugene Ionesco

SUMMARY Two friends, Jean and Berenger, lead very different lives. Jean is neat, hardworking, and cultured, while Berenger drinks too much, is unmotivated at work, and is unkempt. As they talk about their differences at a café, a rhinoceros disrupts the village by running through town, throwing the villagers into a frenzy. Soon, everyone is becoming a rhinoceros, leaving Berenger feeling like an outsider.

ABOUT THE AUTHOR Eugene Ionesco (1912–1994) was born in Romania but lived most of his life in France. His early writing consisted of poetry and critical essays; he began writing drama somewhat late in his career. His plays are from the theater of the absurd movement, which flourished in France after World War II.

Discuss Genre and Set Purpose

DRAMA Drama sometimes presents situations in which characters are confronted with absurd situations. Conflict arises when characters react to these situations. Drama is a way for readers and audiences to understand different ways of making sense of the world.

SET PURPOSE Help students set a purpose for reading, such as what the rhinoceros symbolizes and how different characters react to the situation in the play.

TEXT COMPLEXITY RUBRIC		Rhinoceros DRAMA
Overall Text Complexity		COMPLEX
Quantitative Measure	Lexile	N/A
Qualitative Measures	Text Structure	many shifts in point of view
	Language Conventionality and Clarity	ambiguous language requiring inferences
	Knowledge Demands	fairly complex theme
	Purpose/Levels of Meaning	multiple levels of meaning

SEGMENT 1 ACT I, pp. 3–37

Academic Vocabulary

Read each word with students and discuss its meaning.

syllogism (p. 13) • an argument with a major and a minor premise and a conclusion

pedant (p. 30) • person concerned with knowledge over common sense

FIRST READ ▶ ## Think Through the Text

Have students use text evidence and draw inferences to answer questions.

pp. 3–11 • *What is Jean lecturing Berenger about at the beginning of Act I?* Jean is criticizing Berenger's hygiene, drinking, and work ethic. *What happens during their conversation?* A rhinoceros storms through the village. *How do the villagers react to the rhinoceros?* They are surprised but quickly go back to their conversations and regular lives. ◀RL 3

pp. 22–24 • *What does Jean tell Berenger to do in order to become more cultured and attractive to Daisy?* Jean tells Berenger to visit museums and go to lectures. He also suggests going to a play by Ionesco. ◀RL 1

p. 37 • *How does Berenger behave at the end of the first scene?* He is upset with himself for quarreling with Jean, so he takes a drink and says he is too upset to go to a museum. ◀RL 1

SECOND READ ▶ ## Analyze the Text

• Review pages 3–37 with students. Say: *Something that is absurd is ridiculous. What parts of this section would you describe as absurd?* The rhinoceros trampling through the town is absurd. The way the characters react to the rhino is absurd, too. When Jean tells Berenger to go see a play by Ionesco, this is absurd because that suggestion is embedded in one of Ionesco's plays. ◀RL 1

• Review pages 3–37 with students. Ask: *What do you notice about the dialogue?* Characters often say the same thing in separate conversations and repeat what has been stated. ◀RL 1

• *What is the theme of this section?* The characters' lives are repetitive and meaningless. *How does the author show the theme?* He shows the theme by having characters repeat the same dialogue. They are showing that nothing changes in their meaningless lives, even when a rhinoceros charges through their village. ◀RL 2

Domain Specific Vocabulary

act • a main division of a play

scene • a subdivision of a play that has a fixed setting and continuous time

 ENGLISH LANGUAGE LEARNERS

Use Visuals

Guide students to make a chart of the play's major characters and list adjectives that could describe them.

Then have them orally complete describing sentences such as:

Jean is _____. critical
Berenger is _____. dull
Daisy is _____. attractive
The Logician is _____. annoying

Have students continue the adjective lists as they read the play.

RESPOND TO SEGMENT 1
Classroom Collaboration

Have small groups summarize the events in this act and discuss what is absurd about them. Then have students predict what might happen in the next act.

RESPOND TO SEGMENT 2

Classroom Collaboration

Have students read dialogue from Act II with expression and emotion.

Academic Vocabulary

Read each word with students and discuss its meaning.

pachyderm (p. 40) • large thick-skinned mammal

chivalry (p. 43) • courtesy, thoughtfulness

opiate (p. 45) • something that causes dullness or inaction

wretched (p. 59) • despicable, contemptible

FIRST READ ## Think Through the Text

Have students use text evidence and draw inferences to answer questions.

pp. 38–46 • *Does Berenger seem to take his work seriously? What evidence in the text supports this conclusion?* No, he is late and gets Daisy to help cover it up. *What attitude do the other workers have toward Berenger?* They make fun of his eyewitness account of seeing the rhinoceros. They do not seem to take him seriously. ⬤ RL 1

pp. 52–57 • *How does the first scene end?* The fire brigade comes to rescue the workers from the office amid reports of increasing numbers of rhinoceroses in the village. ⬤ RL 1

pp. 58–71 • *What happens when Berenger goes to visit Jean?* He wants to make amends for their argument about the rhinoceros in Act I but notices a bump on Jean's head, thickening skin, heavy breathing, and a hoarse voice. Jean turns into a rhinoceros. ⬤ RL 1

SECOND READ ## Analyze the Text

• Review pp. 38–57 • *Why do Berenger's and Daisy's coworkers doubt the story about the rhinoceros?* Berenger drinks alcohol, so he does not have the reputation of being reliable. The men may doubt Daisy's version because she is the only woman in the office. Finally, the idea of a rhinoceros charging around a French village is preposterous. ⬤ RL 1

• Have students revisit pages 38–71. *How has Berenger changed by the end of the second act?* Berenger seems more grounded in reality than the other characters. Jean turns into a surly rhinoceros while Berenger tries to help him, which is a role reversal for them. ⬤ RL 3

• Have students revisit pages 38–71. Ask: *What is the theme in this segment of the play?* Sample answer: It is often difficult for people to accept changes. ⬤ RL 2

COMMON CORE **Common Core Connection**

RL 1 cite textual evidence to support analysis of what the text says explicitly as well as inferences drawn; **RL 2** determine a theme or central idea of a text and analyze its development/provide summary; **RL 3** analyze how characters develop/interact with others/advance the plot; **RL 10** read and comprehend literature; **W 2** write informative/explanatory texts; **W 5** develop and strengthen writing by planning, revising, editing, rewriting, or trying a new approach; **SL 4** present information, findings, and supporting evidence clearly, concisely, and logically

Academic Vocabulary

Read each word with students and discuss its meaning.

caprice (p. 74) • unpredictable change

dissociation (p. 82) • separation of mental processes

sublimating (p. 82) • diverting energy from an immediate goal to a more socially acceptable goal

intuitive (p. 85) • having insightful knowledge

capitulating (p. 107) • surrendering

FIRST READ ## Think Through the Text

Have students use text evidence and draw inferences to answer questions.

pp. 71–90 • *What regrets does Berenger have at the beginning of Act III?* He feels that he failed his friend Jean by allowing him to turn into a rhinoceros. *What does Dudard tell Berenger about his guilty feelings?* Jean's change did not come about because of Berenger. It would have happened anyway. He tells him that he is not as important as he might think. **RL 1**

pp. 95–107 • *Why does Berenger want to have children with Daisy?* He thinks that they should repopulate Earth with humans. **RL 3**

SECOND READ ## Analyze the Text

• Review pages 74–75. Ask: *What does Berenger mean when he says that he was more sure of his friend Jean than he was of himself?* At the beginning, Jean is advising him how to live a better life. Jean is very self-confident. Berenger was less sure of himself compared with his friend, which is why it is so devastating for him when Jean becomes a rhinoceros. **RL 3**

• Have students reread pages 81–83. Ask: *Why is Berenger surprised that Mr. Papillon is a rhinoceros?* Berenger saw him as a leader, so it's surprising he has succumbed to the pressure to become a rhinoceros. **RL 3**

• Review pages 38–71. Ask: *What are some possible themes of the play?* resisting or accepting social conformity; the repetition and meaninglessness of everyday life; standing up for what you believe in **RL 2**

Independent/Self-Selected Reading

Have students reread *Rhinoceros* independently to practice analyzing the text on their own, or have them practice the skills using another book, such as:

• *The Bald Soprano* by Eugene Ionesco

• *Waiting for Godot* by Samuel Beckett **RL 10**

WRITE & PRESENT

1. Have small groups discuss and record the possible themes and titles of this play. **RL 2**

2. Ask students to think about the main themes of the entire drama and choose one to explain with specific references to the play. **W 2**

3. Have students share their work with partners and offer suggestions for revising and editing. Students edit their writing based on these suggestions. **W 5**

4. Have students present their final writing to their classmates. Ask students to respond to the themes and ideas from each student's writing. **SL 4**

See Copying Masters, pp. 212–215.

STUDENT CHECKLIST

Writing

☑ Identify at least one theme from the play.

☑ Relate this theme to the symbol of a rhinoceros, using text evidence and words and phrases from the play.

☑ Use complete sentences and developed paragraphs to structure writing.

Speaking & Listening

☑ Read play dialogue with expression.

☑ Present ideas in a meaningful way.

OBJECTIVES

- Describe how characters interact with one another
- Identify the theme of a play
- Interpret symbols and figurative language in drama
- Analyze text using text evidence

Master Harold is broken into three instructional segments.

Options for Reading

Independent Students read the play independently or with a partner and then answer questions posed by the teacher.

Supported Students read a segment aloud with teacher support and answer questions.

 Common Core Connection

RL 1 cite textual evidence to support analysis of what the text says explicitly as well as inferences drawn; **RL 2** determine a theme or central idea of a text/analyze its development/ provide summary; **RL 3** analyze how characters develop and interact with others

"Master Harold" ... and the boys

by Athol Fugard

SUMMARY On a rainy afternoon in a tea room in South Africa, Sam and Willie, two servants, are closing up shop. Soon, Hally, the son of the owner, arrives. The banter is light and friendly until Hally learns that his father, with whom he has a strained relationship, is coming home from the hospital. As tensions heighten, Hally's anger eventually erupts against Sam, potentially destroying their relationship.

ABOUT THE AUTHOR **Athol Fugard** was born in South Africa to an English father and an Afrikaner mother. Many of his plays are drawn from his experiences growing up under the system of apartheid. Since they are critical of that system, Fugard's plays were not produced in South Africa until the 1990s, after the end of apartheid.

Discuss Genre and Set Purpose

DRAMA Remind students that drama includes characters, a setting, and a plot with events that unfold through dialogue and action.

SET PURPOSE Help students set a purpose for reading, such as to examine how race can affect how people interact and to explore how the play is relevant today.

▲ TEXT COMPLEXITY RUBRIC

Overall Text Complexity		*"Master Harold" ... and the boys* DRAMA
		COMPLEX
Quantitative Measure	Lexile	N/A
Qualitative Measures	Text Structure	somewhat complex story concepts
	Language Conventionality and Clarity	some unfamiliar language
	Knowledge Demands	somewhat unfamiliar experience and situation
	Purpose/Levels of Meaning	multiple levels of meaning

Academic Vocabulary

Read each word with students and discuss its meaning.

hiding (p. 7) • beating

barbaric (p. 14) • uncivilized

oscillate (p. 15) • to move back and forth between two points

intrepid (p. 17) • fearless

daunted (p. 17) • intimidated

Inquisition (p. 20) • a series of religious trials in Medieval Europe

ELL ENGLISH LANGUAGE LEARNERS

Use Visuals

Guide students in using the information from the book to create a stage setting for the play. Use concrete objects, such as Hally's table and the telephone, to draw connections between language and real things.

FIRST READ ## Think Through the Text

Have students use text evidence and draw inferences to answer questions.

pp. 4–8 • *Why is Willie dancing at the beginning of the scene?* He's preparing for a dance competition. *What does the interaction between Willie and Sam tell you about their relationship?* Willie looks up to Sam. *How can you tell?* Willie asks Sam for advice; Sam is teaching Willie to dance. **RL 3**

pp. 9–15 • *In what ways does Hally treat Willie and Sam as his friends?* He speaks to them as equals; he lets Sam call him Hally. *How does Hally treat them as servants?* On page 13, Hally yells at Willie and tells him to act his age; he tells Willie and Sam to get back to work. **RL 1, RL 3**

pp. 15–23 • *What does Hally's reaction to how prisoners are beaten tell you about him?* He believes in progress; he believes the world can be a better place. *How does Sam know about the men he and Hally discuss?* He has learned about them from Hally's school books. **RL 1**

SECOND READ ## Analyze the Text

- Review pages 11–14. Ask: *How does Hally feel about his father coming home from the hospital? Support your opinion.* He doesn't want his father to come home. On page 10, he stops short when Sam says he's coming home; on page 12 he says Sam is mistaken; on page 14 he calls home to prove his father isn't there. **RL 1**

- Review pages 19–23. Then ask: *What does the discussion that Hally and Sam have about men of magnitude show about their relationship?* They interact as equals; Hally respects Sam's intelligence, but still treats him as a student; Sam wants to impress Hally. *What do their different choices of important men say about their characters?* Sam's choices of Lincoln and Jesus show him to be more empathic; Hally's choices of Darwin and Tolstoy show him to be more intellectual. **RL 1, RL 2**

RESPOND TO SEGMENT 1

💬 **Classroom Collaboration**

Have partners break this segment into smaller scenes and create a title for each one. For example, pages 4–8 might be called "Dance and Romance." Then have students compare and discuss their titles.

Domain Specific Vocabulary

Boet (p. 4) • familiar term for a male friend; pronounced to rhyme with "foot"

quickstep (p. 4) • a quick and rhythmic dance from the 1920s

gramophone (p. 6) • old-fashioned phonograph

 ENGLISH LANGUAGE LEARNERS

Use Comprehensible Input

Ensure students understand the drama by helping them describe the relationships between the characters in the play.

RESPOND TO SEGMENT 2

 Classroom Collaboration

Have groups of students read scenes aloud and help each other with comprehension and oral expression. Have students trade off roles so everyone has a chance to read.

 Common Core Connection

RL 1 cite textual evidence to support analysis of what the text says explicitly as well as inferences drawn; **RL 2** determine a theme or central idea of a text/analyze its development/ provide summary; **RL 3** analyze how characters develop and interact with others; **RL 10** read and comprehend literature; **W 1** write arguments to support claims; **W 5** develop and strengthen writing by planning, revising, editing, rewriting, or trying a new approach; **SL 4** present information, findings, and supporting evidence clearly, concisely, and logically

---

Academic Vocabulary

Read each word with students and discuss its meaning.

flotsam and jetsam (p. 25) • debris from a shipwreck

audacity (p. 29) • boldness

fiasco (p. 29) • complete failure

perpetual (p. 35) • continuous

despot (p. 38) • ruler with total power

FIRST READ ## Think Through the Text

Have students use text evidence and draw inferences to answer questions.

pp. 24–27 • *Why did Hally spend so much time in Sam and Willie's room when he was a boy?* It was a place to escape his unhappy childhood. *How does Hally describe the experience like a play?* He calls his description of the room stage direction and calls Willie and Sam characters. ▬ RL 1, RL 3

pp. 28–30 • *How did Hally feel when he saw Sam making the kite?* He was curious and excited. *How did he feel when they went to fly the kite?* He was embarrassed; he expected the worst. *How did his feelings change when the kite flew?* He felt proud; he wished there were other kids around to see him. ▬ RL 1, RL 3

pp. 32–38 • *What do you learn about Hally's father during the phone call?* He has lost his leg; he's an alcoholic; he can control Hally's mother. *How does Hally's attitude toward Sam and Willie change after the phone call?* He yells at them and tells them to get back to work. ▬ RL 1, RL 3

SECOND READ ## Analyze the Text

• Review pages 24–26. Ask: *What kind of place was the Jubilee Boarding House?* It was dirty and inexpensive. *What examples from the text support your ideas?* On page 25, Hally says there were bad smells from the kitchen and bathroom; on page 26 Hally describes Sam and Willie's room as cold and gray with broken furniture. ▬ RL 1

• Have students review pages 29–30. Ask: *Why is the story of flying the kite so important to Hally?* It was a happy moment in an unhappy childhood; it made Hally feel proud of himself; it was a time when he and Sam grew very close. ▬ RL 3

Academic Vocabulary

Read each word with students and discuss its meaning.

lenient (p. 39) • tolerant; allowing a lot of freedom

undeterred (p. 41) • staying on course

deportment (p. 45) • the way a person carries themself

hunky-dory (p. 49) • perfectly satisfactory

shambles (p. 51) • complete disorder

FIRST READ ## Think Through the Text

Have students use text evidence and draw inferences to answer questions.

pp. 51–54 • *Why does Sam tell Hally to be careful?* Sam doesn't want Hally to say or do things that he can't take back. *Why does Hally tell Sam to call him "Master Harold"?* to show Sam that he has the power in their relationship **RL 3**

p. 60 • *How does Willie show that he has been affected by Sam's actions?* He says he will apologize to Hilda and stop beating her; he puts his carfare into the jukebox to practice dancing. **RL 2, RL 3**

SECOND READ ## Analyze the Text

- Ask: *How is Sam's description of the dance competition symbolic of what the characters go through in the play?* The characters are all bumping into each other, but the dance floor is a dream world where everything goes smoothly. **RL 2**

- Remind students that Sam warns Hally that he will hurt himself. Ask: *What does Hally do to Sam that ends up hurting himself?* He tells Sam he is only a servant; he says his father is better than Sam because he's white; he spits in Sam's face. **RL 3**

- Ask: *What was the twist ending to the story of flying the kite?* Hally was sitting on a white-only bench. *How does that relate to the theme of the play?* Sam and Hally will always be separated because of the color of their skin. **RL 3**

Independent/Self-Selected Reading

Have students reread *"Master Harold"* ...*and the boys* independently to practice analyzing the text on their own, or have them practice the skills using another text, such as:

- *A Lesson from Aloes* by Athol Fugard

- *Huckleberry Finn* by Mark Twain **RL 10**

Performance Task

WRITE & PRESENT

1. Have students think about and discuss the main themes from the play. **RL 2**

2. Have students write a short essay explaining how one of the themes relates to a symbolic action from the play, such as kite flying or dancing. Encourage students to cite text evidence to defend their ideas. **RL 1, RL 2, W 1**

3. Have students share their work with partners and offer suggestions for revising and editing. Students edit their writing based on these suggestions. **W 5**

4. Have students present their final writing to their classmates. Ask students to respond to the theme analysis from each student's writing. **SL 4**

See Copying Masters, pp. 212–215.

STUDENT CHECKLIST

Writing

☑ Identify at least one theme from the play.

☑ Relate the theme to a symbolic action from the play.

☑ Use complete sentences and developed paragraphs to structure writing.

Speaking & Listening

☑ Read writing aloud with a clear, audible voice.

☑ Present ideas in a meaningful way.

- Describe poetic imagery
- Identify the theme of a poem
- Interpret metaphors in poetry
- Analyze poetry using text evidence

"Sonnet LXXIII"
by William Shakespeare

Options for Reading

Independent Students read the poem first for an initial impression, read it again for deeper meaning, and then finally answer questions posed by the teacher.

Supported Students read the poem twice in pairs or as a group and answer questions with teacher support.

SUMMARY This famous sonnet laments the ravages of time, using metaphors to compare old age to aspects of autumn, late twilight, and a dying fire.

ABOUT THE AUTHOR William Shakespeare (1554–1616) wrote narrative poems, over 150 sonnets, and many dramas.

Discuss Genre and Set Purpose

POETRY Point out to students that "Sonnet LXXIII" is an Elizabethan sonnet, or a poem composed of fourteen lines written in iambic pentameter, where each line has ten syllables. Guide students to note that the poem's structure consists of three quatrains (stanzas made from four lines of verse) and a final couplet (a pair of lines that usually rhyme and have the same meter).

TEXT FOCUS Figurative Language Explain that poets sometimes use metaphors, or the direct comparison of unlike things without using *like*, *as*, *than*, or *resembles*. As you read the poem, have students point out metaphors and identify the things each one compares.

SET PURPOSE Help students set a purpose for reading, such as to analyze the poem's theme and enjoy the language and structure.

Common Core Connection

RL 1 cite textual evidence to support analysis of what the text says explicitly as well as inferences drawn; **RL 2** determine a theme or central idea of a text/analyze its development/ provide summary; **RL 4** determine the meaning of words and phrases, including figurative and connotative meanings; **RL 10** read and comprehend literature; **W 3d** use precise words and phrases, telling details, and sensory language; **W 5** develop and strengthen writing by planning, revising, editing, rewriting, or trying a new approach; **SL 4** present information, findings, and supporting evidence clearly, concisely, and logically

TEXT COMPLEXITY RUBRIC		"Sonnet LXXIII" POETRY
Overall Text Complexity		MORE COMPLEX
Quantitative Measure	Lexile	N/A
Qualitative Measures	Text Structure	complex, unfamiliar poetic structure
	Language Conventionality and Clarity	archaic, unfamiliar language
	Knowledge Demands	complex, sophisticated theme
	Purpose/Levels of Meaning	multiple levels of complex meaning

Academic Vocabulary

Read each word with students and discuss its meaning.

choirs (line 4) • the part of a church where singers stand

doth (line 7) • Old English past tense form of *do*

expire (line 11) • die or stop breathing

FIRST READ ## Think Through the Text

Have students use text evidence and draw inferences to answer questions.

• *How would you characterize the age of the speaker in the poem?* He is entering old age. *To what does the speaker compare old age in the first two quatrains?* He compares it to winter and to day's end. 🔲 RL 1

SECOND READ ## Analyze the Text

• Read the poem aloud. Point out to students that while there are similarities, both winter and twilight are part of cycles that lead to renewal (spring, morning). Ask: *What metaphor in the third quatrain leads to a more solemn conclusion than renewal?* Sample answer: Old age is compared to a dying fire, which, when it is gone, is gone permanently. 🔲 RL 4

• Ask: *What is the speaker telling the listener to do, and where in the poem does this occur?* Sample answer: In lines 13–14, the speaker says that because the listener can tell that the speaker is nearing death, the listener should love the speaker more deeply. *How does this command relate to the theme of the poem?* This relates to the theme of treasuring something because you will lose it soon. 🔲 RL 2

☑ Practice Fluency

EMPHASIZE RHYTHM Stress the importance of concentrating on the rhythm of iambic pentameter when reading a sonnet aloud. Remind students that an iamb is an unstressed syllable followed by a stressed syllable and that *pentameter* means that there are five iambs per line. Have students beat the rhythm with their hands as you read a line aloud. Then read the sonnet aloud together, maintaining the rhythm. 🔲 RL 10

Independent/Self-Selected Reading

If students have demonstrated comprehension of "Sonnet LXXIII," urge them to practice interpreting the sonnet structure using another example by Shakespeare or another author from selections such as:

• *Shakespeare's Sonnets* by William Shakespeare

• *Sonnets from the Portuguese* by Elizabeth Barrett Browning 🔲 RL 10

WRITE & PRESENT

1. Have small groups work together to summarize the poem orally. 🔲 RL 1

2. Ask individuals to write a complete paraphrase of "Sonnet LXXIII" in paragraph form, using modern English while maintaining the use of metaphors. 🔲 W 3d

3. Have students pair-share their paragraphs, offering reactions and suggestions. Have students use each other's suggestions to edit and revise their work. 🔲 W 5

4. Ask volunteers to read their revised paragraphs aloud to the class before submitting them to the teacher. 🔲 SL 4

See Copying Master, pp. 212–215.

STUDENT CHECKLIST

Writing

☑ Analyze the meaning of Elizabethan diction by paraphrasing "Sonnet LXXIII" in paragraph form.

☑ Use metaphors.

☑ Use correct grammar and writing conventions.

Speaking & Listening

☑ Read paragraphs aloud with a clear, audible voice.

☑ Present ideas in a meaningful way.

"Song"
by John Donne

▷ OBJECTIVES

- Describe hyperbole
- Identify the theme of a poem
- Interpret irony in poetry
- Analyze poetry using text evidence

Options for Reading

Independent Students read the poem first for an initial impression and again for deeper meaning, then answer questions posed by the teacher.

Supported Students read the poem twice in pairs or as a group and answer questions with teacher support.

SUMMARY In "Song" (also known by the number 196) the speaker presents several impossible tasks, among them the order to find a woman who is true and fair, and laments that by the time he receives word of such a woman's existence, she will have turned false.

ABOUT THE AUTHOR John Donne (1572–1631) was an English poet, lawyer, and clergyperson in the Church of England. His writings include poetry on the topics of love, religion, and death—or all three at once. He also penned sermons and songs. Donne is often called the greatest English metaphysical poet.

Discuss Genre and Set Purpose

POETRY Students may conclude that "Song" can be interpreted in several ways. Some critics see it as a young man's lighthearted, clever commentary on the fickleness of women. Others claim it is an ironic, humorous piece mocking the Petrarchan poetry of the earlier century, which unrealistically idealized women.

TEXT FOCUS Figurative Language Hyperbole uses great exaggeration or overstatement to make a point.

SET PURPOSE Help students set a purpose for reading, such as to analyze the poem's ironic tone while enjoying humorous hyperbole.

COMMON CORE Common Core Connection

RL 1 cite textual evidence to support analysis of what the text says explicitly as well as inferences drawn; **RL 2** determine a theme or central idea of a text/analyze its development/ provide summary; **RL 4** determine the meaning of words and phrases, including figurative and connotative meanings; **RL 10** read and comprehend literature; **W 4** produce writing in which development, organization, and style are appropriate to task, purpose, and audience; **W 5** develop and strengthen writing by planning, revising, editing, rewriting, or trying a new approach; **SL 1** initiate/participate in a range of collaborative discussions; **SL 6** adapt speech to a variety of contexts and tasks, demonstrating command of formal English

◢ TEXT COMPLEXITY RUBRIC

Overall Text Complexity		"Song" POETRY
		MORE COMPLEX
Quantitative Measure	Lexile	N/A
Qualitative Measures	Text Structure	complex, unfamiliar poetic structure
	Language Conventionality and Clarity	archaic, unfamiliar language
	Knowledge Demands	many references or allusions to other texts
	Purpose/Levels of Meaning	multiple levels of complex meaning

Academic Vocabulary

Read each word with students and discuss its meaning.

cleft (line 4) • split

befell (line15) • happened or happened to

pilgrimage (line 20) • a seeker's journey or search

FIRST READ ## Think Through the Text

Have students use text evidence and draw inferences to answer questions.

• *What is the rhyme scheme of the poem? Stanza 1 is ABAB CC DDD; stanza 2 is EFEF FF GGG; stanza 3 is HIHI JJ FFF.* ⬤ RL 1, RL 4, RL 10

• *What tasks does the speaker challenge the listener to perform? The speaker tells the listener to catch a falling star, impregnate a plant, find past years, learn who gave the devil cloven feet, teach the speaker to hear mermaids, discover how to avoid envy, find what rewards honesty, ride 10,000 days and nights, and find a true and honest woman.* ⬤ RL 4

SECOND READ ## Analyze the Text

• Read the poem aloud. Then ask: *Why might Donne have titled this "Song" and suggested it be sung to music? Sample answer: The sarcastic tone becomes humorous if set to music.* ⬤ RL 1

• *What theme or message is the speaker expressing? Sample answer: Donne is suggesting that the ability to remain free of sin throughout life is as impossible as the fantastical tasks.* **What evidence in the poem supports this theme?** *impossible assignments; references to evil (devil, mandrake, falling star or Lucifer); application of hyperbole followed by the claim that woman, then a symbol of purity, was unfailingly false* ⬤ RL 1

☑ Practice Fluency

EMPHASIZE EXPRESSION Stress the importance of capturing the writer's imperative, ironic tone when reading this poem aloud. Have students practice tone change, taking turns reading aloud various lines in the poem with an ironic tone. ⬤ RL 1, RL 4, RL 10

Independent/Self-Selected Reading

Urge students to practice recognizing Donne's use of language and imagery using another poem from selections such as these:

• *The Complete Poetry and Selected Prose of John Donne* by John Donne

• *John Donne—The Major Works: including Songs and Sonnets and Sermons* by John Donne and John Casey ⬤ RL 10

Performance Task

WRITE & PRESENT

1. Ask students to consider the poem as an exchange between the narrator and his readers or listeners. Direct them to rewrite it in the form of a contemporary dialogue. ⬤ RL 10, SL 1

2. Have pairs consider how to restate each line and write each response by first improvising this conversation. ⬤ RL 2, RL 10, W 5

3. Following their improvisation, help individuals analyze and clarify any confusing imagery. Urge them to conclude with a thematic statement summing up the poem's meaning or message. ⬤ W 4, W 5

4. Have students pair-share their dialogues by assigning the parts and reading them aloud. Direct them to check that all tasks are covered and perform a final revision. ⬤ SL 1

5. Ask paired volunteers to read aloud their resulting dialogues. ⬤ SL 6

See Copying Master, pp. 212–215.

STUDENT CHECKLIST

Writing

☑ Set up the writing as dialogue with appropriate punctuation and grammar.

☑ Use descriptive language and hyperbole.

☑ Conclude with a restatement of the poem's theme.

Speaking & Listening

☑ Read dialogue aloud with a clear, audible voice.

☑ Present ideas in a meaningful way.

"Ozymandias"
by Percy Bysshe Shelley

▶ **OBJECTIVES**

- Identify the theme in a poem
- Analyze the imagery in a poem
- Summarize the events in a literary work

Options for Reading

Independent Students read the poem independently or with a partner and then answer questions posed by the teacher.

Supported Students read the poem and answer questions with teacher support.

SUMMARY In this poem, a traveler describes to the poet some ancient ruins that can be seen in the desert—an old sculpture that has been broken and worn away by time until only its legs and fallen head are left. There are words carved on the statue's pedestal that indicate that this sculpture was of a powerful king who lived long ago.

ABOUT THE POET **Percy Bysshe Shelley** was born in 1792 and grew up in England. He wrote many poems, a novel, a play, and political and religious pamphlets.

Discuss Genre and Set Purpose

POETRY Explain that this poem is a sonnet, or a poem with fourteen lines, each of which has ten syllables. Note that it follows the form of an Italian sonnet by surprising the reader with a change of subject matter at line nine. Then guide students to plot its odd rhyme scheme: *ababacdcedefef*.

TEXT FOCUS **Visual Imagery** Remind students that poetry often presents ideas or themes through imagery or events without directly stating the main idea. Use this poem to show students that examining the things described in a poem can help you figure out its meaning.

SET PURPOSE Help students set a purpose for reading, such as to find out who Ozymandias was and why he was so important.

Common Core Connection

RL 1 cite textual evidence to support analysis of what the text says explicitly as well as inferences drawn; **RL 2** determine a theme or central idea of a text/analyze its development/ provide summary; **RL 4** determine the meaning of words and phrases, including figurative and connotative meanings/analyze impact of word choices; **RL 7** analyze the representation of a subject in two different artistic mediums; **RL 10** read and comprehend literature; **W 2** write informative/explanatory texts; **W 4** produce writing in which development, organization, and style are appropriate to task, purpose, and audience; **SL 6** adapt speech to a variety of contexts and tasks, demonstrating command of formal English

△ TEXT COMPLEXITY RUBRIC		"Ozymandias" POETRY
Overall Text Complexity		**COMPLEX**
Quantitative Measure	Lexile	N/A
Qualitative Measures	Text Structure	complex, unfamiliar poetic structure
	Language Conventionality and Clarity	figurative language and unfamiliar words
	Knowledge Demands	experience includes unfamiliar aspects
	Purpose/Levels of Meaning	multiple levels of meaning

Academic Vocabulary

Read each word with students and discuss its meaning.

visage (line 4) • the features and appearance of a face

pedestal (line 9) • the support or base of a sculpture

colossal (line 13) • extremely large

FIRST READ ## Think Through the Text

Have students use text evidence and draw inferences to answer questions.

• *What has happened to the sculpture?* It has fallen down and broken. The head lies on the ground with the face smashed. **RL 1**

• *How does the traveler know what type of man Ozymandias was?* The traveler studied the expression on the stone face, or what remains of the face. Even though the face is broken, the traveler says that it has an expression of anger and contempt. **RL 1**

• *What would someone see if he or she followed the command to "look on my works"?* The person would not see anything because the traveler says that there is nothing else left standing around the statue. **RL 1**

SECOND READ ## Analyze the Text

• Review the words that are written on the pedestal (lines 10–11). Ask: *What is ironic about these words?* Sample answer: The words suggest that people should be afraid of Ozymandias and his accomplishments, and yet all that is left of him is a broken statue. **RL 4**

• Ask: *What message do you think the poet is expressing through the theme of this poem?* We will all be long forgotten someday. **RL 2**

☑ Practice Fluency

EMPHASIZE EXPRESSION Read the poem aloud, pausing at the end of each line. Then reread with expression, pausing based on sentence structure and phrases. Have students choose which reading makes the most sense and echo-read the poem with you with expression.

Independent/Self-Selected Reading

If students have already demonstrated comprehension of "Ozymandias," have them use another poem to practice skills. Suggested titles:

• "A Satirical Elegy on the Death of a Late Famous General" by Jonathon Swift, from *The Penguin Book of English Verse* edited by Paul Keegan

• *The Penguin Book of the Sonnet: 500 Years of a Classical Tradition in English* by Phillis Levin **RL 10**

WRITE & PRESENT

1. Provide students with examples of other artistic representations of Ramses II, such as photos of the Colossus of Ramses II discovered at the Great Temple of Ptah. Have small groups analyze what is emphasized or absent in different treatments of the pharaoh in these works of art and in Shelley's poem "Ozymandias." **RL 7**

2. Have students write brief expository essays comparing or contrasting how the pharaoh is depicted in the works of art and in the poem. Essays should use examples to support ideas. **W 2**

3. Have students share their work with partners and suggest revisions. Students edit their writing based on suggestions. **W 4**

4. Have students present three main points from their writing orally to the class and then respond to questions from classmates. **SL 6**

See Copying Masters, pp. 212–215.

STUDENT CHECKLIST

Writing

☑ Analyze how different kinds of art represent the same subject.

☑ Write an expository essay that compares two representations.

☑ Revise writing so that it has appropriate style and organization.

Speaking & Listening

☑ Share aloud a viewpoint, giving three main points.

☑ Respond to questions from peers about the ideas.

▷ **OBJECTIVES**

- Identify the rhythm and rhyme patterns in a poem
- Summarize the events described in the poem
- Use text evidence to explore visual imagery

Options for Reading

Independent Students read the poem independently or with a partner and then answer questions posed by the teacher.

Supported Students read a stanza and answer questions with teacher support. Alternatively, students listen as the teacher reads a stanza aloud and then answer questions. Encourage students to read at least a few lines on their own.

"The Raven"

by Edgar Allen Poe

SUMMARY "The Raven" is a poem about a raven that flies into a grieving man's home one evening. The raven speaks one word, *nevermore*. As the man ponders the meaning of this word, he thinks it has to do with his feelings about a woman who died. In the end, the man is despondent, and the bird will not leave the home.

ABOUT THE POET Edgar Allen Poe is best known for his horror stories, written both in poetic and in short story form. Poe also wrote a novel, wrote literary criticism, and edited a literary magazine.

Discuss Genre and Set Purpose

POETRY Tell students that poetry is a form of writing that uses rhythm or meter. Modern poetry also includes poems that do not use meter.

TEXT FOCUS: Rhythm and Rhyme Help students hear the rhythm of the poem by having them clap on the emphasized syllables. Then point out the rhyme scheme.

SET PURPOSE Help students set a purpose for reading, such as to immerse themselves in the imagery, story, and feeling of the poem.

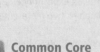

Common Core Connection

RL 1 cite textual evidence to support analysis of what the text says explicitly as well as inferences drawn; **RL 2** determine a theme or central idea of a text/analyze its development/ provide summary; **RL 3** analyze how characters develop and interact with others; **RL 5** analyze how author's choices create mystery, tension, or surprise; **RL 10** read and comprehend literature; **W 3** write narratives; **W 5** develop and strengthen writing by planning, revising, editing, rewriting, or trying a new approach; **SL 5** make strategic use of digital media in presentations

▲ **TEXT COMPLEXITY RUBRIC**

Overall Text Complexity		"The Raven" POETRY
		COMPLEX
Quantitative Measure	Lexile	N/A
Qualitative Measures	Text Structure	familiar poetic structure
	Language Conventionality and Clarity	figurative language and unfamiliar words
	Knowledge Demands	experience includes unfamiliar aspects
	Purpose/Levels of Meaning	multiple levels of meaning

Academic Vocabulary

Read each word with students and discuss its meaning.

surcease (line 10) • the process of ending

dirges (line 65) • songs or music played at a funeral

melancholy (line 65) • sadness

ominous (line 70) • hinting that something bad is going to happen

FIRST READ Think Through the Text

Have students use text evidence to answer questions.

- *What is the speaker doing before the Raven comes into the house?* *He is reading late in the night, trying to take his mind off of his grief.* ◗RL 1

- *How does the Raven enter the house?* *The speaker keeps hearing a noise outside. When he opens the shutter, the Raven flies in.* ◗RL 1

- *What is the final question the speaker asks the Raven?* *He asks if his soul will be able to clasp Lenore again in Heaven.* *How does he react to the Raven's answer?* *He gets mad and tells the Raven to leave because he thinks the Raven is saying he will never see Lenore again.* ◗RL 3

SECOND READ Analyze the Text

- Ask: *How do the rhythm and rhyme help make the story more powerful or affect the overall mood?* *They create a repetitious beat, making the reader feel like he or she is trapped in the room experiencing the same moment of grief over and over like a throbbing wound.* ◗RL 5

- Ask: *What idea is expressed by having the poem end with the Raven still sitting in the room?* *The Raven represents the man's grief and sorrow. He will never get over the death of Lenore. His sadness will always be with him.* ◗RL 2

- Ask: *What are some themes of the poem?* *lost love, sorrow, grief* ◗RL 2

☑ Practice Fluency

EMPHASIZE RHYTHM Read the first stanza of the poem aloud flatly, ignoring the rhythm. Then reread the stanza, using the rhythm. Have students explain why poetry is often best enjoyed when read aloud.

Independent/Self-Selected Reading

If students have already demonstrated comprehension of "The Raven," have them use another poem to practice skills. Suggested titles:

- *Complete Stories and Poems of Edgar Allen Poe* by Edgar Allen Poe

- *The Rime of the Ancient Mariner and Other Poems* by Samuel Taylor Coleridge ◗RL 10

WRITE & PRESENT

1. Have small groups discuss what they think of the speaker and how they or others might respond to him if he told them his story as a prose tale. ◗RL 3

2. Have each student write an individual narrative that describes what might happen when the speaker tells his story to a friend. Narratives should include details about the setting, the characters, and the dialogue. ◗W 3

3. Have students share their work with partners and suggest revisions and edits. Students edit their writing based on these suggestions. ◗W 5

4. Have students choose background music or visual images that fit their narratives. Then have students use the digital media as they read their stories aloud to the class. ◗SL 5

See Copying Masters, pp. 212–215.

STUDENT CHECKLIST

Writing

☑ Clearly describe how people might respond to the poem's speaker.

☑ Write a narrative that portrays what happens when the narrator talks to others about the Raven.

☑ Strengthen writing by revising it.

Speaking & Listening

☑ Read writing aloud with a clear, audible voice.

☑ Choose digital media that best fits the ideas or theme of a spoken presentation.

OBJECTIVES

- Identify the meaning of a poem
- Identify elements of poetry
- Identify figurative language
- Analyze text using text evidence

Options for Reading

Independent Students read the poem independently, uninterrupted, and then answer questions posed by the teacher.

Supported Students read the entire poem aloud and then reread each quatrain, or stanza, on its own and answer questions with teacher support.

"We Grow Accustomed to the Dark"
by Emily Dickinson

SUMMARY This poem uses a familiar four-line pattern (quatrain) to explore the discomfort of facing darkness: real darkness and the concept of darkness, such as fear of the unknown or loss.

ABOUT THE AUTHOR Emily Dickinson was an American poet. Her poetry is still admired for her inventive use of language, imagery, punctuation, and capitalization.

Discuss Genre and Set Purpose

POETRY Remind students that specific features make this a poem: short lines, stanzas, meter, rhythm, imagery, and figurative language.

TEXT FOCUS Figurative Language Tell students that figurative language communicates ideas beyond the literal meaning of words. As you read, ask students to identify figurative language. ◖RL 4

SET PURPOSE Help students set a purpose for reading the poem, such as analyzing the poet's use of figurative language and imagery.

Common Core Connection

RL 1 cite textual evidence to support analysis of what the text says explicitly as well as inferences drawn; **RL 2** determine a theme or central idea of a text and analyze its development; **RL 4** determine the meaning of words and phrases, including figurative and connotative meanings; **RL 5** analyze how author's choices create mystery, tension, or surprise; **RL 10** read and comprehend literature; **W 3** write narratives; **W 3d** use precise words and phrases, telling details, and sensory language; **W 5** develop and strengthen writing by planning, revising, editing, rewriting, or trying a new approach; **SL 1** initiate/participate in a range of collaborative discussions

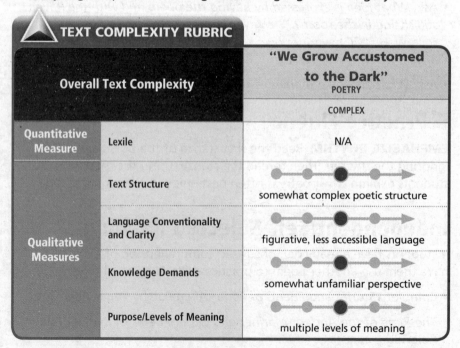

TEXT COMPLEXITY RUBRIC		"We Grow Accustomed to the Dark" POETRY
Overall Text Complexity		COMPLEX
Quantitative Measure	Lexile	N/A
Qualitative Measures	Text Structure	somewhat complex poetic structure
	Language Conventionality and Clarity	figurative, less accessible language
	Knowledge Demands	somewhat unfamiliar perspective
	Purpose/Levels of Meaning	multiple levels of meaning

Academic Vocabulary

Read each word with students and discuss its meaning.

accustomed (line 1) • used to

disclose (line 11) • show; reveal

alters (line 17) • changes

FIRST READ **Think Through the Text**

Have students use text evidence and draw inferences to answer questions.

• *In lines 5–8, Dickinson uses imagery to describe what sensation?* what it feels like when lights suddenly go out *How does the poet describe it?* You are unsteady, but then your eyes get used to the darkness. **RL 1**

• *What startling concrete image does Dickinson use to convey the difficulty of facing the dark?* walking headfirst into a tree **RL 4**

• *What is the effect of the unusual use of capital letters and dashes?* They call attention to the uncertainty one feels in the dark. They also emphasize words, suggest a pause, and help set the poem's rhythm. **RL 5**

SECOND READ **Analyze the Text**

• Read the poem aloud for meaning without stopping at line endings. Ask: *What are the types of darkness the poet refers to in line 9?* Sample answers: any scary experience; the unknown **RL 1, RL 4**

• Ask: *What can change to make things nearly all right again?* The situation itself can change or the way you view it can change. *Which lines in the poem support your ideas?* lines 17–20 **RL 2, RL 10**

• Explain to students that Dickinson used figurative language to make a comparison in this poem. Ask: *What is being compared?* Walking out into the dark is compared to facing a difficult or unknown situation. *What do you think the image in line 10 describes?* how people can't think clearly when they are afraid of the unknown **RL 4**

☑ Practice Fluency

EMPHASIZE EXPRESSION Have students read the poem aloud for meaning and expression. Suggest alternative approaches such as not pausing at dashes or running lines together as they read.

Independent/Self-Selected Reading

Have students select other poems from other anthologies independently to explore unconventional styles. **RL 10**

• *Red Bird* by Mary Oliver

• *Dickinson: Selected Poems and Commentaries* by Helen Vendler

WRITE & PRESENT

1. Have small groups refer to the text to discuss the imagery that appeals to the five senses (seeing, hearing, speaking, listening, touching). Ask students to think about how the imagery conveys the poet's ideas. **RL 1, RL 4**

2. Have students write a comparison of Dickinson's view of confronting the unknown with how they faced an unsettling experience, such as moving to a new school. Encourage students to use figurative language and imagery as they describe the experience and their response. **W 3, W 3d**

3. Have students share their work with partners and offer suggestions for revising and editing. Students edit their writing based on these suggestions. **W 5**

4. Have students present their final writing to their classmates. Ask students to respond to the themes and ideas from each student's writing. **SL 1**

See *Copying Masters*, pp. 212–215.

STUDENT CHECKLIST

Writing

☑ In writing, compare Dickinson's description with how you faced an unknown situation.

☑ Use figurative language.

☑ Use correct language conventions.

Speaking & Listening

☑ Participate effectively in a collaborative discussion.

☑ Present ideas in a meaningful way.

▶ OBJECTIVES

- Describe poetic imagery
- Identify the theme of a poem
- Interpret alliteration and rhyme in poetry
- Analyze poetry using text evidence

Options for Reading

Independent Students read the poem first for an initial impression, then again for deeper meaning, and then finally answer questions posed by the teacher.

Supported Students read the poem twice in pairs or as a group and answer questions with teacher support.

"The Loveliest of Trees"

by A. E. Housman

SUMMARY This poem composed of rhymed couplets uses a simple natural image to express the belief that because life is short, we should experience the beauty of nature during all seasons.

ABOUT THE AUTHOR A. E. Housman (1859–1936) was a British poet and scholar. While spending his career as a professor of Latin studies at University College, London, and later, Cambridge, he composed several volumes of lyric poetry that were noted for a restrained simplicity of style and pessimistic tone.

Discuss Genre and Set Purpose

POETRY Point out to students that "The Loveliest of Trees" is a lyric poem. Poets write lyric poetry by observing something in nature that leads to the expression of an idea or emotion.

TEXT FOCUS Figurative Language Alliteration is the meaningful use of repeated beginning sounds in words that are close together.

SET PURPOSE Help students set a purpose for reading, such as to analyze the poem's theme while enjoying its meter and rhyme.

COMMON CORE Common Core Connection

RL 1 cite textual evidence to support analysis of what the text says explicitly as well as inferences drawn; **RL 2** determine a theme or central idea of a text/analyze its development/ provide summary; **RL 4** determine the meaning of words and phrases, including figurative and connotative meanings; **RL 10** read and comprehend literature; **W 3d** use precise words and phrases, telling details, and sensory language; **W 5** develop and strengthen writing by planning, revising, editing, rewriting, or trying a new approach; **SL 4** present information clearly, concisely, and logically

▲ TEXT COMPLEXITY RUBRIC

Overall Text Complexity		"The Loveliest of Trees" POETRY
		MORE COMPLEX
Quantitative Measure	Lexile	N/A
Qualitative Measures	Text Structure	simple, familiar poetic structure
	Language Conventionality and Clarity	longer descriptions
	Knowledge Demands	fairly complex theme, somewhat unfamiliar perspective
	Purpose/Levels of Meaning	single level of complex meaning

Academic Vocabulary

Read each word with students and discuss its meaning.

bough (line 2) • a major limb or branch on a tree

Eastertide (line 4) • the weeks around the Christian holiday of Easter, usually early in the spring

threescore (line 5) • a period of 60 years

score (line 7) • a period of 20 years

WRITE & PRESENT

1. Have pairs discuss the visual imagery used in this poem, for example, the changing look of the cherry tree. Encourage them to explain their own ideas and understanding of the images based on the text. Then have each student brainstorm a list of natural images that have particular personal meaning. **RL 4**

2. Following the model of "Loveliest of Trees," have students compose a two- or three-stanza poem with rhyming couplets in which they introduce and describe a natural image, note its impact, and draw a conclusion that reveals an underlying theme. Students should include at least two examples of alliteration. **W 3d**

3. Have students pair-share their poems, offering reactions and editing suggestions. **W 5**

4. Ask volunteers to read their revised poems aloud. **SL 4**

See Copying Masters, pp. 212–215.

FIRST READ # Think Through the Text

Have students use text evidence and draw inferences to answer questions.

• *How old is the speaker, and how much time does he believe he has left to appreciate nature?* *In line 5, the speaker refers to the lifespan of 70 years, and in the next line, he notes that 20 of his years have passed. The speaker is 20 and believes he has 50 more years.* **RL 1**

SECOND READ # Analyze the Text

• Read the poem aloud. *What is the poem's rhyme scheme and structure?* *The poem's rhyme scheme is aa, bb, cc, dd, ee, ff—six rhyming couplets divided into three stanzas.* **RL 4**

• Ask: *What theme or message is the speaker expressing in this poem?* *Life is too brief to miss any chances to enjoy the pleasures of nature. What evidence supports this theme? In lines 5–8, the speaker addresses the brevity of life, and in lines 9–12, he says what he will do.* **RL 2**

• Review the poem's form with students. *How does the style and form of the poem reinforce its theme?* *The short lines, simple word choices, and sing-song rhythm all reinforce that life is too short.* **RL 2, RL 4**

☑ Practice Fluency

EMPHASIZE RHYTHM Stress the importance of concentrating on rhythm when reading a rhyming poem aloud. Have students read the first stanza without rhythm. Then read it together again with emphasis on the beat and rhyme. **RL 10**

Independent/Self-Selected Reading

If students have demonstrated comprehension of "The Loveliest of Trees," urge them to practice recognizing alliteration and lyricism using another poem by Housman from selections such as these:

• *A Shropshire Lad* by A. E. Housman

• *The Collected Poems of A. E. Housman* by A. E. Housman **RL 10**

STUDENT CHECKLIST

Writing

☑ Introduce a central image from nature, describe it, and draw a conclusion that reveals a central theme.

☑ Use descriptive language and alliteration.

☑ Check rhythm and rhyme.

Speaking & Listening

☑ Read poetry aloud with a clear, audible voice.

☑ Present ideas in a meaningful way.

DOMAIN: Literature
LESSON TOPIC: Rhythm

▶ OBJECTIVES

- Analyze text using evidence
- Analyze word choices
- Analyze rhythm and rhyming patterns
- Identify the theme of a poem

Options for Reading

Independent Students read the poem independently and then read stanzas aloud with a partner and answer questions posed by the teacher.

Supported The teacher reads the entire poem once and then students read it by stanzas and answer questions with teacher support.

"Lift Every Voice and Sing"

by James Weldon Johnson

SUMMARY "Lift Every Voice and Sing" celebrates the African American spirit. It reflects on the historical experiences of many African Americans, their religious roots, and their hope for the American value system.

ABOUT THE AUTHOR James Weldon Johnson was born in 1871 in Florida, shortly after the end of the Civil War. An award-winning educator, lawyer, diplomat, poet, and songwriter, he was also a civil rights activist and leader.

Discuss Genre and Set Purpose

POETRY Remind students that one of the pleasures of reading poetry is to experience the patterns of rhythms and words created by the poet to express ideas and emotions.

TEXT FOCUS Rhythm and Rhyme Explain to students that rhythm refers to the arrangement of stressed and unstressed syllables and, along with rhyme, brings out the musical qualities of language.

SET PURPOSE Help students set a purpose for reading the poem, such as discovering the influence of rhythm, or meter, and rhyme on the ideas and emotions conveyed by the poem.

COMMON CORE — Common Core Connection

RL 1 cite textual evidence to support analysis of what the text says explicitly as well as inferences drawn; **RL 2** determine a theme or central idea of a text/analyze its development/provide summary; **RL 4** determine the meaning of words and phrases, including figurative and connotative meanings/analyze impact of word choices; **RL 5** analyze how author's choices create mystery, tension, or surprise; **RL 10** read and comprehend literature; **W 2** write informative/explanatory texts; **W 2b** develop topic with facts, definitions, details, quotations, or other information and examples; **W 2d** use precise language and domain-specific vocabulary; **W 5** develop and strengthen writing by planning, revising, editing, rewriting, or trying a new approach; **SL 4** present information, findings, and supporting evidence clearly, concisely, and logically

△ TEXT COMPLEXITY RUBRIC

Overall Text Complexity		"Lift Every Voice and Sing" POETRY
		COMPLEX
Quantitative Measure	Lexile	N/A
Qualitative Measures	Text Structure	simple, familiar poetic structure
	Language Conventionality and Clarity	figurative, symbolic language
	Knowledge Demands	cultural and literary knowledge useful
	Purpose/Levels of Meaning	multiple levels of meaning

Academic Vocabulary

Read each word with students and discuss its meaning.

harmonies (line 3) • agreements
resounding (line 6) • echoing, booming
chastening (line 12) • punishing

FIRST READ ## Think Through the Text

Have students use text evidence and draw inferences to answer questions.

- *Lines 7 and 12 contain references to what specific aspects of history?* years of slavery, unfair treatment, and physical abuse ⬤RL 1, RL 4

- *The poet is optimistic about the future, so why did he choose a harsh image in line 18 as a remembrance of the past?* It is a reminder of the violence that accompanied slavery and racism. *Which words indicate hope?* rejoicing, faith, hope, rising sun, bright star *How do these words create tension in the poem?* They bring up opposing images. ⬤RL 5

- *What path is the speaker describing in the last stanza?* the path to justice, religious commitment, the best values of the country ⬤RL 2, RL 10

SECOND READ ## Analyze the Text

- Have students reread the poem aloud. Ask them to describe the structure of the poem. *It has three stanzas of increasing lengths: 10, 11, and 12 lines.* ⬤RL 4

- Ask: *Why are there slight variations in the poem's rhythm, or meter, and accented syllables?* to keep the poem from becoming tedious; to give the poem liveliness and create interest for the reader ⬤RL 5

- Read the title aloud. Ask: *Who is every voice, as in the title of the poem?* Every voice in the world that supports equality for all. ⬤RL 5

- Ask: *What do you think are the themes of this poem?* celebration, remembrance, persistence, perseverance, faith, hope ⬤RL 5

☑ Practice Fluency

EMPHASIZE RHYTHM Remind students to listen for the rhythm and to emphasize the beat when they read poetry. Have students read each stanza of the poem with emphasis on the meter and the rhymes.

Independent/Self-Selected Reading

Have students select other poems independently to practice analyzing poetry on their own.

- *The Book of American Negro Poetry* by James Weldon Johnson

- *Here in Harlem: Poems in Many Voices* by Dean Myers ⬤RL 10

WRITE & PRESENT

1. Ask students to think about the structure, rhythm and meter, and rhyming patterns in the poem. Have them write an essay in which they discuss how these elements help convey the ideas and emotions of the poem. ⬤W 2

2. Encourage students to cite specific text evidence to support their ideas. Help students understand the rhythm by counting the beats in each line (6, 6, 10, 6, 6, 10, 14, 14, 6, 6 or 12, 10). Note that *listening* and *chastening* are pronounced as two-syllable words to make the pattern work. ⬤W 2b, W 2d

3. Have students share their work with partners and offer suggestions for revising and editing. Students edit their writing based on these suggestions. ⬤W 5

4. Have students present their final writing to their classmates. Ask students to respond to the ideas from each student's writing. ⬤SL 4

See Copying Masters, pp. 212–215.

STUDENT CHECKLIST

Writing

☑ Identify the rhyme scheme and at least one aspect of the poem's rhythm.

☑ Explain how the rhythm and rhyme scheme help bring out the ideas and emotions conveyed in the poem.

Speaking & Listening

☑ Present ideas and supporting evidence in a clear and meaningful way.

OBJECTIVES

- Describe poetic imagery
- Identify the theme of a poem
- Interpret allusion in poetry
- Analyze poetry using text evidence

"Yet Do I Marvel"
by Countee Cullen

Options for Reading

Independent Students read the poem first for an initial impression and then again for deeper meaning, and then answer questions posed by the teacher.

Supported Students read the poem aloud twice in pairs or as a group and answer questions with teacher support.

SUMMARY This 14-line lyrical sonnet presents several contradictory situations that test religious faith, the last being that a particular race is the focus of suppression and prejudice. In the ending couplet, however, the speaker concludes with the realization that a person so tormented still has the artistic yearnings of all humans.

ABOUT THE AUTHOR **Countee Cullen** (1903–1946) was a writer of the Harlem Renaissance movement. After winning a citywide poetry contest in high school, Cullen graduated from New York University and later earned a master's degree from Harvard University.

Discuss Genre and Set Purpose

POETRY Tell students that "Yet Do I Marvel" is a lyric sonnet filled with imagery. Remind them that allusions are references to someone or something that is widely known, such as from mythology or the Bible.

TEXT FOCUS **Visual Imagery** Explain that a poet uses words to create visual imagery that conveys a thought or feeling. ▬RL 4

SET PURPOSE Help students set a purpose for reading, such as to analyze the poem's imagery and to identify the theme.

COMMON CORE **Common Core Connection**

RL 1 cite textual evidence to support analysis of what the text says explicitly as well as inferences drawn; **RL 2** determine a theme or central idea of a text/analyze its development/ provide summary; **RL 4** determine the meaning of words and phrases, including figurative and connotative meanings/analyze impact of word choices; **RL 10** read and comprehend literature; **W 1e** provide a concluding statement or section; **W 2b** develop topic with facts, definitions, details, quotations, or other information and examples; **W 3d** use precise words and phrases, telling details, and sensory language; **W 4** produce writing in which development, organization, and style are appropriate to task, purpose, and audience; **W 5** develop and strengthen writing by planning, revising, editing, rewriting, or trying a new approach; **W 9** draw evidence from literary or informational texts; **SL 1** initiate/ participate in a range of collaborative discussions; **SL 6** adapt speech to a variety of contexts and tasks, demonstrating command of formal English

TEXT COMPLEXITY RUBRIC

Overall Text Complexity		"Yet Do I Marvel" POETRY
		MORE COMPLEX
Quantitative Measure	Lexile	N/A
Qualitative Measures	Text Structure	somewhat complex poetic structure
	Language Conventionality and Clarity	figurative, less accessible language
	Knowledge Demands	some cultural and literary knowledge useful, one or two references or allusions to other texts
	Purpose/Levels of Meaning	single level of complex meaning

Academic Vocabulary

Read each word with students and discuss its meaning.

quibble (line 2) • to make trivial objections to win an argument

fickle (line 6) • changeable; inconstant

catechism (line 10) • a question-and-answer summary of religious beliefs

FIRST READ Think Through the Text

Have students use text evidence and draw inferences to answer questions.

• Read lines 1–4. Ask: *What paradox, or situation that seems to contradict itself, is first described? Although he believes that God is kind, the poet wonders why He lets the mole remain blind.* ⬤ RL 1, RL 2

• *What are some words or phrases the poet uses to create sympathetic images in lines 1–8? Sample answer:* little, buried, fickle ⬤ RL 1, RL 4

SECOND READ Analyze the Text

• Reread the poem aloud. Ask: *Why do you think God's brain and hand are described as "awful"? Sample answer: to show that God is powerful in both positive and negative ways* ⬤ RL 4

• Reread the final couplet with students. *What surprising final paradox does the speaker reveal? Sample answer: God would make a poet who also happens to experience racial prejudice and then expect him to write joyfully.* ⬤ RL 1, RL 2, RL 4, RL 10

• *What is the connotation of the words* marvel *and* curious *in line 13? They have a positive connotation; the speaker is glad to be a poet.* ⬤ RL 4

☑ Practice Fluency

EMPHASIZE RHYTHM Read the poem through once without pausing, and then have students reread the poem, emphasizing the beat and pausing at the completion of an image or thought. ⬤ RL 10

Independent/Self-Selected Reading

If students have demonstrated comprehension of "Yet Do I Marvel," urge them to practice recognizing lyrical sonnets and allusions and in other poems by Cullen from selections such as these:

• *My Soul's High Song: The Collected Writings of Countee Cullen, Voice of the Harlem Renaissance* by Countee Cullen

• *Caroling Dusk: An Anthology of Verse by Black Poets of the Twenties* by Countee Cullen ⬤ RL 10

WRITE & PRESENT

1. Have students write a paragraph interpreting "Yet Do I Marvel" discussing the poem's theme and how it makes them feel. ⬤ W 5

2. Help individuals write a topic sentence that includes the title, author, and a brief statement of theme. ⬤ RL 2, W 2a, W 4

3. Guide students to explain their interpretations in supporting sentences. ⬤ RL 2, W 3d, W 9

4. Have students conclude with how the poem makes them feel. Have them add one sentence saying whether they liked the poem and why. ⬤ W 1e, W 2b, W 3d

5. Have triads comment on and peer edit each other's work before rewriting. Ask volunteers to read their paragraphs aloud. ⬤ W 5, SL 1, SL 6

See Copying Masters, pp. 212–215.

STUDENT CHECKLIST

Writing

☑ Write an interpretative analysis.

☑ Provide supporting details from the poem.

☑ Use correct grammar and writing conventions.

Speaking & Listening

☑ Participate effectively in a collaborative discussion.

☑ Read an essay aloud with a clear, audible voice.

OBJECTIVES

- Identify the theme of a poem
- Interpret allusions in poetry
- Identify irony in a poem
- Analyze poetry using text evidence

Options for Reading

Independent Students read the poem independently for an initial impression and then answer questions posed by the teacher.

Supported Students read the poem twice in pairs or as a group and answer questions with teacher support.

"Musée des Beaux Arts"

by W. H. Auden

SUMMARY This poem reflects on "Landscape with the Fall of Icarus," a painting by Pieter Brueghel that shows a lovely spring day with Icarus plunging into the sea in the background. This leads the speaker in the poem to think about how all human suffering is surrounded by the ordinary activities of daily life.

ABOUT THE AUTHOR W. H. Auden (1907–1973) is widely regarded as one of the greatest English language poets of the twentieth century, a writer whose technical skill and ability to write in every verse form is virtually unequaled. His style ranges from the ironic to the dramatic.

Discuss Genre and Set Purpose

POETRY Explain to students that the poem is technically complex, with ten syllables in each of the first three lines and a complicated rhyme scheme.

TEXT FOCUS Allusions The poem refers to Greek mythology, sixteenth-century Belgium, martyrdom, old master painters, and Christian beliefs, as well as contemporary events.

SET PURPOSE Help students set a purpose for reading, such as to understand how the poem's allusions and irony help suggest its theme.

Common Core Connection

RL 1 cite textual evidence to support analysis of what the text says explicitly as well as inferences drawn; **RL 2** determine a theme or central idea of a text/analyze its development/provide summary; **RL 7** analyze the representation of a subject or a key scene in two different artistic mediums; **RL 9** analyze how author draws on/transforms source material in a specific work; **RL 10** read and comprehend literature; **W 1** write arguments to support claims; **W 5** develop and strengthen writing by planning, revising, editing, rewriting, or trying a new approach; **SL 1** initiate/participate in a range of collaborative discussions

TEXT COMPLEXITY RUBRIC

Overall Text Complexity		"Musée des Beaux Arts" POETRY
		MORE COMPLEX
Quantitative Measure	Lexile	N/A
Qualitative Measures	Text Structure	somewhat complex poetic structure
	Language Conventionality and Clarity	some figurative language and unfamiliar words
	Knowledge Demands	fairly complex theme
	Purpose/Levels of Meaning	multiple levels of complex meaning

Academic Vocabulary

Read each word with students and discuss its meaning.

reverently (line 5) • with reverence; very respectfully

martyrdom (line 10) • enduring terrible suffering rather than renouncing beliefs

ploughman (line 15) • a farm laborer behind a plow

forsaken (line 16) • deserted or abandoned

FIRST READ ## Think Through the Text

Have students use text evidence and draw inferences to answer questions.

• *About what are the Old Masters never wrong?* In lines 1–2, the speaker says the painters were never wrong about suffering. **RL 1**

• *What ironic actions does the speaker refer to while a torturer is making a martyr suffer?* In lines 12–13, a dog behaves like a dog and the torturer's horse scratches its posterior on a tree. **RL 2**

SECOND READ ## Analyze the Text

• Read the poem aloud. Then ask: *What is the rhyme scheme in this poem?* There are rhyming lines but no formal rhyme scheme. *How does this reinforce the poem's theme?* Like the poem's rhymes, human suffering may be random and unnoticed by others. **RL 2**

• Ask: *What theme or message is the speaker expressing in this poem?* Sample answer: Like an indifferent horse or dogs going about their business, people pay little attention to disaster. *How does the image of the ploughman in the painting support this theme?* In lines 15–18, the ploughman doesn't even look up as Icarus falls to his death. **RL 2, RL 9**

☑ Practice Fluency

EMPHASIZE RATE Stress the importance of concentrating on reading rate in a poem using enjambment (a thought runs on beyond the end of a line). Discuss the pace at which a sentence is read with a natural pause at the end of the thought. **RL 10**

Independent/Self-Selected Reading

If students have demonstrated comprehension of "Musée des Beaux Arts," urge them to practice recognizing allusion using another poem by Auden or from selections such as these:

• *Collected Poems* by W. H. Auden and Edward Mendelson

• *Pictures from Brueghel and Other Poems* by William Carlos Williams **RL 10**

WRITE & PRESENT

1. Have students view Brueghel's "Landscape with the Fall of Icarus" online or in a book and analyze the painting from the perspective of the speaker in Auden's poem. Have them use their analysis of the painting to argue for or against a theme in the poem, such as that daily life continues without noticing the suffering of individuals. **RL 7, RL 9**

2. Help students develop their argument in support of the theme as it relates to the artwork alluded to in the poem and present it in a short essay. **W 1**

3. Have them support their point of view with evidence from the poem. **RL 1, W 1**

4. Have students share their essays with partners and offer suggestions for revising and editing. Students edit their writing based on these suggestions. **W 5**

5. Ask volunteers to read their essays aloud. **SL 1**

See Copying Masters, pp. 212–215.

STUDENT CHECKLIST

Writing

☑ Determine a central theme of a poem based on a painting alluded to in the poem.

☑ Develop an argument with supporting evidence.

Speaking & Listening

☑ Read an essay aloud with a clear, audible voice.

☑ Present ideas in a meaningful way.

OBJECTIVES

- Analyze text using text evidence
- Apply knowledge from outside the text to help analyze meaning and theme
- Describe how word choices and line breaks convey meaning in poetry

Options for Reading

Independent Students read the poem silently and aloud, independently or with the teacher, and then answer questions posed by the teacher.

Supported Students read a few lines and answer questions with teacher support. Students then reread the lines independently or with a partner. Encourage students to read at least a few lines on their own.

COMMON CORE **Common Core Connection**

RL 1 cite textual evidence to support analysis of what the text says explicitly as well as inferences drawn; **RL 2** determine a theme or central idea of a text/analyze its development/ provide summary; **RL 4** determine the meaning of words and phrases, including figurative and connotative meanings/analyze impact of word choices; **RL 10** read and comprehend literature; **W 1c** use words, phrases, and clauses to link major sections of text, create cohesion, and clarify relationships; **W 3d** use precise words and phrases, telling details, and sensory language; **W 4** produce writing in which development, organization, and style are appropriate to task, purpose, and audience; **W 5** develop and strengthen writing by planning, revising, editing, rewriting, or trying a new approach; **SL 1** initiate/participate in a range of collaborative discussions

"Women"
by Alice Walker

SUMMARY With short, free verse lines, the poet immortalizes a generation of African American women who focused on obtaining an education for their children. Images in the poem of domestic work are intertwined with images of strength and protest to show how such women contributed to the struggle for civil rights.

ABOUT THE POET **Alice Walker** was born in Georgia in 1944. She went to Spelman College and Sarah Lawrence College and worked to register black voters in the South during the civil rights movement. She received the Pulitzer Prize and the National Book Award for her novel *The Color Purple*.

Discuss Genre and Set Purpose

POETRY Tell students that poets use words arranged in unusual ways to create images, moods, and feelings. Poets of free verse use stressed and unstressed syllables, sound devices, and line breaks to create rhythm.

TEXT FOCUS Line Breaks Explain to students that poets break lines of poetry to develop, enhance, or create layers of meaning. Line breaks may occur at the end of a grammatical unit or in the middle of one for emphasis or to signal a pause.

SET PURPOSE Guide students to set a purpose for reading, such as paying attention to how the poet uses line breaks to help convey meaning.

▲ TEXT COMPLEXITY RUBRIC

Overall Text Complexity		"Women" POETRY COMPLEX
Quantitative Measure	Lexile	N/A
Qualitative Measures	Text Structure	free verse poetic structure
	Language Conventionality and Clarity	some unfamiliar words or phrases
	Knowledge Demands	some specialized knowledge required
	Purpose/Levels of Meaning	implied, somewhat easy to identify from context with guidance

> **Academic Vocabulary**
>
> Read each word with students and discuss its meaning.
>
> **stout** (line 3) • sturdy or marked by determination
>
> **battered** (line 7) • pounded repeatedly, smashed

FIRST READ ## Think Through the Text

Have students use text evidence and draw inferences to answer questions.

- *To whom are the women compared in lines 12–18?* *The women are like army leaders or generals.* *What historical issues are part of this poem?* *the civil rights movement in the United States* ⬛ **RL 4**

- *For what and for whom are these women fighting?* *They are fighting for books and desks, or education, for their children.* *Which lines tell you this?* *lines 19–21* ⬛ **RL 1, RL 2, RL 10**

SECOND READ ## Analyze the Text

- Read the poem aloud to students. *Describe the visual images that you get from the poem.* *Sample answer: They wear scarves on their heads while doing domestic chores like ironing or cooking. They live their daily lives with determination like generals and soldiers.* ⬛ **RL 1**

- Have students pay attention to the line breaks as you reread lines 5–20 aloud. Ask: *What do the line breaks and single-word lines cause you to do as you read?* *stop and start reading; pause* *What impact do the line breaks have on your understanding of the poem?* *They emphasize certain words and call attention to the women's actions.* ⬛ **RL 4, RL 10**

- Have students reread lines 22–26. Discuss what the women knew and didn't know. Ask: *What book or page could the women identify without knowing it themselves?* *Sample answer: The women might not have been well educated, but they knew that a good education would enable their children to achieve civil rights.* ⬛ **RL 1, RL 2, RL 10**

☑ Practice Fluency

EMPHASIZE EXPRESSION Ask students to read the poem aloud with a varying emphasis on the one-word lines. Students can practice raising and lowering the pitch of their voices, reading faster or slower, or even reading more loudly or more quietly. Have students discuss how their expression when reading can change meanings. ⬛ **RL 4, RL 10**

Independent/Self-Selected Reading

If students have already demonstrated comprehension of "Women," have them select other poetry to read, such as:

- *Absolute Trust in the Goodness of the Earth* by Alice Walker

- *Mother Love: Poems* by Rita Dove ⬛ **RL 10**

WRITE & PRESENT

1. Have small groups discuss how the line breaks and word choices in the poem help to create images that reveal the women's character. ⬛ **RL 4, RL 10**

2. Ask students to think about why the women in the poem were fighting. Have students write a poem that describes a woman they know who influences their lives. Remind them to use line breaks as a way to convey meaning and create an impact. ⬛ **W 1c, W 3d, W 4**

3. Have students share their work with the small group and offer feedback for revising and editing. Students edit their writing. ⬛ **W 5**

4. Have students read their revised poems aloud. Ask students to respond to each other's word choices and use of line breaks. ⬛ **SL 1**

See Copying Masters, pp. 212–215.

STUDENT CHECKLIST

Writing

☑ Write an explanation for the line breaks used in your poem.

☑ Use quotations from the poem correctly.

☑ Use proper conventions in your writing.

Speaking & Listening

☑ Participate respectfully in a classroom discussion about "Women."

☑ Ask and answer questions about the poem's subject matter, the poem's line breaks, and the poet's word choice.

☑ Describe details in your own writing or drawing that relate to the content of "Women."

OBJECTIVES

- Explain the meaning of a poem
- Explore the use of metaphor
- Explore the use of visual imagery through figurative language
- Examine repetition in poetry
- Analyze text using text evidence

Options for Reading

Independent Students read the poem independently or with a partner and then answer questions posed by the teacher.

Supported Students read each stanza separately and answer questions with teacher support.

"I Am Offering This Poem"

by Jimmy Santiago Baca

SUMMARY The poet uses repetition and vivid sensory images to describe the love he is offering to the addressee of the poem and to convey the importance of love in life.

ABOUT THE POET Jimmy Santiago Baca learned to read and began to write poetry while spending five years in prison. Inspired to help others in need, he runs a charity that organizes writing workshops for everyone from schoolchildren to prisoners.

Discuss Genre and Set Purpose

POETRY Have students look at the poem. Note that this poem is free verse, which does not rhyme. Point out that the poem's lines are grouped into stanzas, each punctuated by a repeated phrase.

TEXT FOCUS Visual Imagery Explain that poets use vivid words and sensory images, as well as figurative language, to help the reader picture the things being described and to increase the enjoyment of the poem.

SET PURPOSE Encourage students to set a purpose for reading the poem, such as to examine the different descriptive images the poet uses.

COMMON CORE Connection

RL 1 cite textual evidence to support analysis of what the text says explicitly as well as inferences drawn; **RL 2** determine and provide a summary of a theme or central idea of a text; **RL 4** determine the meaning of words and phrases, including figurative meanings; **RL 10** read and comprehend literature; **W 2b** develop topic with facts, details, quotations, or other information and examples; **W 5** develop and strengthen writing by planning, revising, editing, rewriting, or trying a new approach; **SL 4** present findings clearly, concisely, and logically

TEXT COMPLEXITY RUBRIC

Overall Text Complexity		"I Am Offering This Poem" POETRY
		ACCESSIBLE
Quantitative Measure	Lexile	N/A
Qualitative Measures	Text Structure	less familiar poetic structure
	Language Conventionality and Clarity	some figurative language
	Knowledge Demands	everyday knowledge required
	Purpose/Levels of Meaning	implied, but easy to identify from context

Academic Vocabulary

Read each word with students and discuss its meaning.

mature (p. 52) • completely grown to adulthood

hogan (p. 52) • a type of house built by the Navajo Indians

dense (p. 52) • thickly and closely packed together

FIRST READ ## Think Through the Text

Have students use text evidence and draw inferences to answer questions.

- *To what does the poet compare the poem in the second stanza?* to a pot full of corn and to a scarf RL 4

- *What kind of figurative language are these comparisons?* metaphors *How do you know?* Each comparison consists of two things, but they do not use the words *like* or *as*. RL 4

- *How does the poet use repetition in this poem?* After each stanza, he repeats the phrase "I love you." RL 1

SECOND READ ## Analyze the Text

- *How does the poet use references to warmth in the imagery of this poem?* All of the things to which he compares the poem he is offering—a coat, thick socks, a pot full of corn, a scarf, and a fire—are things that will keep you warm. *What do you think the poet means by making these comparisons?* He is saying that a poem full of love will keep a person warm, or make him or her feel loved. RL 4

- Ask students to review the last stanza of the poem. Ask: *What is the theme of this poem?* Sample answer: Knowing that one is loved is all a person needs to live. RL 2

☑ Analyze the Text

EMPHASIZE RATE Explain to students that it is important to read the words of a poem filled with symbolism at a steady but slower rate so that readers have time to think about the interpretation. Model how to read the poem at a slower rate. Then have students choral-read the poem with you. RL 2

Independent/Self-Selected Reading

If students have already demonstrated comprehension of "I Am Offering This Poem," have them use another poem to practice skills. Suggested titles:

- *The Dream Keeper and Other Poems* by Langston Hughes

- *Partly Cloudy: Poems of Love and Longing* by Gary Soto RL 10

WRITE & PRESENT

1. Have small groups review the symbolism in "I Am Offering This Poem" and discuss their interpretations of the poet's message. RL 2

2. Have students write an opinion paragraph that identifies the theme of the poem and how they used metaphors and other figurative language to figure it out. Remind them to support their ideas with details from the poem and their understanding of figurative language. W 2b

3. Have students exchange paragraphs and offer suggestions for revising and editing. Suggest that students improve their writing based on these suggestions. W 5

4. Have students share their writing with the class. SL 4

See Copying Masters, pp. 212–215.

STUDENT CHECKLIST

Writing

☑ Write an opinion paragraph that identifies the theme of the poem.

☑ Develop and strengthen writing by revising and editing.

☑ Use correct language conventions.

Speaking & Listening

☑ Participate effectively in a collaborative discussion.

☑ Present writing to the class, speaking clearly at an understandable pace.

▶ **OBJECTIVES**

- Determine the central idea of a text
- Determine author's purpose
- Analyze text using text evidence

Options for Reading

Independent Students read the text independently or with a partner and then answer questions posed by the teacher.

Supported Students read the text and answer questions with teacher support.

"Speech to the Second Virginia Convention"

by Patrick Henry

SUMMARY In this speech to the second Virginia Convention in 1775, often referred to as the "Give me liberty or give me death speech," Patrick Henry argues for the colonists to fight against British tyranny.

ABOUT THE AUTHOR Patrick Henry was born in Virginia in 1736. He was a lawyer and famous orator. He is best known for championing the revolutionary cause.

Discuss Genre and Set Purpose

INFORMATIONAL TEXT Remind students that an informational text conveys information about a topic and often includes an argument or claim. Discuss how Henry expresses his ideas in this speech.

SET PURPOSE Help students set a purpose for reading, such as to determine the central message in Henry's speech.

COMMON CORE **Common Core Connection**

RI 2 determine a central idea/analyze its development/provide summary; **RI 6** determine author's point of view or purpose/analyze how author uses rhetoric; **RI 9** analyze seminal U.S. documents of historical and literary significance; **W 2** write informative/explanatory texts; **W 5** develop and strengthen writing by planning, revising, editing, rewriting, or trying a new approach; **SL 4** present information, findings, and supporting evidence clearly, concisely, and logically

▲ TEXT COMPLEXITY RUBRIC

Overall Text Complexity		"Speech to the Second Virginia Convention" INFORMATIONAL TEXT
		COMPLEX
Quantitative Measure	Lexile	1010L
Qualitative Measures	Text Structure	somewhat complex social studies concepts
	Language Conventionality and Clarity	figurative, symbolic language
	Knowledge Demands	specialized knowledge required
	Purpose/Levels of Meaning	implied, but easy to infer

COMMON CORE

Academic Vocabulary

Read each word with students and discuss its meaning.

apt (p. 34) • to be inclined to do something

arduous (p. 34)• requiring great exertion or effort

comports (p. 34) • to be in agreement

subjugation (p. 35) • the act, fact, or process of bringing under control

supplication (p. 35) • an appeal; a petition; a request

FIRST READ ## Think Through the Text

Have students use text evidence and draw inferences to answer questions.

pp. 34–36 • *What is Patrick Henry's opinion about the British government?* It intends to use force to decrease the colonists' rights. *What is the evidence for this?* He says that while the British may act peacefully when responding to the colonists' petitions, they are moving toward war to try to force the colonists into submission. ▬RI 6

pp. 34–36 • *What is Henry's main argument?* He is calling for Virginia's militia to take action against the British. *What evidence does he use to support his argument?* Sample answer: Henry says that the British are preparing for war. He says that if the people stand by idly, Great Britain will forcefully enslave them. ▬RI 2

SECOND READ ## Analyze the Text

• *What rhetorical and literary devices does Henry use throughout his argument?* Sample answer: He asks rhetorical questions to prompt thinking. He also uses figurative language and imagery to show that the colonists are in danger of becoming slaves to Great Britain. In addition, he uses restatement to convey his message in different ways. ▬RI 2

• *What is the theme of Henry's speech?* liberty *How does Henry develop this theme?* In the beginning of the speech, he says that the colonists are in a struggle for liberty. The body of his speech focuses on Great Britain's effort to take away their freedoms. Then, he ends his speech with the memorable phrase, "Give me liberty or give me death." ▬RI 2

Independent/Self-Selected Reading

Have students reread the "Speech to the Second Virginia Convention" independently to practice analyzing the text on their own, or have them practice the skills using another text, such as:

• "Speech in the Convention" by Benjamin Franklin

• "Shall Liberty or Empire Be Sought?" by Patrick Henry ▬RI 9

Performance Task

WRITE & PRESENT

1. Have students think about and discuss Patrick Henry's main argument and reasoning. ▬RI 2

2. Have each student write a short essay that analyzes Henry's main argument and evaluates his reasoning. ▬W 2

3. Have students share their work with partners and offer suggestions for revising and editing. Students edit their writing based on these suggestions. ▬W 5

4. Have students present their final writing to their classmates. Ask students to respond to ideas from each student's writing. ▬SL 4

See Copying Masters, pp. 212–215.

STUDENT CHECKLIST

Writing

☑ Identify the main argument of the speech.

☑ Evaluate Henry's reasoning.

☑ Use complete sentences and developed paragraphs to structure writing.

Speaking & Listening

☑ Read writing aloud with a clear, audible voice.

☑ Present ideas in a meaningful way.

"Speech to the Second Virginia Convention" • **113**

▷ OBJECTIVES

- Determine author's purpose
- Determine the theme or central idea of a text
- Analyze text using text evidence

"Farewell Address"
by George Washington

"Farewell Address" is broken into three instructional segments.

SEGMENTS

SEGMENT 1 . . . . .pp. 5–17
SEGMENT 2 . . . . . . .pp. 18–23
SEGMENT 3 . . . . . . .pp. 24–34

Options for Reading

Independent Students read the text independently or with a partner and then answer questions posed by the teacher.

Supported Students read a segment and answer questions with teacher support.

SUMMARY At the end of his second term as President of the United States, George Washington wrote this letter to the American people, explaining his decision not to run for a third term as President and to retire from political life. In his letter, Washington offers his ideas and opinions about a variety of topics, including the Constitution, political parties, religion, and foreign relations.

ABOUT THE AUTHOR **George Washington,** one of the founders of the United States, led the Continental Army during the American Revolution. In 1788, Washington was elected the first President of the United States. He served two terms as President before retiring to his home in Mount Vernon, Virginia. He died on December 14, 1799.

Discuss Genre and Set Purpose

INFORMATIONAL TEXT Have students preview the text and identify the characteristics of the letter. Discuss how authors express their points of view using facts and details.

SET PURPOSE Help students set a purpose for reading, such as identifying the author's purpose for writing a letter to the American people.

Common Core Connection

RI 1 cite textual evidence to support analysis of what the text says explicitly as well as inferences drawn; **RI 2** determine a central idea/analyze its development/provide summary; **RI 6** determine author's point of view or purpose/analyze how author uses rhetoric

▲ TEXT COMPLEXITY RUBRIC		"Farewell Address" INFORMATIONAL TEXT
Overall Text Complexity		**COMPLEX**
Quantitative Measure	Lexile	1490L
Qualitative Measures	Text Structure	complex social studies concepts
	Language Conventionality and Clarity	many unfamiliar or high academic words; complex and varied sentence structure
	Knowledge Demands	some specialized knowledge required
	Purpose/Levels of Meaning	multiple purposes; multiple levels of complex meaning

Academic Vocabulary

Read each word with students and discuss its meaning.

apprise (p. 5) • inform; advise

solicitude (p. 9) • concern

maxims (p. 24) • principles or rules of conduct

insidious (p. 28) • deceitful

delineated (p. 32) • described or outlined with precision

actuated (p. 34) • put into action

Domain Specific Vocabulary

suffrages (p. 6) • votes given in favor of a candidate

parties (p. 14) • organizations established to gain political power

ELL ENGLISH LANGUAGE LEARNERS

Use Comprehensible Input

Substitute difficult vocabulary and paraphrase critical ideas expressed in the text. For example, say: *A resolution is a decision. In the first paragraph, Washington explains his decision about running again for President. Does he say he will or will not run for President again?*

FIRST READ ## Think Through the Text

Have students use text evidence and draw inferences to answer questions.

p. 5 • *To whom is Washington speaking in this letter?* the American people ◖RI 6

pp. 5–6 • *What is Washington's resolution?* He is not running for President for a third term. *Why had Washington abandoned the idea of retiring after his first term as President?* The United States was in a difficult situation with foreign nations, and everyone closest to him advised him to run again. ◖RI 2

p. 9 • *Why does Washington decide to offer the American people recommendations in his farewell letter?* He is concerned for their welfare. ◖RI 6

pp. 14–15 • *What concerns Washington about characterizing political parties by geographical lines, such as northern and southern, Atlantic and western?* People may start to believe that there is a difference of local interests and views, therefore alienating citizens from one another. ◖RI 6

RESPOND TO SEGMENT 1

 Classroom Collaboration

Have small groups summarize the main points in this segment and ask questions about parts of the text that are unclear.

SECOND READ ## Analyze the Text

• Review pages 6–7 with students. Ask: *What evidence from the text suggests that the American people's opinion about his retirement is important to Washington?* Sample answer: He details his decision-making process to the American people, explaining that their concerns led him to run for a second term. ◖RI 1

• Review pages 9–17 with students. Then ask: *What is a major theme in this part of the letter?* unity *What examples from the text support your idea?* Sample answer: Washington says that patriotism for America should outweigh any local allegiences. He also explains that each part of the country is dependent on the other for success in manufacturing and commerce. ◖RI 2

Domain Specific Vocabulary

Constitution (p. 16) • the fundamental law of the United States, which went into effect in 1789

despotism (p. 19) • absolute power or control; tyranny

 ENGLISH LANGUAGE LEARNERS

Use Peer Supported Learning

Pair students to read and discuss the text. Have them take turns explaining the main points of each paragraph to their partners.

RESPOND TO SEGMENT 2

 Classroom Collaboration

Have small groups work together to summarize what they have read. Have them ask questions about parts of the text that are unclear.

 Common Core Connection

RI 1 cite textual evidence to support analysis of what the text says explicitly as well as inferences drawn; **RI 2** determine a central idea/analyze its development/provide summary; **RI 4** determine the meaning of words and phrases, including figurative, connotative, and technical meanings/analyze impact of word choices; **RI 10** read and comprehend literary nonfiction; **W 2** write informative/explanatory texts; **W 5** develop and strengthen writing by planning, revising, editing, rewriting, or trying a new approach; **W 6** use technology to produce, publish, and update writing products; **SL 4** present information, findings, and supporting evidence clearly, concisely, and logically

FIRST READ **Think Through the Text**

Have students use text evidence and draw inferences to answer questions.

pp. 19–20 • *What is Washington's opinion about political parties?* They can have a negative effect on the country. *What examples from the text support your ideas?* Sample answer: Washington says that parties create animosity between different parts of the country. ◼ RI 1

p. 23 • *Why does Washington believe in the promotion of educational institutions?* He believes that the transmission of knowledge is important so public opinion will be enlightened. ◼ RI 1

SECOND READ **Analyze the Text**

• Review page 18 with students. Ask: *What is Washington's advice about preserving the integrity of the U.S. government?* resist changing its principles *What does Washington say is the best test of existing laws?* experience ◼ RI 1

• Have students revisit pages 22–23. Ask: *According to Washington, what two concepts are most important to political prosperity?* religion and morality *What reasons does he give to support the claim?* Sample answer: Washington asks whether we would have any security if religious obligations were not part of the oaths of the justice system. ◼ RI 1

• Ask: *What is a central idea of this segment?* preserving the prosperity of the country *What examples from the text support your idea?* Washington warns against the dangers of political parties dividing the country. He also advises against changing the Constitution without testing the laws with time and experience. ◼ RI 2

FIRST READ   Think Through the Text

Have students use text evidence and draw inferences to answer questions.

pp. 24–25 • *What is George Washington's opinion about taxes?* *Washington says that in order to have revenue, people must pay taxes. They are not pleasant, but necessary.* ◖RI 1

pp. 25–26 • *What does Washington mean by habitual hatred or fondness for another country?* *He means having a hatred or fondness for another country that becomes customary and permanent, without looking at the current motives for the relationship between the United States and the other country.* ◖RI 4

SECOND READ   Analyze the Text

- Review pages 25–31. Then ask: *What is Washington's main argument regarding foreign attachments?* *Washington believes that the United States should not make permanent attachments with any one country. Instead, he says, the United States should try to have just and friendly relations with all countries.* **Provide an example from the text that supports your ideas.** *Sample answer: Washington warns against an attachment to Europe because its primary interests do not align with the United States. So why, he asks, should we entangle ourselves in their destiny?* ◖RI 1, RI 2

- Review pages 32–33 with students. Ask: *Why does Washington mention his proclamation of April 22, 1793?* *Sample answer: His neutral position in the war in Europe aligns with his main argument of distancing the country from foreign attachments that are not beneficial to its interests.* ◖RI 1

Independent/Self-Selected Reading

Have students reread "Farewell Address" independently to practice analyzing the text on their own, or have them practice the skills using another text, such as:

- *George Washington: A Biography in His Own Words* by George Washington

- *The Monroe Doctrine: Empire and Nation in Nineteenth-Century America* by Jay Sexton ◖RI 10

Performance Task

WRITE & PRESENT

1. Have small groups discuss Washington's ideas about the country's alliances with foreign governments. ◖RI 2

2. Have students compare Washington's ideas about these types of alliances in a written essay. Encourage students to cite text evidence to support their comparisons. ◖W 2

3. Have students share their work with partners and offer suggestions for revising and editing. Students edit their writing based on these suggestions. ◖W 5

4. Have students present their final writing to their classmates. Ask students to respond to the comparisons in each student's writing. ◖SL 4

5. Individual students turn in their final drafts to the teacher. ◖W 6

See Copying Masters, pp. 212–215.

STUDENT CHECKLIST

Writing

☑ Identify Washington's ideas about foreign attachments.

☑ Compare Washington's ideas about attachments with other foreign policy statements. Use text evidence and quotes from the text.

☑ Use complete sentences and developed paragraphs to structure writing.

Speaking & Listening

☑ Read writing aloud with a clear, audible voice.

☑ Present ideas in a meaningful way.

▶ OBJECTIVES

- Determine the central idea of a text
- Determine author's purpose
- Analyze text using text evidence

Options for Reading

Independent Students read the text independently or with a partner and then answer questions posed by the teacher.

Supported Students read the text and answer questions with teacher support.

"Gettysburg Address"

by Abraham Lincoln

SUMMARY Abraham Lincoln delivered this address on November 19, 1863, during the American Civil War, at the dedication of the National Cemetery in Gettysburg, Pennsylvania. Lincoln's speech honored the fallen Union soldiers who had defeated the Confederate Army four months before in the Battle of Gettysburg.

ABOUT THE AUTHOR Abraham Lincoln became the 16th President of the United States in 1860. He fought to end slavery and keep the Southern states from seceding from the nation during the American Civil War. In 1864, the nation reelected Lincoln to a second term. He served until his assassination on April 15, 1865.

Discuss Genre and Set Purpose

INFORMATIONAL TEXT Remind students that an informational text conveys information about a topic and often includes an argument or claim. Explain that the author supports his or her argument or claim with facts, details, and opinions. It is up to the reader to evaluate the information presented in order to draw his or her own conclusions.

SET PURPOSE Help students set a purpose for reading, such as to find the central message in Lincoln's speech.

COMMON CORE Common Core Connection

RI 1 cite textual evidence to support analysis of what the text says explicitly as well as inferences drawn; **RI 2** determine a central idea/analyze its development/provide summary; **RI 6** determine author's point of view or purpose/analyze how author uses rhetoric; **RI 9** analyze seminal U.S. documents of historical and literary significance; **W 2** write informative/explanatory texts; **W 5** develop and strengthen writing by planning, revising, editing, rewriting, or trying a new approach; **SL 4** present information, findings, and supporting evidence clearly, concisely, and logically

▲ TEXT COMPLEXITY RUBRIC

Overall Text Complexity		"Gettysburg Address" INFORMATIONAL TEXT
		ACCESSIBLE
Quantitative Measure	Lexile	1440L
Qualitative Measures	Text Structure	clearly stated and sequential organization of main ideas and details
	Language Conventionality and Clarity	some unfamiliar language
	Knowledge Demands	some specialized knowledge required
	Purpose/Levels of Meaning	single level of complex meaning

Academic Vocabulary

Read each word with students and discuss its meaning.

fourscore (line 1) • four times twenty; eighty

proposition (line 3) • something stated or affirmed

endure (line 6) • sustain without impairment or yielding

consecrate (line 12) • to make or declare sacred

devotion (line 20) • earnest attachment to a cause

vain (line 23) • without significance or value

FIRST READ ## Think Through the Text

Have students use text evidence and draw inferences to answer questions.

Lines 1–3 • *What is Lincoln referring to in the opening lines of his speech?* He is referring to the Founding Fathers and the adoption of the Declaration of Independence in 1776. *Why?* to remind the American people what the Union Army is fighting for ▰RI 1

Lines 4–26 • *What is Abraham Lincoln's main purpose for giving this speech?* He is honoring the fallen Union soldiers who fought against the Confederate Army in the Battle of Gettysburg. *What text evidence supports your ideas?* Sample answer: Lincoln explains that they are gathered together to dedicate a part of the field as the final resting place to those who died to save the nation. ▰RI 6

SECOND READ ## Analyze the Text

• *What is Lincoln's central message to those gathered for the dedication of the National Cemetery in Gettysburg?* Do not let the Union soldiers' deaths be in vain. ▰RI 2

• *What background knowledge helped you better understand Lincoln's dedication?* The Civil War was fought between the Union, or the Northern states in support of the federal government of the United States, and the Confederacy, or the Southern slave states that wanted to secede from the country. ▰RI 9

Independent/Self-Selected Reading

Have students reread Lincoln's "Gettysburg Address" independently to practice analyzing the text on their own, or have them practice the skills using another speech, such as:

• "The Man with the Muck Rake" Speech by Theodore Roosevelt

• "National Day of Prayer and Remembrance" Speech by George W. Bush ▰RI 9

Performance Task

WRITE & PRESENT

1. Have small groups discuss the purpose and central message of Lincoln's speech. ▰RI 2

2. Have students write about how Lincoln used this dedication to refocus people's attention on the purpose of the Civil War. Encourage students to cite text evidence to defend their ideas. ▰W 2

3. Have students share their work with partners and offer suggestions for revising and editing. Students edit their writing based on these suggestions. ▰W 5

4. Have students present their final writing to their classmates. Ask students to respond to the themes and ideas from each student's writing. ▰SL 4

See Copying Masters, pp. 212–215.

STUDENT CHECKLIST

Writing

☑ Identify the central message of the speech.

☑ Use text evidence to identify how Lincoln refocused people's attention on the purpose of the war.

☑ Use complete sentences and developed paragraphs to structure writing.

Speaking & Listening

☑ Read writing aloud with a clear, audible voice.

☑ Present ideas in a meaningful way.

▶ **OBJECTIVES**

- Determine a central idea
- Analyze a seminal U.S. document
- Analyze how author unfolds an analysis or series of events or ideas
- Analyze text using text evidence

"Second Inaugural Address" is broken into three instructional segments.

Options for Reading

Independent Students read the selection independently or with a partner and then answer questions posed by the teacher.

Supported Students read a segment and answer questions with teacher support.

COMMON CORE **Common Core Connection**

RI 1 cite textual evidence to support analysis of what the text says explicitly as well as inferences drawn; **RI 2** determine a central idea/analyze its development/provide summary; **RI 3** analyze how an author unfolds an analysis or series of ideas or events; **RI 9** analyze seminal U.S. documents of historical and literary significance

"Second Inaugural Address"

by Abraham Lincoln

SUMMARY On March 4, 1865, President Abraham Lincoln delivered his second inaugural address to the American people. He compared the state of the country with where it was four years previously when he made his first inaugural address. Lincoln then offered his hope that the war would soon end.

ABOUT THE AUTHOR Abraham Lincoln (1809–1865) served as President of the United States from 1861–1865. The Civil War started during his first term in office. Lincoln opposed slavery and worked to preserve the reunification of the states. The war ended on March 28, 1865, just after the start of his second term. Lincoln was assassinated on April 14, 1865.

Discuss Genre and Set Purpose

INFORMATIONAL TEXTS: ENGLISH/LANGUAGE ARTS Preview the selection with students. Help them identify characteristics of informational texts, such as the names of people and places, dates, and specific events.

SET PURPOSE Help students set a purpose for reading, such as to find information about the content of the second inaugural address.

▲ **TEXT COMPLEXITY RUBRIC**

Overall Text Complexity		"Second Inaugural Address" INFORMATIONAL TEXT
		COMPLEX
Quantitative Measure	Lexile	1490L
Qualitative Measures	Text Structure	somewhat complex civics concepts
	Language Conventionality and Clarity	figurative, symbolic language; complex and varied sentence structure; sophisticated descriptions
	Knowledge Demands	specialized knowledge required
	Purpose/Levels of Meaning	single topic, explicitly stated

Academic Vocabulary

Read each word with students and discuss its meaning.

expiration (p. 40) • end

engrosses (p. 41) • occupies

ventured (p. 41) • offered

impending (p. 41) • imminent or threatening

avert (p. 41) • prevent from happening

FIRST READ ▶ **Think Through the Text**

Have students use text evidence and draw inferences to answer questions.

p. 40 • *Is Lincoln's second inaugural address longer or shorter than his first one was?* shorter RI 1

pp. 40–41 • *What is Lincoln's reason for the difference in length between the two addresses?* The public is aware of what is going on, and there is nothing new to report. RI 1

p. 41 • *How does Lincoln feel about the future?* He feels encouraged and hopeful. RI 1, RI 2

p. 41 • *What event was about to start when Lincoln made his first inaugural address?* The Civil War was about to start. RI 1

SECOND READ ▶ **Analyze the Text**

- Review pages 40–41. Ask: *What is the occasion for this speech?* Lincoln has been elected to a second term as President. **To whom is it addressed?** It is addressed to the people of the United States. RI 9

- Review pages 40–41. Ask: *How does Lincoln start his examination of the ideas that led to the Civil War?* He refers back to his first inaugural address and compares the state of the country then with the current situation. RI 9

- Review pages 40–41. Ask: *Is Lincoln going to discuss the progress of the war in this speech?* no *What examples from the text support your answer?* He says that people already know that the war is going on and have heard about its progress from others. He says he will not attempt to say what the outcome might be. RI 1, RI 3

ELL **ENGLISH LANGUAGE LEARNERS**

Use Peer Supported Learning

Have students work in small groups. Tell each group to make a two-column chart listing Lincoln's main points and the facts he uses to develop them. Then have groups share their charts. Tell them to add information from other groups to their own charts.

RESPOND TO SEGMENT 1

💬 **Classroom Collaboration**

Have partners create a summary of the main ideas in this segment. Then have students raise questions that might be answered in the next segment.

Domain Specific Vocabulary

inaugural (p. 41) • having to do with the ceremony of swearing in a public official

arms (p. 41) • weapons and other equipment used for fighting wars

 ENGLISH LANGUAGE LEARNERS

Use Comprehensible Input

Ensure students understand the main points by asking questions such as: *What was going on in the United States when Lincoln was President?* and *What does Lincoln give as the cause of the war?*

 RESPOND TO SEGMENT 2

Classroom Collaboration

Have small groups work together to summarize what they have read. Have them ask questions about what they don't understand.

 Common Core Connection

RI 1 cite textual evidence to support analysis of what the text says explicitly as well as inferences drawn; **RI 3** analyze how an author unfolds an analysis or series of ideas or events; **RI 9** analyze seminal U.S. documents of historical and literary significance; **RI 10** read and comprehend literary nonfiction; **W 2** write informative/explanatory texts; **W 5** develop and strengthen writing by planning, revising, editing, rewriting, or trying a new approach; **SL 4** present information, findings, and supporting evidence clearly, concisely, and logically

Academic Vocabulary

Read each word with students and discuss its meaning.

insurgent (p. 42) • politically rebellious

deprecated (p. 42) • condemned

perpetuate (p. 43) • make something last

duration (p. 43) • length of time something lasts

fundamental (p. 43) • basic, essential

FIRST READ ## Think Through the Text

Have students use text evidence and draw inferences to answer questions.

p. 42 • *According to Lincoln, what were some people trying to do at the time of his first inaugural address?* They were trying to destroy the Union. **RI 1**

pp. 42–43 • *According to Lincoln, what did most people believe was the cause of the war?* slavery in the southern states **RI 1**

pp. 42–43 • *What did neither side expect about the war?* Neither side expected it to go on for so long. **RI 1**

SECOND READ ## Analyze the Text

- Review page 42 with students. Ask: *How does Lincoln portray the people who oppose him?* He describes them as rebels who don't care about keeping the country intact. **RI 3**

- Have students revisit pages 42–43. Ask: *What is President Lincoln doing in this section of the address?* He is reminding his listeners about the cause of the war as well as pointing out each side's role regarding the practice of slavery. **RI 1, RI 9**

- Review the last sentence on page 43. Ask: *What is Lincoln's purpose with this sentence?* He reminds his listeners that both sides have God in common. **RI 1, RI 9**

Academic Vocabulary

Read each word with students and discuss its meaning.

providence (p. 46) • God's guidance

discern (p. 45) • tell the difference

ascribe (p. 45) • credit

unrequited (p. 45) • not shared

malice (p. 46) • hatred

FIRST READ ## Think Through the Text

Have students use text evidence and draw inferences to answer questions.

p. 44 • *What does Lincoln have to say about the prayers from both sides of the country? Neither side's prayers were completely answered.* ◉ RI 1

p. 45 • *According to Lincoln, why has God given the war to the North and South? It is punishment for the practice of slavery.* ◉ RI 1

p. 46 • *What is Lincoln's view about both sides? He has no hatred of either side. He wants both sides to heal.* ◉ RI 1

SECOND READ ## Analyze the Text

• Reread pages 44–45. Ask: *What point does Lincoln make in this section of his address? He wonders if God brought the war to the United States to help the country get rid of slavery.* ◉ RI 9

• Reread page 45. Ask: *How does Lincoln show his desire for unity? He uses plural pronouns to show that he wants both sides to come together.* ◉ RI 9

Independent/Self-Selected Reading

Have students reread "Second Inaugural Address" independently to practice analyzing the text on their own, or have them practice the skills using another text, such as:

• *The 1864 Presidential Election: A War Weary Nation Reelects President Abraham Lincoln* by Wendy Vierow

• *1864: Lincoln at the Gates of History* by Charles Bracelen Flood ◉ RI 10

Performance Task

WRITE & PRESENT

1. Have small groups analyze how Lincoln unfolds his examination of the ideas that led to the Civil War, paying attention to the order in which the points are made, how Lincoln introduces and develops his points, and the connections drawn between them. ◉ RI 9

2. Ask students to think about the structure Lincoln uses in his address. Have them write a paragraph that describes how Lincoln unfolds his ideas. Encourage students to cite text evidence. ◉ W 2

3. Have students share their work with partners and offer suggestions for revising and editing. Students edit their writing based on these suggestions. ◉ W 5

4. Have students present their final writing to their classmates. Ask students to respond to the themes and ideas from each student's writing. ◉ SL 4

See Copying Masters, pp. 212–215.

STUDENT CHECKLIST

Writing

☑ Analyze how Lincoln unfolds his ideas.

☑ Explain how Lincoln explains and develops his points.

Speaking & Listening

☑ Read writing aloud with a clear, audible voice.

☑ Present ideas in a meaningful way.

▷ OBJECTIVES

- Determine a central idea
- Analyze seminal U.S. document
- Analyze how author unfolds an analysis or series of events or ideas
- Analyze text using text evidence

"State of the Union Address" is broken into three instructional segments.

Options for Reading

Independent Students read the selection independently or with a partner and then answer questions posed by the teacher.

Supported Students read a segment and answer questions with teacher support.

Common Core Connection

RI 1 cite textual evidence to support analysis of what the text says explicitly as well as inferences drawn; **RI 2** determine a central idea/analyze its development/provide summary; **RI 4** determine the meaning of words and phrases, including figurative, connotative, and technical meanings/analyze impact of word choice; **RI 9** analyze seminal U.S. documents of historical and literary significance

"State of the Union Address"

by Franklin Delano Roosevelt

SUMMARY On January 6, 1941, President Franklin Delano Roosevelt delivered his State of the Union Address, the annual presidential speech presented to Congress to report on the country's most pressing issues. In his speech, Roosevelt stressed the importance of the United States helping other democracies in their battles against dictators. Roosevelt presented thoughts about the basic things citizens expected as well as the freedoms he believed everyone in the world should have.

ABOUT THE AUTHOR Franklin Delano Roosevelt (1882–1945) served as President of the United States from 1933–1945. He initially wanted to keep the United States out of World War II, but he still wanted to help the nations under attack. After Pearl Harbor was attacked in 1941, Roosevelt prepared the country to go to war.

Discuss Genre and Set Purpose

INFORMATIONAL TEXT Preview the selection with students. Help them identify characteristics of informational texts, such as names of people and places, dates, and specific events.

SET PURPOSE Help students set a purpose for reading, such as to find information about the content of the State of the Union address.

▲ TEXT COMPLEXITY RUBRIC

Overall Text Complexity		"State of the Union Address" INFORMATIONAL TEXT COMPLEX
Quantitative Measure	Lexile	1280L
Qualitative Measures	Text Structure	somewhat complex civics concepts
	Language Conventionality and Clarity	some unfamiliar or academic words
	Knowledge Demands	specialized knowledge required
	Purpose/Levels of Meaning	single topic, explicitly stated

Academic Vocabulary

Read each word with students and discuss its meaning.

unprecedented (p. 89) • never before seen or experienced

vindicate (p. 90) • to uphold or justify

tyranny (p. 90) • an oppressive or cruel government

propaganda (p. 91) • heavily biased publicity meant to sway opinions

FIRST READ ## Think Through the Text

Have students use text evidence and draw inferences to answer questions.

p. 89 • *According to President Roosevelt, what is so unusual about this particular time in the history of the United States?* America is facing the most serious threat to its security from another country. ● RI 1

p. 90 • *What has historically been the country's position on isolation from other countries?* The country has not been in favor of being isolated from other countries. ● RI 1

pp. 90–91 • *What are some of the threats to democracy?* the use of weapons and misleading publicity, or propaganda ● RL 1

pp. 90–91 • *What might happen if the countries that are fighting the tyrants lose?* The continents of Asia, Europe, Africa, and Australia would come under rule by the dictators. ● RL 1

SECOND READ ## Analyze the Text

• Review page 89. Ask: *Who is giving the speech?* President Franklin D. Roosevelt is giving the speech. *To whom is it addressed?* It is addressed to the members of Congress. ● RI 9

• Review pages 89–90. Ask: *What does President Roosevelt mean when he refers to points on a compass?* He means that the war between different regions of the U.S. is over, and the country is all one again. ● RI 4

• Ask: *What do you think is a major theme of this segment?* A major theme is the danger that the United States faces from tyranny and dictators. *What examples from the text support your ideas?* The Peace of Versailles is not being upheld. Dictators and tyrants are trying to take over four continents. ● RI 1, RI 2

 ENGLISH LANGUAGE LEARNERS

Use Sentence Frames

Guide students to generate adjectives that could describe the situation as described by the President. Then have them orally complete sentence frames such as the following:

The dictators are _____.
oppressive *The United States needs to be _____.* helpful *Progress has been _____.* slow

RESPOND TO SEGMENT 1

Classroom Collaboration

Have partners create a summary of the main ideas in this segment. Then have students raise questions that might be answered in the next segment.

Domain Specific Vocabulary

dictator (p. 91) • a ruler who uses force to completely control a country

armament (p. 91) • weapons and other equipment used for fighting wars

 ENGLISH LANGUAGE LEARNERS

Use Comprehensible Input

Ensure students understand the theme of the speech by asking questions such as: *What is happening on four continents?* and *Why does President Roosevelt think the United States should help democracies?*

 RESPOND TO SEGMENT 2

Classroom Collaboration

Have small groups work together to summarize what they have read. Have them ask questions about what they don't understand.

 Common Core Connection

RI 1 cite textual evidence to support analysis of what the text says explicitly as well as inferences drawn; **RI 2** determine a central idea/analyze its development/provide summary; **RI 9** analyze seminal U.S. documents of historical and literary significance; **RI 10** read and comprehend literary nonfiction; **WS 2** write informative/explanatory texts; **WS 5** develop and strengthen writing by planning, revising, editing, rewriting, or trying a new approach; **SL 4** present information, findings, and supporting evidence clearly, concisely, and logically

Academic Vocabulary

Read each word with students and discuss its meaning.

dupes (p. 92) • victims of deceit

peril (p. 92) • danger

partisanship (p. 92) • supporting only one side

acquiesce (p. 93) • agree in a passive way

appropriations (p. 94) • money for a particular purpose

FIRST READ ## Think Through the Text

Have students use text evidence and draw inferences to answer questions.

p. 92 • *What might happen first if the United States were invaded?*
Enemy agents and their helpers here would take over important places. ⬛RI 1

p. 92 • *On what should the country now place the most emphasis?*
fighting the overseas tyrants ⬛RI 1

pp. 93–94 • *How does the President want manufacturing to change?*
He wants to change from peacetime to wartime manufacturing by increasing the production of weapons and other war materials. ⬛RI 1

SECOND READ ## Analyze the Text

- Review page 92 with students. Ask: *Why is this State of the Union address so unusual? There has never before been such a threat of invasion or the loss of democracy.* ⬛RI 9

- Have students revisit pages 92–94. Ask: *What is President Roosevelt doing in this section of the address? He is laying out his vision for the foreign policy of the United States. He is asking for cooperation from Congress.* ⬛RI 9

- Ask: *What is a major theme of this segment? the priority of defending the United States What examples from the text support your ideas? The President calls for a nonpartisan commitment to defense. He asks Congress to approve money to increase arms production and to supply arms to foreign democracies.* ⬛RI 1, RI 2

Academic Vocabulary

Read each word with students and discuss its meaning.

stimulating (p. 95) • encouraging, inspiring

stamina (p. 95) • energy and strength to keep doing something

abiding (p. 96) • long-lasting

millennium (p. 97) • a time period of one thousand years

antithesis (p. 97) • direct opposite

FIRST READ Think Through the Text

Have students use text evidence and draw inferences to answer questions.

p. 95 • *What evidence does Roosevelt cite that the dictators will strike first?* They struck first in Norway, Belgium, and the Netherlands. ◼RI 1

pp. 95–96 • *What are the things people should expect from a democracy?* People should expect equal opportunities, jobs, financial and medical security, civil liberty, and an improved standard of living. ◼RI 1

pp. 95–96 • *What are the four freedoms?* freedom of speech and of religion, freedom from want and from fear ◼RI 1

SECOND READ Analyze the Text

• Reread the last four paragraphs of the address on page 97. Then ask: *What is Roosevelt's purpose in this section of the address?* He is telling Congress that they have the immediate opportunity and responsibility to defend and spread the democratic way of life. ◼RI 9

• Ask: *What do you think is the theme of the whole address? Why?* Sample answer: preparing the nation for war—President Roosevelt describes the danger, predicts what might happen if it is not confronted, and outlines a defense strategy. ◼RI 1, RI 2

Independent/Self-Selected Reading

Have students reread "State of the Union Address" independently to practice analyzing the text on their own, or have them practice the skills using another book, such as:

• *1001 Things Everyone Should Know about World War II* by Frank E. Vandiver

• *World War II: The Definitive Visual History* by DK Publishers ◼RI 10

WRITE & PRESENT

1. Have small groups discuss the main theme of the address. ◼RI 2

2. Ask students to think about the main theme of the address. Have students write about how the theme is developed throughout the address. Encourage students to cite text evidence to defend their ideas. ◼W 2

3. Have students share their work with partners and offer suggestions for revising and editing. Students edit their writing based on these suggestions. ◼W 5

4. Have students present their final writing to their classmates. Ask students to respond to the themes and ideas from each student's writing. ◼SL 4

See Copying Masters, pp. 212–215.

STUDENT CHECKLIST

Writing

☑ Identify the theme from the address.

☑ Explain how the theme is developed, using text evidence and quotes from the address.

☑ Use complete sentences and developed paragraphs to structure writing.

Speaking & Listening

☑ Read writing aloud with a clear, audible voice.

☑ Present ideas in a meaningful way.

▶ OBJECTIVES
- Determine author's purpose
- Evaluate author's argument
- Analyze text using text evidence

Options for Reading

Independent Students read the text independently or with a partner and then answer questions posed by the teacher.

Supported Students read the text and answer questions with teacher support.

"Spirit of Liberty" Speech
by Judge Learned Hand

SUMMARY Judge Learned Hand delivered his "Spirit of Liberty" speech on May 21, 1944, during World War II, to celebrate "I AM an American Day." In his address, Hand discusses the idea of liberty and defines the spirit of liberty in America.

ABOUT THE AUTHOR Judge Learned Hand was born in 1872 in Albany, New York. He followed in his father's footsteps and became a lawyer, earning a degree from Harvard Law School. In 1909, Hand was appointed federal district judge for the Southern District of New York by President William Howard Taft. He then served on the United States Circuit Court of Appeals for the Second Judicial Circuit until his death in 1961.

Discuss Genre and Set Purpose

INFORMATIONAL TEXT Remind students that an informational text conveys information about a topic and often includes an argument or claim. Explain that the author supports his or her argument or claim with facts, details, and opinions. It is up to the reader to evaluate the information presented in order to come to his or her own conclusions.

SET PURPOSE Help students set a purpose for reading, such as to identify how Hand defines the spirit of liberty.

Common Core Connection

RI 1 cite textual evidence to support analysis of what the text says explicitly as well as inferences drawn; **RI 2** determine a central idea/analyze its development/provide summary; **RI 3** analyze how author unfolds an analysis or series of ideas or events; **RI 4** determine the meaning of words and phrases, including figurative, connotative, and technical meanings/analyze impact of word choices; **RI 9** analyze seminal U.S. documents of historical and literary significance; **W 2** write informative/explanatory texts; **W 5** develop and strengthen writing by planning, revising, editing, rewriting, or trying a new approach; **SL 4** present information, findings, and supporting evidence clearly, concisely, and logically

▲ TEXT COMPLEXITY RUBRIC

Overall Text Complexity		"The Spirit of Liberty" Speech INFORMATIONAL TEXT COMPLEX
Quantitative Measure	Lexile	1080L
Qualitative Measures	Text Structure	more difficult social studies concepts
	Language Conventionality and Clarity	less straightforward sentence structure
	Knowledge Demands	some specialized knowledge required
	Purpose/Levels of Meaning	implied, but easy to infer

Academic Vocabulary

Read each word with students and discuss its meaning.

affirm (p. 1) • to state or assert positively

conviction (p. 1) • a fixed or firm belief

oppression (p. 1) • injustice; hardship

bias (p. 1) • belief in one way; partiality

aspirations (p. 1) • goals; hopes

FIRST READ ## Think Through the Text

Have students use text evidence and draw inferences to answer questions.

- *Why, according to Hand, are Americans a "picked group"?* *Americans, or their ancestors, had to choose to come to America, braving the dangers of a strange land.* **RI 4**

- *According to Hand, why did people come to America?* *They sought liberty.* *How does Hand define* liberty? *freedom from oppression, freedom from want, freedom from ourselves* **RI 4**

- *What is Hand's claim about the relationship between liberty and the law?* *Liberty cannot be saved or helped by the law. It must live in the hearts of men and women.* **RI 2**

SECOND READ ## Analyze the Text

- *How does Hand use repetition in his speech?* *He repeats the idea that no constitution, law, or court can help or save liberty to support his claim that it must live in the hearts of men and women.* **RI 1, RI 3**

- *In your own words, what is Hand's argument about the role of the spirit of liberty in America?* *Sample answer: It should be the beacon or standard of America's promise.* *What evidence does Hand present to support this argument?* *Sample answer: The spirit of liberty is what men are fighting and dying for in the war.* **RI 2**

- *What do you think is the central idea or main argument of Hand's speech?* *Sample answer: Americans have a common cause and common interest to fight for the liberty of all Americans.* **RI 2**

Independent/Self-Selected Reading

Have students reread "The Spirit of Liberty" speech independently to practice analyzing the text on their own, or have them practice the skills using another text, such as:

- "Pearl Harbor Address to the Nation" by Franklin Delano Roosevelt

- "Inaugural Address" by John Fitzgerald Kennedy **RI 9**

Performance Task

WRITE & PRESENT

1. Have small groups discuss Hand's argument and specific claims about the spirit of liberty. **RI 2**

2. Ask students to think about and assess Hand's evidence and reasoning. Have students write an essay evaluating Hand's argument and claims about the spirit of liberty. Encourage students to cite text evidence to defend their ideas. **W 2**

3. Have students share their work with partners and offer suggestions for revising and editing. Students edit their writing based on these suggestions. **W 5**

4. Have students present their final writing to their classmates. Ask students to respond to ideas from each student's writing. **SL 4**

See Copying Masters, pp. 212–215.

STUDENT CHECKLIST

Writing

☑ Identify the main argument and at least one claim from the speech.

☑ Evaluate the evidence and reasoning used to support the argument and claims presented in the speech.

☑ Use complete sentences and developed paragraphs to structure writing.

Speaking & Listening

☑ Read writing aloud using a clear, audible voice.

☑ Present ideas in a meaningful way.

▶ OBJECTIVES

- Identify the theme of the text
- Determine and compare the author's points of view
- Determine the purpose of the text
- Determine the purpose of irony

Options for Reading

Independent Students read the text independently or with a partner and then answer questions posed by the teacher.

Supported Students read a segment and answer questions with teacher support.

"Declaration of Conscience"
by Margaret Chase Smith

SUMMARY Margaret Chase Smith wrote "A Declaration of Conscience" during a difficult time in American history. Senator Joseph McCarthy intimidated many colleagues and citizens by labeling them fascists and communists. In spite of great risk, on June 1, 1950, Margaret Chase Smith addressed President Truman at a Congressional hearing and read her "Declaration of Conscience."

ABOUT THE AUTHOR **Margaret Chase Smith** was a Republican Congresswoman from Maine who held offices both in the House of Representatives and the United States Senate. People remember her for her length of service and her fearless stand against Senator Joseph McCarthy's smear campaigns.

Discuss Genre and Set Purpose

INFORMATIONAL TEXT Remind students that an informational text conveys information about a topic and often includes an argument or claim.

SET PURPOSE Help students set a purpose for reading, such as to understand why Senator Smith was so distressed that she took the chance of criticizing her colleagues.

COMMON CORE Connection

RI 1 cite textual evidence to support analysis of what the text says explicitly as well as inferences drawn; **RI 2** determine a central idea/analyze its development/provide summary; **RI 4** determine the meaning of words and phrases, including figurative, connotative, and technical meanings/analyze impact of word choices; **RI 6** determine author's point of view or purpose/analyze how author uses rhetoric; **RI 10** read and comprehend literary nonfiction; **W 1** write arguments to support claims; **W 2f** provide a concluding statement or section; **W 5** develop and strengthen writing by planning, revising, editing, rewriting, or trying a new approach; **SL 4** present information, findings, and supporting evidence clearly, concisely, and logically

▲ TEXT COMPLEXITY RUBRIC

Overall Text Complexity		"Declaration of Conscience" INFORMATIONAL TEXT
		COMPLEX
Quantitative Measure	Lexile	1310L
Qualitative Measures	Text Structure	organization of main ideas and details is complex but largely explicit
	Language Conventionality and Clarity	figurative, less accessible language
	Knowledge Demands	increased amount of cultural and literary knowledge useful
	Purpose/Levels of Meaning	single level of complex meaning

Academic Vocabulary

Read each word with students and discuss its meaning.

national condition (p. 1) • national state

deliberative body (p. 1) • thinking, judging group

impute (p. 2) • charge (v.)

calumny (p. 4) • lies; slander

rendezvous (p. 5) • meeting place

vilification (p. 5) • belittling; debasing

FIRST READ **Think Through the Text**

Have students use text evidence and draw inferences to answer questions.

- *What is Senator Smith's point of view?* *She has many points of view. She spoke as a Republican, as a woman, as a senator, and as an American.* **RI 6**

- *What does the text say about why Senator Smith is so concerned about the reputation of the Senate?* *because it has become hateful* **RI 1**

- *Why are the rights mentioned in the "Declaration" so important?* *They are freedoms valued in the United States because they protect citizens against bullying—in school hallways or on the Senate floor.* **RI 2**

- *Discuss the four behaviors to which Smith refers.* *Sample answers: Fear paralyzes people; ignorance leads to poor decisions; bigotry is based on ignorance; smearing runs counter to the idea of fairness.* **RI 2**

SECOND READ **Analyze the Text**

- Remind students that repeating phrases is a rhetorical device authors use for various reasons. Say: *Senator Smith repeats some phrases in her declaration. Why does she do this?* *to create tension and impact* **RI 1**

- Remind students that irony or sarcasm is a literary device used to create tension or surprise. *Why is the title ironic?* *It reminds the reader of "The Declaration of Independence."* **RI 4**

- *What do you think is the theme of the text? Why?* *Sample answer: Even in a democracy, freedom of speech needs to be tempered by civility. It does not give one license to attack others personally.* **RI 2**

Independent/Self-Selected Reading

Have students reread "Declaration of Conscience" independently to practice analyzing the text on their own, or have them practice the skills using another book, such as:

- *American Heritage Book of Great Speeches* edited by Suzanne McIntire

- *Ain't I a Woman?* by Sojourner Truth **RI 10**

Performance Task

WRITE & PRESENT

1. Have small groups discuss and explain Smith's viewpoints. **RI 6**

2. Ask students to discuss the idea of character assassination and write an essay from the point of view of someone who is under unfair attack. They should create tension, include irony, repeated phrases, and a strong conclusion. **W 1, W 2f**

3. Have students share their work with partners and offer suggestions for revising and editing. Students edit their writing based on these suggestions. **W 5**

4. Have students present their final writing to their classmates. Ask students to respond to the themes and ideas from each student's writing. **SL 4**

See Copying Masters, pp. 212–215.

STUDENT CHECKLIST

Writing

☑ Identify the use of irony and tension in their essays.

☑ Relate the theme of freedom of speech to freedom from attack.

☑ Use complete sentences and developed paragraphs to structure writing.

Speaking & Listening

☑ Participate in a range of collaborative discussions.

☑ Present ideas in a meaningful way.

▶ OBJECTIVES

- Analyze text using text evidence
- Analyze the development of an author's ideas
- Analyze an argument

Options for Reading

Independent Students read the letter independently and then answer questions posed by the teacher.

Supported Students read the letter with partners and then answer questions posed by the teacher.

"Letter from Birmingham Jail"

by Martin Luther King Jr.

SUMMARY Martin Luther King Jr. wrote this letter on April 16, 1963, while in prison for disobeying an Alabama state court order against demonstrating in Birmingham. In response to the white clergymen who criticized him for his actions, King wrote that African Americans had to demonstrate against injustice and that moderate whites were hindering them more than racists.

ABOUT THE AUTHOR Civil rights leader and clergyman **Martin Luther King Jr.** spoke and wrote in support of the rights of African Americans until his assassination in 1968. Known for his oratorical skills, King also wrote five books and an anthology of sixteen of his sermons.

Discuss Genre and Set Purpose

INFORMATIONAL TEXT Point out to students that the date and the salutation are clues that the text is a letter. Explain that it was an "open" letter written in response to a public statement from eight white clergymen. Discuss how the public and the clergymen were the audience for the letter.

SET PURPOSE Help students set a purpose for reading, such as to find out how King develops and refines his ideas.

COMMON CORE Common Core Connection

RI 1 cite textual evidence to support analysis of what the text says explicitly as well as inferences drawn; **RI 2** determine a central idea/analyze its development; **RI 5** analyze how author's ideas or claims are developed and refined; **RI 8** delineate/evaluate the argument and specific claims in a text; **RI 9** analyze seminal U.S. documents of historical and literary significance; **W 1** write arguments to support claims; **W 4** produce writing in which development, organization, and style are appropriate to task, purpose, and audience; **W 5** develop and strengthen writing by planning, revising, editing, rewriting, or trying a new approach; **SL 1** initiate/participate in a range of collaborative discussions; **SL 4** present supporting evidence clearly, concisely, and logically

▲ TEXT COMPLEXITY RUBRIC

Overall Text Complexity		"Letter from Birmingham Jail" INFORMATIONAL TEXT
		ACCESSIBLE
Quantitative Measure	Lexile	1200L
Qualitative Measures	Text Structure	complex sentence structures
	Language Conventionality and Clarity	some unfamiliar or academic words
	Knowledge Demands	historical and civics knowledge required
	Purpose/Levels of Meaning	easy to identify from context

Academic Vocabulary

Read each word with students and discuss its meaning.

alternative (p. 5) • a choice or option

status quo (p. 10) • the existing state of affairs

advocate (p. 13) • to speak or write in support of

moderate (p. 17) • a person holding views that are not extreme

conformity (p. 30) • behavior in accordance with socially accepted standards

---

FIRST READ ## Think Through the Text

Have students use text evidence and draw inferences to answer questions.

pp. 5–7 • *What four basic steps does King follow in a nonviolent campaign?* collection of the facts, negotiation, self-purification, direct action *What does self-purification consist of?* workshops on being nonviolent; asking whether one could be hit without retaliating and endure jail *What would this demand of the demonstrators?* commitment, courage **RI 1**

pp. 7, 10 • *Why does King conclude that he has no alternative but to take direct action and demonstrate?* The city's white power structure still believes in segregation; business leaders did not keep their promises; privileged groups do not give up their privileges unless other (that is, nonprivileged) groups demand it. **RI 5**

SECOND READ ## Analyze the Text

• *How does King distinguish a just law from an unjust law?* A just law adheres to natural law or God's law, while an unjust law does not. *How does he support this definition and his claim that the demonstrators can disobey laws?* by citing philosophers such as St. Augustine and St. Thomas Aquinas **RI 2**

• Ask: *Why was it important for King to include biblical references?* because his main audience was Christian clergymen *How else does he strengthen his argument throughout the letter?* by citing philosophers such as Socrates and Martin Buber, and American statesmen **RI 8**

Independent/Self-Selected Reading

Have students reread "Letter from Birmingham Jail" independently to practice analyzing the text on their own, or have them practice the skills using another text, such as:

• "On the Duty of Civil Disobedience" by Henry David Thoreau

• Address to the Nation on Civil Rights, June 11, 1963 by John F. Kennedy **RI 9**

WRITE & PRESENT

1. Have small groups discuss King's distinction between just and unjust laws and analyze his claim that people have a moral responsibility to break unjust laws. **RI 5, SL 1**

2. Have each student determine his or her stance on the issue of just and unjust laws. Using ideas from the discussion and examples of their own, students should draft argumentative essays arguing their position. **W 1, W 4**

3. Have students exchange drafts of their essays and peer-review for revising. Then have them edit their revised drafts. **W 5**

4. Students present their essays in small groups. **SL 4**

See Copying Masters, pp. 212–215.

STUDENT CHECKLIST

Writing

☑ Write an argument to support a claim.

☑ Use an appropriate organization and style.

☑ Use language conventions.

Speaking & Listening

☑ Participate effectively in a collaborative discussion.

☑ Demonstrate an understanding of the text.

☑ Present supporting evidence clearly, concisely, and logically.

▶ OBJECTIVES

- Analyze text using text evidence
- Determine author's purpose
- Determine author's point of view
- Analyze author's use of rhetoric

"I Have a Dream"
by Martin Luther King, Jr.

Options for Reading

Independent Students read the speech independently (suggest they "hear" the words as they read) and then answer questions posed by the teacher.

Supported Students read the speech aloud in a group with the teacher and then answer questions posed by the teacher.

SUMMARY Martin Luther King, Jr., delivered his famous "I Have a Dream" speech to a crowd of about 250,000 who had gathered to demonstrate for civil rights. King speaks of the debt of equal opportunity owed to African Americans, of the injustice of segregation and police brutality suffered by African Americans, and of his dream that one day racism will no longer exist in America.

ABOUT THE AUTHOR Martin Luther King, Jr., civil rights leader, advocate of nonviolence, and clergyman, spoke and wrote in support of the rights of African Americans until his assassination in 1968. King won the Nobel Peace Prize in 1964.

Discuss Genre and Set Purpose

INFORMATIONAL TEXT Have students skim the speech for clues to its genre. Discuss how the use of the first-person pronoun *I* and the historical and social references to the Constitution, Declaration of Independence, and the Negro suggest that the text is nonfiction and is a historical personal statement of belief.

SET PURPOSE Help students set a purpose for reading, such as to determine King's purpose in creating this text.

COMMON CORE **Common Core Connection**

RL 2 determine a central idea/analyze its development/provide summary; **RI 4** determine the meaning of words and phrases, including figurative, connotative, and technical meanings/ analyze impact of word choices; **RI 5** analyze how author's ideas or claims are developed and refined; **RI 6** determine author's point of view or purpose/analyze how author uses rhetoric; **RI 9** analyze seminal U.S. documents of historical and literary significance; **W 4** produce writing in which development, organization, and style are appropriate to task, purpose, and audience; **W 2** write informative/explanatory texts; **W 5** develop and strengthen writing by planning, revising, editing, rewriting, or trying a new approach; **W 9** draw evidence form literary or informational texts; **SL 1** initiate/participate in a range of collaborative discussions; **SL 4** present supporting evidence clearly, concisely, and logically

◢ TEXT COMPLEXITY RUBRIC

Overall Text Complexity		"I Have a Dream" INFORMATIONAL TEXT
		ACCESSIBLE
Quantitative Measure	Lexile	1180L
Qualitative Measures	Text Structure	complex sentence structures
	Language Conventionality and Clarity	some unfamiliar or academic words
	Knowledge Demands	historical and civics knowledge required
	Purpose/Levels of Meaning	easy to identify from context

Academic Vocabulary

Read each word with students and discuss its meaning.

promissory (p. 38) • stating a promise or an obligation

urgency (p. 38) • a state requiring immediate action

legitimate (p. 39) • lawful; conforming to accepted principles

degenerate (p. 40) • to sink or decline

FIRST READ ## Think Through the Text

Have students use text evidence and draw inferences to answer questions.

pp. 37–38 • *What does King mean when he says that the demonstrators have come to Washington to cash a check?* He means that they are owed their rights and have come to claim them. *On what basis does he make the claim that African Americans are owed these rights?* the Constitution and the Declaration of Independence ▬ RI 4

pp. 37, 39–41 • *What evidence does King cite to describe the lack of rights African Americans still experience?* poverty in the midst of prosperity, police brutality, segregation, and discrimination *What action does King advocate?* to continue demonstrating nonviolently; to work with white Americans ▬ RI 5

pp. 42–43 • *What was King's dream in 1963?* that racial injustice will end and all Americans will be equal ▬ RI 2

SECOND READ ## Analyze the Text

• Ask: *What was King's purpose or purposes in making this speech?* to motivate and inspire; to inform the nation of African Americans' reasons for continuing to demonstrate ▬ RI 6

• *What point of view does King take on the issue of civil rights?* He and other African Americans will not be satisfied until their rights are achieved. ▬ RI 6

• *What are some rhetorical and literary devices King uses to advance his purpose?* repetition, hyperbole, allusion, metaphor (e.g. "island of poverty") ▬ RI 6

Independent/Self-Selected Reading

Have students reread "I Have a Dream" independently to practice analyzing the text on their own, or have them practice the skills using another text, such as:

• "Universal Declaration of Human Rights" by General Assembly of the United Nations

• "On Women's Right to Vote" by Susan B. Anthony ▬ RI 9

WRITE & PRESENT

1. Have small groups analyze the different rhetorical devices King used in his speech. Ask students to record their examples on a chart. ▬ RI 6, SL 1

2. Have each student select a rhetorical device that King used and write a short essay that explains his use of the device, offers examples, and analyzes how King used the device to inspire his audience and advance his position. ▬ W 2, W 9

3. Have students share their work with partners and offer suggestions for revising and editing. Students edit their writing based on these suggestions. ▬ W 5

4. Students present their essays in small groups. ▬ SL 4

See Copying Masters, pp. 212–215.

STUDENT CHECKLIST

Writing

☑ Write an essay analyzing use of a rhetorical device.

☑ Draw evidence from the text.

☑ Use language conventions.

Speaking & Listening

☑ Participate effectively in a collaborative discussion.

☑ Demonstrate an understanding of the text.

☑ Present supporting evidence clearly, concisely, and logically.

☑ Read writing aloud with a clear, audible voice.

OBJECTIVES

- Recognize the impact of major events in the author's life
- Make inferences based on text evidence
- Analyze how the author unfolds events

I Know Why the Caged Bird Sings is broken into three instructional segments.

SEGMENTS

SEGMENT 1 . . . . pp. 1–87
SEGMENT 2 . . . . . . pp. 87–197
SEGMENT 3 . . . . . pp. 197–285

Options for Reading

Independent Students read the book independently or with a partner and then answer questions posed by the teacher.

Supported Students read a segment and answer questions with teacher support.

 **Common Core Connection**

RI 1 cite textual evidence to support analysis of what the text says explicitly as well as inferences drawn; **RI 3** analyze how author unfolds a series of events

I Know Why the Caged Bird Sings

by Maya Angelou

SUMMARY This is an autobiography of the early part of Maya Angelou's life in the 1930s and '40s. Born Marguerite Johnson, at age three she and her older brother, Bailey, were sent to live with their grandmother. This book takes us through Angelou's life until the age of sixteen.

ABOUT THE AUTHOR Maya Angelou is a renowned poet and writer. This is the first of six autobiographical volumes. It was nominated for a National Book Award and adapted for television. She was involved in the civil rights movement, working with Martin Luther King Jr. In 1993, she composed the poem "On the Pulse of Morning," which she read at the inauguration of President Bill Clinton.

Discuss Genre and Set Purpose

INFORMATIONAL TEXT Have students briefly page through the book. Discuss with students that although this is an autobiography, it has many aspects of fictional writing, such as thematic development.

SET PURPOSE Help students set a purpose for reading, such as to learn more about the early life of Maya Angelou.

TEXT COMPLEXITY RUBRIC

Overall Text Complexity		I Know Why the Caged Bird Sings INFORMATIONAL TEXT
		COMPLEX
Quantitative Measure	Lexile	1070L
Qualitative Measures	Text Structure	genre traits less common to informational texts
	Language Conventionality and Clarity	increased, clearly assigned dialogue
	Knowledge Demands	some cultural knowledge useful
	Purpose/Levels of Meaning	implied, but easy to infer

SEGMENT 1 pp. 1–87

Academic Vocabulary

Read each word with students and discuss its meaning.

rancor (p. 12) • bitterness

heinous (p. 19) • monstrous

anachronism (p. 21) • a person, thing, idea, or custom that seems to belong to a different time in history

sobriquet (p. 47) • nickname

chifforobe (p. 47) • wardrobe; a tall piece of furniture with drawers and hanging space for clothes

Domain Specific Vocabulary

cotton gin (p. 7) short for cotton engine, it is a machine that separates cotton fiber from its seed

Klan (p. 18) Klu Klux Klan—a far-right organization that advocates white supremacy

serf (p. 18) a member of the lowest feudal class forced to do labor, akin to a slave

lynched (p. 19) put to death by hanging by mob action and without legal authority

---

FIRST READ ## Think Through the Text

Have students use text evidence and draw inferences to answer questions.

pp. 6–7 *How does Maya come to live in Stamps, Arkansas?* She and her brother, Bailey, are sent by train from California. Her parents' marriage was ending, and her father sent them to live with his mother. ◾ RI 3

pp. 23–25 *What is Maya's attitude toward white people? Cite text evidence to support your ideas.* Since Maya lives in a segregated town, she doesn't see white people as real. They are different. They are strange creatures who lived in a sort of un-life. ◾ RI 1

pp. 51–52 *What happens that surprises Maya?* Her parents in California send her a gift. *Why does this surprise her?* Maya assumes her parents are dead. She doesn't understand how her mother could be happy living without her children. She often imagines her mother's funeral. ◾ RI 3

SECOND READ ## Analyze the Text

• Have students look back on pages 52–59. *What major event occurs?* Maya's father comes to Stamps and takes her and Bailey to live with their mother in St. Louis. *How does Maya feel about this?* She says her world would never be the same. She is afraid of her father but is also impressed by how handsome he is and how well he speaks. ◾ RI 3

• Review pages 75–87. Ask: *How did Maya's reaction to Mr. Freeman's assault change over time?* At first Maya won't tell anyone what happened because she is afraid that Mr. Freeman will kill Bailey. Once Bailey tells her that he can't be killed, on page 81, she tells the truth. *How did Maya feel about the trial and verdict?* Maya feels that she lied when she didn't admit that Mr. Freeman touched her before. She reasons that she is responsible for his conviction and, ultimately, his death. *Why does Maya stop speaking after Mr. Freeman's death?* She thinks that her speaking to people could lead to their deaths. ◾ RI 3

ELL ### ENGLISH LANGUAGE LEARNERS

Use Sentence Frames

Have students fill in sentence frames to review what has happened so far:

First, Maya moves to _____. Stamps, Arkansas *She lives with her* _____. grandmother *Then she moves to* _____. St. Louis *There she lives with her* _____. mother *Last, she moves back to* _____ *to live with her* _____ *again.* Stamps; grandmother

---

RESPOND TO SEGMENT 1

 Classroom Collaboration

Have small groups work together to create a summary of the important events in Maya's life in this segment. Ask students to put the events on a timeline.

Domain Specific Vocabulary

white lightning (p. 133)
• illegally made alcohol

Joe Louis (p. 133) •
known as the
Brown Bomber, a
professional boxer and
world heavyweight
champion from 1937
to 1949

calaboose (p. 194) a jail

 ENGLISH LANGUAGE LEARNERS

Use Comprehensible Input

Ensure students understand
the events in Maya's life by
asking questions, such as:
*How does Mrs. Flowers help
Maya? Why do Maya and
Bailey move to California?*

 RESPOND TO SEGMENT 2

Classroom Collaboration

Have small groups work
together to summarize what
has happened to Maya in
this segment. Have them ask
questions about what they
don't understand.

 Common Core Connection

RI 1 cite textual evidence to support analysis
of what the text says explicitly as well as
inferences drawn; **RI 2** provide a summary;
RI 3 analyze how author unfolds a series of
events; **RI 10** read and comprehend literary
nonfiction; **W 4** produce writing in which
development, organization, and style are
appropriate to task, purpose, and audience;
W 5 develop and strengthen writing by
planning, revising, editing, rewriting, or trying
a new approach; **SL 1b** set rules for collegial
discussion and decision-making, clear goals and
deadlines, and individual roles; **SL 4** present
supporting evidence clearly and concisely

Academic Vocabulary

Read each word with students and discuss its meaning.

affluent (p. 118) • rich
commensurate (p. 118) • matching or equal
blasphemous (p. 121) • expressing or involving disrespect for God
metamorphosis (p. 154) • transformation
onerous (p. 157) • burdensome or difficult
solicitous (p. 159) • caring and attentive

FIRST READ ▶ **Think Through the Text**

Have students use text evidence and draw inferences to answer
questions.

pp. 91–102 *Explain the relationship between Maya and Mrs. Flowers.
Why did Maya call her a life line (page 91)? When Maya returned to
Stamps, she continued not to speak to anyone but Bailey. Momma asked
Mrs. Flowers to intervene. She gave Maya books and showed her the
power of the spoken word as she read aloud. Maya liked the way Mrs.
Flowers said her name (Marguerite) and felt liked and respected for
being herself. Mrs. Flowers helped Maya to speak again and gave her a
new lease on life.* **RI 3**

pp. 191–197 • *Why does Maya move to California? After the incident
where Bailey had to help with the dead man, Momma decided it was
better for Maya and Bailey to live in California with their mother.* **RI 1**

SECOND READ ▶ **Analyze the Text**

• Review pages 165–182 with students. Say: *Trace Maya's feelings during
the graduation ceremony. Why do her feelings change? At first, Maya
is happy, but when Mr. Donleavy talks to the class, she feels
completely deflated. She feels that she has been put in her place as a
black person who will never amount to anything. Finally, on page 180,
when Henry Reed turns to the students and sings what Maya describes
as "the Negro national anthem," she feels she has heard the words
for the first time and feels proud to be black.* **RI 3**

• Have students look back on pages 182–191. Ask: *What does the
incident with the dentist tell you about Momma's character? It shows
that she is very strong. She stands up to a white man and demands
money from him after he insults her and refuses to help Maya.* **How
does Maya imagine Momma?** *We see her imagining an overpowering
Momma who can rectify any situation.* **RI 3**

Academic Vocabulary

Read each word with students and discuss its meaning.

traverse (p. 199) • to move through an area

clemency (p. 204) • showing mercy

cajoled (p. 223) • persuaded gently

filial (p. 241) • a child's feeling toward a parent

aphorisms (p. 264) • sayings

FIRST READ **Think Through the Text**

Have students use text evidence and draw inferences to answer questions.

pp. 206–210 • *How does the way Maya feels about San Francisco change how she feels about herself? What examples from the text support your ideas?* She loves San Francisco and feels like she belongs there. On page 209, she says she became free of fear. **RI 1**

pp. 221–239 • *Where does Maya go on vacation?* She visits her father in Los Angeles. *What significant events take place?* She goes to Mexico with her father. He gets drunk, and she has to figure out how to drive home. **RI 2**

pp. 259–268 • *What job did Maya get?* She became a streetcar conductor. *Why is that significant?* She was the first African American conductor. *What does Maya's pursuit of the job tell you about her personality?* She is persistent. **RI 3**

SECOND READ **Analyze the Text**

- Revisit pages 247–251. Ask: *How did being homeless change Maya?* She felt more secure; she felt like she belonged to the human race and became more tolerant of different people. **RI 10**

- Review pages 279–285 with students. Ask: *How does Maya's mother help her learn an important lesson about herself?* Maya's mother shows Maya that she does know how to be a good mother. **RI 3**

Independent/Self-Selected Reading

Have students reread *I Know Why the Caged Bird Sings* independently to practice analyzing the text on their own, or have them practice the skills using another book, such as:

- *Their Eyes Were Watching God* by Zora Neale Hurston

- *Black Boy* by Richard Wright **RI 10**

WRITE & PRESENT

1. Have small groups refer to the text to discuss pivotal events in Maya's life. Ask students to think about how these events lead to her self-discovery. **RI 3**

2. Individual students select different events and write an analysis of how they changed the way Maya saw herself. Encourage students to cite text evidence to support their analyses. **RI 1, SL 1b, W 4**

3. Small groups reconvene to share their work and suggest revisions. Students edit their writing based on these suggestions. **W 5**

4. Students present their final papers to classmates. **SL 4**

5. Individual students turn in their final drafts to the teacher. **W 4**

See Copying Masters, pp. 212–215.

STUDENT CHECKLIST

Writing

☑ Write about one main pivotal event.

☑ Use text evidence to support your analysis of the effect of this event.

☑ Use complete sentences and developed paragraphs to structure writing.

Speaking & Listening

☑ Participate effectively in collaborative discussions.

☑ Speak clearly at an understandable pace.

▶ OBJECTIVES

- Determine the central idea of a text
- Determine author's purpose
- Analyze text using text evidence

Options for Reading

Independent Students read the text independently or with a partner and then answer questions posed by the teacher.

Supported Students read the text and answer questions with teacher support.

"Hope, Despair and Memory"

by Elie Wiesel

SUMMARY Elie Wiesel delivered this speech in December of 1986 after receiving the Nobel Peace Prize. In this speech, Wiesel examines how memory can bring both hope and despair, but emphasizes that people must remember the most horrible atrocities so that they do not repeat them.

ABOUT THE AUTHOR **Elie Wiesel,** born in Romania in 1928, is a Holocaust survivor, an award winning novelist, a journalist, and a human rights activist. In 1958, his first book, *Night*, was published.

Discuss Genre and Set Purpose

INFORMATIONAL TEXT Remind students that an informational text conveys information about a topic and often includes an argument or claim. Explain that the author supports his or her argument or claim with facts, details, and opinions. It is up to the reader to evaluate the information presented in order to draw conclusions. Discuss how Wiesel expresses his ideas in this speech to the Nobel committee.

SET PURPOSE Help students set a purpose for reading, such as to find the central message in Wiesel's speech.

Common Core Connection

RI 1 cite textual evidence to support analysis of what the text says explicitly as well as inferences drawn; **RI 2** determine a central idea/analyze its development/provide summary; **RI 6** determine author's point of view or purpose/determine how an author uses rhetoric; **RI 10** read and comprehend literary nonfiction; **W 1** write arguments to support claims; **W 5** develop and strengthen writing by planning, revising, editing, rewriting, or trying a new approach; **SL 4** present information, findings, and supporting evidence clearly, concisely, and logically

▲ TEXT COMPLEXITY RUBRIC

Overall Text Complexity		"Hope, Despair and Memory" INFORMATIONAL TEXT COMPLEX
Quantitative Measure	Lexile	900L
Qualitative Measures	Text Structure	less conventional problem/solution structure
	Language Conventionality and Clarity	some unfamiliar and/or academic language
	Knowledge Demands	a number of references to other texts
	Purpose/Levels of Meaning	Implied, but easy to identify from text

Academic Vocabulary

Read each word with students and discuss its meaning.

aberration (p. 175) • a departure from what is normal or desired

xenophobia (p. 175) • an intense fear of foreigners

incumbent (p. 176) • necessary as a result of an obligation

abhorrence (p. 176) • hatred

propitious (p. 177) • favorable and likely to lead to success

repugnant (p. 179) • offensive and completely unacceptable

FIRST READ ## Think Through the Text

Have students use text evidence and draw inferences to answer questions.

p. 174 • *Why does Wiesel begin his speech with a story?* The story provides an analogy to the theme of his speech. It shows the importance and the power of remembering. **RI 6**

p. 175 • *To what event is Wiesel referring?* He is referring to the Holocaust and his own experiences in concentration camps. *What text evidence supports your ideas?* Sample answer: He says they were prisoners. He mentions long processions vanishing into flames, which refers to the gas chambers. **RI 1**

pp. 177–178 • *Wiesel says we have failed to learn the lessons of the Holocaust. Why?* He names a number of things that at the time were indications of failure, such as apartheid and terrorism. **RI 1**

SECOND READ ## Analyze the Text

- *What is Wiesel's central message?* Sample answer: Although memories can be painful, they can also bring hope that we will learn from the past and not repeat the same mistakes. **RI 2**

- *What does Wiesel want the listener to do?* Wiesel believes that even though we may not be able to prevent an injustice, we must rise up to protest against it. **RI 6**

Independent/Self-Selected Reading

Have students reread "Hope, Despair and Memory" independently to practice analyzing the text on their own, or have them practice the skills using another text, such as:

- *Night* by Elie Wiesel

- "Day of Affirmation Address at Cape Town University" ("A Tiny Ripple of Hope") by Robert F. Kennedy **RI 10**

WRITE & PRESENT

1. Have small groups discuss the purpose and central message of Wiesel's speech. **RI 2, RI 6**

2. Ask students to write a persuasive essay on the importance of protesting injustice. Encourage students to cite text evidence to defend their ideas. **W 1**

3. Have students share their work with partners and offer suggestions for revising and editing. Students edit their writing based on these suggestions. **W 5**

4. Students present their final papers to classmates. **SL 4**

See Copying Masters, pp. 212–215.

STUDENT CHECKLIST

Writing

☑ Identify the central message of the speech.

☑ Write a persuasive essay using text evidence to support your ideas.

☑ Use complete sentences and developed paragraphs to structure writing.

Speaking & Listening

☑ Read writing aloud with a clear, audible voice.

☑ Present ideas in a meaningful way.

▷ OBJECTIVES

- Analyze text using text evidence
- Explain the theme and how the speaker develops it
- Describe how audience can affect a speaker's purpose

Options for Reading

Independent Students read the speech independently and then answer questions posed by the teacher.

Supported Students read the speech and answer questions with teacher support.

"Speech at Moscow State University"

by Ronald Reagan

SUMMARY This moving speech was delivered to a student group in Moscow in May of 1988 by President Ronald Reagan. Reagan's focus is to bring a message of freedom to the Soviet people.

ABOUT THE AUTHOR Ronald Wilson Reagan (1911–2004) was the fortieth President of the United States. Prior to entering politics, Reagan was a film actor. He is considered one of the most influential conservative Republicans in United States history.

Discuss Genre and Set Purpose

NONFICTION Students should recall that speeches are rhetorical situations where the speaker is often persuading the audience to take some action or adopt an idea.

SET PURPOSE Help students set a purpose for reading, such as to learn what made the speech significant in history.

Common Core Connection

RI 1 cite textual evidence to support analysis of what the text says explicitly as well as inferences drawn; **RI 2** determine a central idea/analyze its development/provide summary; **RI 3** analyze how author unfolds an analysis or series of ideas or events; **RI 4** determine the meaning of words and phrases, including figurative, connotative, and technical meanings/ analyze impact of word choices; **RI 5** analyze how author's ideas or claims are developed and refined; **RI 6** determine author's point of view or purpose/analyze how author uses rhetoric; **RI 10** read and comprehend literary nonfiction; **W 2** write informative/explanatory texts; **W 4** produce writing in which development, organization, and style are appropriate to task, purpose, and audience; **W 5** develop and strengthen writing by planning, revising, editing, rewriting, or trying a new approach; **SL 1** initiate/participate in a range of collaborative discussions; **SL 4** present information, findings, and supporting evidence clearly, concisely, and logically

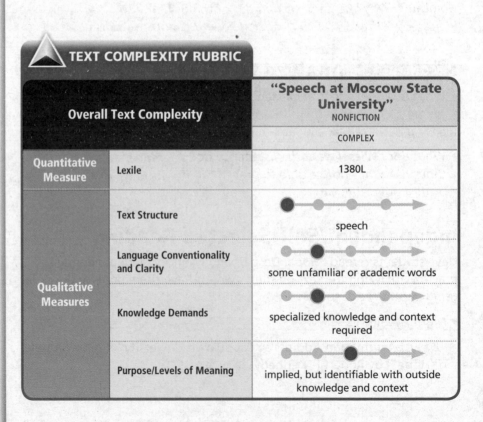

TEXT COMPLEXITY RUBRIC		"Speech at Moscow State University" NONFICTION
Overall Text Complexity		COMPLEX
Quantitative Measure	Lexile	1380L
Qualitative Measures	Text Structure	speech
	Language Conventionality and Clarity	some unfamiliar or academic words
	Knowledge Demands	specialized knowledge and context required
	Purpose/Levels of Meaning	implied, but identifiable with outside knowledge and context

Academic Vocabulary

Read each word with students and discuss its meaning.

ingenious (p. 606) • cleverly original

monopoly (p. 609) • exclusive controls

unintrusive (p. 609) • not intruding

cudgel (p. 609) • a short stick or club

FIRST READ   Think Through the Text

Have students use text evidence and draw inferences to answer questions.

p. 605 • *What revolution is Reagan referring to at the start of his speech?* He is talking about the technological, or computer, revolution. ◼ RI 4

pp. 606–607 • *What does Reagan say technology needs in order to grow?* Reagan says that we must have freedom in order for technology to reach its potential. ◼ RI 1, RI 5

SECOND READ   Analyze the Text

- Review page 606. Ask: *Why does Reagan compare the change from the Industrial Revolution to the technological revolution to a chrysalis?* Sample answer: Reagan is comparing the Industrial Revolution to the caterpillar and the technological revolution to the butterfly; what we once thought was innovative and revolutionary (industry) is now confining but morphing into ideas that have no limits (through technology). ◼ RI 1, RI 4

- Review pages 607–608. Ask: *Why do you think President Reagan spends so much time explaining the many freedoms that Americans enjoy?* Since the people of the Soviet Union did not have the same rights as Americans, Reagan wanted to explain what these concepts meant in practice, hoping to spread democracy and freedom. ◼ RI 1, RI 3, RI 5

- Review pages 607–610. Ask: *What do you think President Reagan's goal is for his speech to the students?* Sample answer: President Reagan wants to get the students interested in having more freedom in their country. He wants to make freedom attractive to them so that the future will bring more open communication between the United States and the Soviet Union. ◼ RI 2, RI 6

Independent/Self-Selected Reading

Have students reread the "Speech at Moscow State University" independently to practice analyzing the text on their own, or have them practice the skills using another speech, such as:

- Remarks at the Rudolph Wilde Platz in Berlin by President John F. Kennedy, transcript available at the JFK Presidential Library

- Remarks for the United Nations Fourth World Conference on Women, by Hillary Rodham Clinton, 1995 ◼ RI 10

Performance Task

WRITE & PRESENT

1. Have students think about and discuss the theme of freedom in the speech. ◼ RI 2, RI 5, RI 6

2. Have students write an essay analyzing how Reagan unfolds the theme of freedom in his speech. Remind them to cite evidence from the speech in their essays. ◼ RI 1, RI 5, W 2, W 4

3. Have students share their essays in groups, offering suggestions for revision. Students should edit their writing based on the group's feedback. ◼ W 5

4. Have students develop group presentations to share their essays. Ask students to respond to the ideas in each presentation. ◼ SL 1, SL 4

See Copying Masters, pp. 212–215.

STUDENT CHECKLIST

Writing

☑ Explain the development of the theme in the speech.

☑ Identify examples of text that support the explanation.

☑ Use complete sentences and developed paragraphs to structure writing.

Speaking & Listening

☑ Read writing aloud with a clear, audible voice.

☑ Present ideas in a meaningful way.

▷ OBJECTIVES

- Analyze text using text evidence
- Identify the author's purpose and point of view in an essay
- Describe how essays can reflect history and cultural values

Options for Reading

Independent Students read the essay independently and then answer questions posed by the teacher.

Supported Students read the essay and answer questions with teacher support.

"A Quilt of a Country"

by Anna Quindlen

SUMMARY In "A Quilt of a Country," Anna Quindlen tries to reconcile the unity of the United States with the diverse nature of the population. Quindlen is writing in response to the September 11, 2011, terrorist attacks, and the fact that the nation went through a period of intense unification, while simultaneously, reports of intolerance against Arab Americans were in the news.

ABOUT THE AUTHOR Anna Quindlen is an American writer who has also written columns for the *New York Times* and *Newsweek*. She won a Pulitzer Prize for commentary writing in 1992.

Discuss Genre and Set Purpose

NONFICTION Remind students that an essay is a short piece of informational text that often appears in magazines. It is focused on a particular topic and often includes the author's personal views.

SET PURPOSE Help students set a purpose for reading such as to discover what the author thinks about how diversity influences how we perceive historical events.

Common Core Connection

RI 1 cite textual evidence to support analysis of what the text says explicitly as well as inferences drawn; **RI 2** determine a central idea/analyze its development/provide summary; **RI 4** determine the meaning of words and phrases, including figurative, connotative, and technical meanings/analyze impact of word choices; **RI 5** analyze how author's ideas or claims are developed and refined; **RI 6** determine author's point of view or purpose/analyze how author uses rhetoric; **RI 10** read and comprehend literary nonfiction; **W 2** write informative/explanatory texts; **W 4** produce writing in which development, organization, and style are appropriate to task, purpose, and audience; **W 5** develop and strengthen writing by planning, revising, editing, rewriting, or trying a new approach; **SL 1** initiate/participate in a range of collaborative discussions; **SL 4** present information, findings, and supporting evidence clearly, concisely, and logically

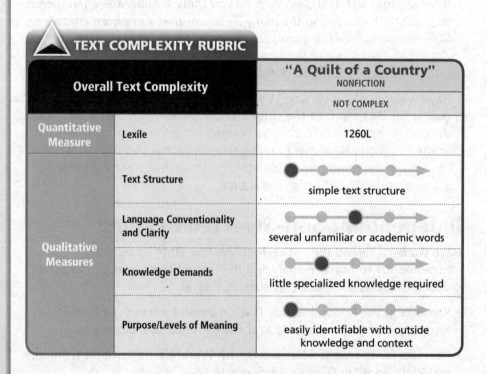

TEXT COMPLEXITY RUBRIC

Overall Text Complexity		"A Quilt of a Country" NONFICTION
		NOT COMPLEX
Quantitative Measure	Lexile	1260L
Qualitative Measures	Text Structure	simple text structure
	Language Conventionality and Clarity	several unfamiliar or academic words
	Knowledge Demands	little specialized knowledge required
	Purpose/Levels of Meaning	easily identifiable with outside knowledge and context

Academic Vocabulary

Read each word with students and discuss its meaning.

improbable (p. 1) • unlikely

pluralistic (p. 1) • when different groups coexist

tenuously (p. 2) • thinly

coalescing (p. 2) • blending together

FIRST READ Think Through the Text

Have students use text evidence and draw inferences to answer questions.

p. 1 • *What is the significance of the title?* Sample answer: The title compares the United States with a pieced quilt since it is a nation of various immigrants coming together to create a whole nation. **RI 1, RI 2, RI 4**

p. 1 • *To what tragedy is Quindlen referring?* the 9/11 terrorist attacks **RL 1**

SECOND READ Analyze the Text

• Explain that Francine Nolan and Portnoy are fictional characters; John Cheever is an author. Cheever wrote, and these characters inhabit, stories with characters from different ethnic and racial groups living in the same location. Ask: *Why does Quindlen mention Nolan, Portnoy, and Cheever?* These examples support the idea of America as a diverse nation whose people take pride in their individual identities. **RI 1, RI 2, RI 5**

• Review page 2. *Ask: What point is Quindlen making by drawing a parallel between immigrants from years ago and immigrants today?* She is saying that recent immigrants deserve the same tolerance as immigrants who came from Europe. **RI 5, RI 6**

• Review page 2. Ask: *What does Quindlen think is unique about America?* People from all over the world come together to form one united country; she says this is an unlikely occurrence, but when it happens, it is extraordinary. **RI 1, RI 2, RI 10**

Independent/Self-Selected Reading

Have students reread "A Quilt of a Country" independently to practice analyzing the text on their own, or have them practice the skills using another essay, such as:

• "The Real Meaning of 9/11" by Jeffrey Goldberg

• "Citizenship in Emergency" by Elaine Scarry **RI 10**

WRITE & PRESENT

1. Have students think about and discuss the purpose and point of view of the essay. **RI 2, RI 5, RI 6**

2. Have students write an essay determining Quindlen's purpose and point of view. Remind them to cite evidence from the text in their writing. **RI 1, RI 6, W 2, W 4**

3. Have partners share their essays, offering suggestions for revision. Students should discuss their ideas and edit them based on feedback from their partners. **W 5**

4. Have students share their final writing with the class. Ask students to respond to the ideas in each student's writing. **SL 1, SL 4**

See Copying Masters, pp. 212–215.

STUDENT CHECKLIST

Writing

☑ Determine the purpose and point of view of the author.

☑ Use formal language conventions in essay writing.

Speaking & Listening

☑ Read writing aloud with a clear, audible voice.

☑ Participate effectively in class discussions.

☑ Ask and answer questions about text details.

▶ OBJECTIVES

- Analyze seminal U.S. documents of historical significance
- Determine author's point of view or purpose
- Analyze text using text evidence

This excerpt from *Bury My Heart at Wounded Knee* is broken into three instructional segments.

Options for Reading

Independent Students read the book independently or with a partner and then answer questions posed by the teacher.

Supported Students read a segment and answer questions with teacher support.

Common Core Connection

RI 1 cite textual evidence to support analysis of what the text says explicitly as well as inferences drawn; **RI 3** analyze how author unfolds an analysis or series of ideas or events; **RI 6** determine author's point of view or purpose/analyze how author uses rhetoric

from *Bury My Heart at Wounded Knee*

by Dee Brown

SUMMARY This history of the treatment of American Indians by the United States government begins in the East, as the first white settlers arrive in the New World. It ends with the massacre of hundreds of men, women, and children at Wounded Knee in 1890. Relying heavily on accounts from American Indians, the book is a stark reminder of the toll in human life and dignity brought about by broken promises.

ABOUT THE AUTHOR Dee Brown was raised in Arkansas and knew many American Indians as a youth. He questioned the myth of their savagery. As a librarian and later a professor of library science, he had access to numerous historical materials. He wrote several books but is best remembered for his groundbreaking work, *Bury My Heart at Wounded Knee*. He died in 2002, having retired to Arkansas.

Discuss Genre and Set Purpose

INFORMATIONAL TEXT Remind students that informational text includes facts but may also have a strong point of view.

SET PURPOSE Help students set a purpose for reading, such as to analyze relations between whites and American Indians over time.

▲ TEXT COMPLEXITY RUBRIC		from *Bury My Heart at Wounded Knee* INFORMATIONAL TEXT
Overall Text Complexity		COMPLEX
Quantitative Measure	Lexile	1080L
Qualitative Measures	Text Structure	somewhat complex concepts
	Language Conventionality and Clarity	increased unfamiliar or academic words
	Knowledge Demands	multiple perspectives
	Purpose/Levels of Meaning	implied, but easy to infer

SEGMENT 1 pp. 1–36

Academic Vocabulary

Read each word with students and discuss its meaning.

dialects (p. 1) • different forms of a language

extinction (p. 4) • the act of disappearing forever

tenacious (p. 11) • persistent or determined

destitute (p. 28) • state of extreme need

genuinely (p. 34) • honestly or truly

ELL **ENGLISH LANGUAGE LEARNERS**

Use Visuals

Ask students to examine the portraits and photos in Segment 1. Have them draw their own portraits of historical American Indians or indigenous people in their native country. Encourage students to use gestures or words to describe their drawings.

FIRST READ ## Think Through the Text

Have students use text evidence and draw inferences to answer questions.

p. 5 • *Who is Sharp Knife?* He is Andrew Jackson, the President of the United States in 1829. *What was his first recommendation to Congress regarding American Indians?* He recommended that all American Indians be moved west of the Mississippi River and that these lands be granted to them forever. RI 1

pp. 6–12 • *During the mid-1800s, how did the eastern tribes differ from the western tribes?* The eastern tribes were defeated and demoralized by their contact with white settlers. The western tribes were largely warlike and independent. ▬RI 1

pp. 14–15 • *Contrast the treatment of Mexicans and Navahos in New Mexico by Americans.* Americans protected the Mexicans because they considered them American citizens. They punished the Navahos for retaliating against the Mexicans, although the Mexicans were in the wrong. ▬RI 3

pp. 30–33 • *What were conditions like on the Bosque Redondo reservation?* The land was wretched and unfit for farming. The water was bad. All the trees were cut down. People were underfed and forced to take shelter in holes in the ground. Disease was rampant. ▬RI 3

RESPOND TO SEGMENT 1

💬 **Classroom Collaboration**

Have partners create timelines using the events discussed in this segment. Encourage students to use computers to make their timelines and to add to their work as they read later segments.

SECOND READ ## Analyze the Text

• Review pages 1–12. Ask: *How did relations between whites and American Indians change from the time of Columbus to the mid-1800s?* Relations deteriorated. First, the two groups were friendly. Then they began fighting over land and became increasingly suspicious of each other. ▬RI 3

• Review pages 20–33. *Does the author admire General James Carleton? Cite examples to explain your answer.* No, the author does not admire the general. The author thinks the general is haughty in his relations with American Indians (pages 21, 31), dishonest in his dealings with tribes (pages 26, 32), and obsessive in his quest to move the American Indians to the reservation (pages 25, 33). ▬RI 6

Domain Specific Vocabulary

breechclouts (p. 39) • cloth that covers the loins

tepees (p. 58) • cone-shaped tents that are easily transported

ENGLISH LANGUAGE LEARNERS

Use Peer Supported Learning

Place students of different abilities in small groups during the classroom collaboration. Encourage more advanced group members to offer guidance and feedback to beginning learners.

RESPOND TO SEGMENT 2

Classroom Collaboration

Encourage small groups to work together to summarize what they have read. Have them ask questions to clarify any concepts they don't understand.

Common Core Connection

RI 1 cite textual evidence to support analysis of what the text says explicitly as well as inferences drawn; **RI 3** analyze how author unfolds an analysis or series of ideas or events; **RI 5** analyze how author's ideas or claims are developed and refined; **RI 6** determine author's point of view or purpose/analyze how author uses rhetoric; **RI 9** analyze seminal U.S. documents of historical and literary significance; **RI 10** read and comprehend literary nonfiction; **W 2** write informative/ explanatory texts; **W 5** develop and strengthen writing by planning, revising, editing, rewriting, or trying a new approach; **SL 1** initiate/ participate in a range of collaborative discussions

Academic Vocabulary

Read each word with students and discuss its meaning.

annuities (p. 38) • fixed sums of money paid to people each year

neutral (p. 46) • not taking sides in a dispute

barricade (p. 48) • a structure that obstructs an enemy

dictum (p. 54) • a formal announcement

obsequious (p. 58) • slavish, fawning

FIRST READ Think Through the Text

Have students use text evidence and draw inferences to answer questions.

pp. 38–39 • *According to Big Eagle, why did many American Indians dislike whites?* Whites acted as though they were better than American Indians, which was particularly galling to the proud Sioux. Also, some whites abused American Indian women. RI 9

pp. 51–52 • *Why did most other Sioux leaders refuse to support Little Crow's war?* Little Crow had failed to drive the soldiers from Fort Ridgely. Also, some undisciplined young warriors had attacked and murdered defenseless settlers. Although Little Crow despised these attacks, he knew his war had brought them on. RI 3

pp. 58–59 • *Use examples to describe the author's view of the Indian trials.* The author did not approve of how the trials were handled. He points out that the Indians did not receive defense counsel and that witnesses convicted Indians based on mere hearsay. RI 6

SECOND READ Analyze the Text

• Review pages 39–40 with students. Ask: *Why did the Indians want the agents to give them food from the warehouse?* The crops had failed, and the Indians were starving. Plus, it was not the Indians' fault that they did not have money for the stored food—the government had not sent their annuities yet. *How did agency officials respond?* They refused at first, then relented when the Indians broke into the warehouse. *What broken promise made the Indians leave the council in anger?* The agent promised to issue food to other starving Santees, and instead the agent and traders insulted the Indians and refused to distribute the food. RI 1

• Have students revisit page 64. Ask: *How did reactions vary among Americans following the trial of Shakopee and Medicine Bottle?* Sample answer: The St. Paul Pioneer noted that no evidence existed to convict the men but also added that their deaths would not be a serious injustice. The Minnesota legislature gave a bonus to McKenzie for illegally drugging and dragging the captives back to America. RI 3

Academic Vocabulary

Read each word with students and discuss its meaning.

relinquish (p. 67) • to give up

circular (p. 74) • a letter sent out to a large group

rations (p. 83) • fixed amounts of food or other resources

alliance (p. 96) • union of allies

expedition (p. 98) • a journey with a purpose

FIRST READ # Think Through the Text

Have students use text evidence and draw inferences to answer questions.

pp. 70–71 • *Why did Lean Bear take along his medal and government papers?* He thought they would prove he was a friend of the United States. *What happened?* He was shot and killed by the soldiers. ▬RI 1

pp. 87–94 • *What strikes you most about the massacre of Sand Creek?* Sample answer: People rushed to stand under the American flag for protection and were brutally murdered. *What was one consequence of the massacre?* As pointed out on page 94, all peace-loving chiefs were killed or lost power. Indians were determined to fight the whites. ▬RI 9

p. 102 • *What does the author feel was the real reason for the massacre?* The author writes that the Indians' loss of the territory of Colorado was the real reason for the massacre. ▬RI 6

SECOND READ # Analyze the Text

• Review pages 76–77 with students. Then ask: *How did having a face-to-face conversation with One-Eye and Eagle Head change Wynkoop's perception of Indians?* Before the conversation, he thought of Indians as lacking feeling and being cruel. Afterward, he called them superior beings. ▬RI 3

• Review pages 87–91 with students. Ask: *How does the author make the massacre of Sand Creek seem real?* He uses firsthand accounts that describe the atrocities committed by the soldiers, along with the heart-wrenching belief by some Indians that they would not be harmed. ▬RI 5

Independent/Self-Selected Reading

Have students reread this excerpt from *Bury My Heart at Wounded Knee* independently to practice analyzing the text on their own, or have them practice the skills using another book, such as:

• *Voices of Wounded Knee* by William S. E. Coleman

• *Black Elk Speaks: Being the Life Story of a Holy Man of the Oglala Sioux* by John G. Neihardt ▬RI 10

Performance Task

WRITE & PRESENT

1. Place students in groups and discuss the author's point of view concerning the Sand Creek massacre. Which details did he include and emphasize? ▬RI 6

2. Have each student write a short essay describing the author's point of view. Encourage students to cite text evidence to defend their ideas. ▬W 2

3. Have students share their work with partners and offer suggestions for revising and editing. Students should edit their writing based on these suggestions. ▬W 5

4. Have students present their final writing to the class before turning it in. Ask other students to listen respectfully and ask questions for clarification. ▬SL 1

See Copying Masters, pp. 212–215.

STUDENT CHECKLIST

Writing

☑ Identify author's point of view of the Sand Creek massacre.

☑ Use text evidence and quotes to support writing.

☑ Use complete sentences and revise writing as needed.

Speaking & Listening

☑ Read writing aloud with a clear, audible voice.

☑ Listen respectfully to others and ask questions.

OBJECTIVES

- Identify the author's view in a text
- Analyze the information and examples presented in a text
- Explain the meaning of figurative language

This excerpt from *Son of the Morning Star: Custer and the Little Big Horn* is broken into three instructional segments.

SEGMENTS

Options for Reading

Independent Students read the book independently and then answer questions posed by the teacher.

Supported Students read smaller segments within each section with teacher support.

from *Son of the Morning Star*

by Evan S. Connell

SUMMARY Evan S. Connell uses letters and other primary source documents to recreate Custer and his army's defeat at the Battle of the Little Big Horn. The book describes the lives and character of many of the main persons involved.

ABOUT THE AUTHOR **Evan S. Connell** wrote novels, poetry, short stories, and biographies. His works include both fiction and nonfiction. In 2000, he won the Lannan Literary Award for Lifetime Achievement.

Discuss Genre and Set Purpose

INFORMATIONAL TEXT Explain that informational texts about history present the facts about a historic event or historic person(s). In this book, the writer reveals the controversy over various facts, describing conflicting information and explaining why certain sources of information are considered more reliable than others.

SET PURPOSE Help students set a purpose for reading, such as to find out what the soldiers and Native Americans were really like and what they actually experienced.

Common Core Connection

RI 1 cite textual evidence to support analysis of what the text says explicitly as well as inferences drawn; **RI 3** analyze how author unfolds an analysis or series of ideas or events; **RI 4** determine the meaning of words and phrases, including figurative, connotative, and technical meanings/analyze impact of word choices; **RI 5** analyze how author's ideas or claims are developed and refined; **RI 6** determine author's point of view or purpose/analyze how author uses rhetoric

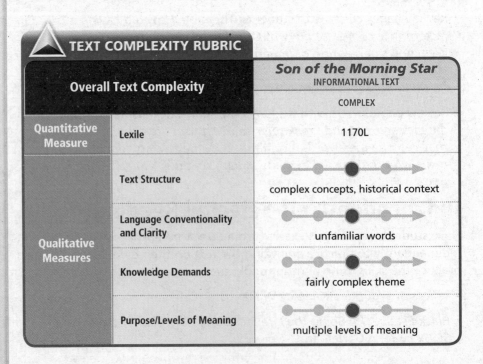

TEXT COMPLEXITY RUBRIC

Overall Text Complexity		*Son of the Morning Star* INFORMATIONAL TEXT
		COMPLEX
Quantitative Measure	Lexile	1170L
Qualitative Measures	Text Structure	complex concepts, historical context
	Language Conventionality and Clarity	unfamiliar words
	Knowledge Demands	fairly complex theme
	Purpose/Levels of Meaning	multiple levels of meaning

> ### Academic Vocabulary
>
> Read each word with students and discuss its meaning.
>
> **dubious** (p. 29) • unreliable, questionable
>
> **sinister** (p. 30) • evil, hinting at something bad happening
>
> **contemptuous** (p. 46) • showing no respect for someone or something
>
> **circumspect** (p. 49) • secretive, discreet
>
> **preposterous** (p. 57) • hard to believe, absurd, outlandish

Idioms and Expressions

Explain the phrase about shadows creeping across the document on page 29. Discuss how shadows can symbolize darkness or hiding. Use and explain the idiom, *hiding in the shadows*. Help students to recognize that the writer is trying to say that there are problems with the document.

Have students create a book of idioms and expressions they encounter in the text. Then have students work with fluent speakers to ask about what the expression means. Students should write an explanation of the phrase along with examples of when the phrase might be used.

FIRST READ **Think Through the Text**

Have students use text evidence and draw inferences to answer questions.

pp. 28–30 • *What does the writer mean when he mentions shadows creeping across the document?* The document does not seem to be legitimate. It was probably not written by the people who actually served with Custer. *What are some examples of those "shadows"?* There were signatures from men who did not know how to write, and an FBI investigation showed some signatures to be forgeries. ▬RI 1, RI 5, RI 6

p. 32 • *What are some of the reasons that Benteen disliked Custer?* Custer was younger than Benteen and had a higher rank. Custer was assigned the division that had belonged to a Third Cavalry commandant Benteen liked. Custer was boastful. ▬RI 1

p. 57 • *What is a Gatling?* It is a type of gun. This one was so heavy it could be pulled by a horse. *What did some of the soldiers think of the Gatling?* It was dangerous and difficult to carry. ▬RI 4

SECOND READ **Analyze the Text**

- Review pages 33–35. Ask: *How is the account of Benteen different from traditional historic accounts of American soldiers?* This account describes Benteen's failures, including the details of his court-martial. *Why do you think that Connell includes many of these types of details in the book?* Sample answer: He wants to paint a more complete picture of the men and tell what really happened. ▬RI 5, RI 6

- Review pages 56–57 with students. Then ask: *Why does the author include excerpts from letters?* Sample answer: This shows what the men were thinking. It also allows the men to "speak for themselves," rather than the writer using his words to describe it. ▬RI 5, RI 6

- Review the last five paragraphs on page 60 with students. Ask: *How does the last sentence on page 60 show that the writer is coming from a modern perspective looking back?* This statement shows that he would not expect soldiers to really be so lighthearted on the actual battlefield. ▬RI 3, RI 6

RESPOND TO SEGMENT 1

 Classroom Collaboration

Have partners discuss the different sources of information the writer uses to determine what happened (letters, government documents, personal accounts, other history books). Direct partners to name at least one strength and one weakness of using each type of source.

Domain Specific Vocabulary

Read each word with students and discuss its meaning.

adjutants (p. 75) • assisting officers

tacticians (p. 80) • people who study war strategies

 ENGLISH LANGUAGE LEARNERS

Comprehensible Input

Ask yes/no questions for students with beginning language skills and provide sentence frames for more advanced speakers. Sample sentence frames:
The gold rush brought _____ to Native Americans. The gold rush was harmful to Native Americans because _____.

 RESPOND TO SEGMENT 2

Classroom Collaboration

Have small groups work together to summarize what they have read. Have them ask questions about what they don't understand.

 Common Core Connection

RI 2 determine a central idea/analyze its development/provide summary; **RI 4** determine the meaning of words and phrases; **RI 5** analyze how author's ideas or claims are developed and refined; **RI 6** determine author's point of view or purpose/analyze how author uses rhetoric; **RI 10** read and comprehend literary nonfiction; **W 2** write informative/explanatory texts; **W 5** develop and strengthen writing by planning, revising, editing, rewriting, or trying a new approach; **SL 4** present information, findings, and supporting evidence clearly, concisely, and logically

Academic Vocabulary

Read each word with students and discuss its meaning.

impetuous (p. 63) • impulsive, quick to act

palimpsest (p. 68) • parchment with many different texts written on it, with one erased so another could be written

malicious (p. 73) • mean-spirited

acerbic (p. 75) • unsympathetic and harsh (in terms of criticism)

reticent (p. 83) • quiet, not speaking much

FIRST READ ## Think Through the Text

Have students use text evidence and draw inferences to answer questions.

pp. 63–64 • *What were some of the effects of the gold rush on the Native Americans living in the area?* cholera, more demands for land and increased attacks from whites ▪RI 1

p. 73 • *What context clues help you define the word* erroneous *in the second full paragraph on page 73?* misinterpretation; the message should have been; honest mistake ▪RI 4

p. 76 • *What does the author say would have been Sitting Bull's reason to call off the attack?* He knew that attacking them would only bring on more attacks against his own people. ▪RI 1

p. 80 • *How did historians use metal detectors to help them figure out what happened?* They found where bullets and metal equipment had been laying on the ground and reconstructed the scene. ▪RI 1

SECOND READ ## Analyze the Text

• Have students review pages 67–68. Ask: *What do the differing stories about how Crazy Horse got his name suggest about history?* Sample answer: History can be lost. It is limited by the stories that people tell and/or by what they write down at the time. ▪RI 1, RI 5, RI 6

• Review page 72 with students. Ask: *Why do you think that people labeled photographs as Crazy Horse even though the photos were not of him?* They wanted to be able to say they had seen him. ▪RI 1

• Review pages 81–82 with students. Ask: *What does the author mean when he mentions that there was ineradicable debris that was characteristic of industrial nations?* Sample answer: pollution, manufacturing, cities and urban areas *How would you summarize what Chief Joseph said?* Sample answer: The Native Americans are a free people and the whites have no authority over us. The whites are asking us to do what they are not willing to do themselves. ▪RI 2

Academic Vocabulary

Read each word with students and discuss its meaning.

incorruptible (p. 105) • not willing to accept a bribe

fortuitously (p. 107) • fortunately, luckily

circuitous (p. 114) • in a roundabout way, not direct

ensconced (p. 119) • settled; perched

FIRST READ ## Think Through the Text

Have students use text evidence and draw inferences to answer questions.

p. 106 • *What does the author mean when he writes that Custer was more like an actor than a playwright?* Custer simply responded to what came his way. He was not the one who made plans or devised strategies. He acted on others' ideas. ⊂RI 4, RI 5, RI 6

pp. 118–119 • *Were you surprised by the way that Custer and Rosser behaved on and off the battlefield? Why or why not?* Sample answer: It is somewhat shocking that they acted like friends when they were not on the battlefield, but were actually mortal enemies who were trying to kill each other. *How does this illustrate the nature of the Civil War?* It shows how this war set brother against brother. ⊂RI 2

SECOND READ ## Analyze the Text

• Ask: *What is the author's view of Custer?* Custer was a ruthless and cruel man. He was selfish and took many chances that cost the lives of the men who served under him. ⊂RI 1, RI 6

• On page 106, the author writes about how the view of historical events change as societal values change. *In what ways does this hold true for the people and events described in this book?* Sample answer: Today, people recognize that the actions taken against the Native Americans were acts of genocide and are inhumane and inexcusable. This is a different view than that held by many white Americans at the time. *How does the quote on page 132 show this?* The author clearly connects the words of Custer to those of Hitler. ⊂RI 2, RI 5

Independent/Self-Selected Reading

Have students reread the excerpt from *Son of the Morning Star: Custer and the Little Big Horn* independently to practice analyzing the text on their own, or have them practice the skills using another book, such as:

• *History of the Second Seminole War 1835–1842* by John K. Mahon

• *Archaeological Perspectives on the Battle of the Little Bighorn* by Scott, Fox, Connor, and Harmon ⊂RI 10

Performance Task

WRITE & PRESENT

1. Have groups discuss what this book suggests about how and why history changes over time. ⊂RI 1, RI 5, RI 6

2. Have students write brief essays explaining how the author shows that our understanding of history can change long after events have occurred. Students should provide examples from the text in their essays. ⊂RI 1, RI 5, RI 6, W 2

3. Have students share their work with partners and suggest revisions and edits. Students edit their writing based on these suggestions. ⊂W 5

4. Have students present their final writing to the class by giving an oral presentation that is organized around the main examples they chose. ⊂SL 4

See Copying Masters, pp. 212–215.

STUDENT CHECKLIST

Writing

☑ Analyze what the author implies about how and why history changes.

☑ Write an essay using examples from the text.

☑ Strengthen writing by revising it.

Speaking & Listening

☑ Present ideas in an organized and logical way.

☑ Demonstrate command of formal spoken English.

OBJECTIVES

- Determine and analyze the development of central ideas
- Read and comprehend literary nonfiction
- Analyze text using text evidence

This excerpt from *The Story of Art* is broken into three instructional segments.

SEGMENTS

Options for Reading

Independent Students read the text independently or with a partner and then answer questions posed by the teacher.

Supported Students read a segment and answer questions with teacher support.

COMMON CORE Common Core Connection

RI 1 cite textual evidence to support analysis of what the text says explicitly as well as inferences drawn; **RI 2** determine a central idea/analyze its development/provide summary; **RI 3** analyze how author unfolds an analysis or series of ideas or events; **RI 5** analyze how author's ideas or claims are developed and refined

from *The Story of Art*

by E. H. Gombrich

SUMMARY *The Story of Art* traces the development and impact of art on humans, beginning with the first rough sketches on cave walls. The text discusses the contributions of different cultures to art and the changing purpose of art over time. The book also cites examples of art from each of the cultures or periods discussed.

ABOUT THE AUTHOR **Ernst Hans Gombrich** was born in Vienna, Austria, in 1909. His mother's interest in music meant that he was exposed at an early age to many leading artists and intellectuals. He attended Vienna University before immigrating to Britain in the 1930s. His influential work, *The Story of Art,* made art accessible to millions. He is considered one of Britain's most famous art historians and received numerous honors, including the Order of the British Empire, before his death in 2001.

Discuss Genre and Set Purpose

INFORMATIONAL TEXT Remind students that informational text is nonfiction. It provides in-depth information about topics. Have students predict what they will learn in this book.

SET PURPOSE Help students set a purpose for reading, such as to compare and contrast how different cultures approach art.

TEXT COMPLEXITY RUBRIC

Overall Text Complexity		from *The Story of Art* INFORMATIONAL TEXT
		COMPLEX
Quantitative Measure	Lexile	1250L
Qualitative Measures	Text Structure	organization of main ideas and details is complex, but largely explicit
	Language Conventionality and Clarity	ambiguous language requiring inferences
	Knowledge Demands	some specialized knowledge required
	Purpose/Levels of Meaning	implied, but easy to infer

Academic Vocabulary

Read each word with students and discuss its meaning.

weathered (p. 49) • worn away

elaborate (p. 50) • detailed, complex

incantations (p. 50) • the chantings of words to make magic

fleeting (p. 50) • lasting for a very short time

train (p. 51) • a group of assistants

FIRST READ ## Think Through the Text

Have students use text evidence and draw inferences to answer questions.

p. 49 • *Why does the author think the art of Egypt is important to Western readers?* He believes that Western art is heavily influenced by Greek art and that Greek art, in turn, was heavily influenced by Egyptian art. 🔊 RI 3

p. 50 • *What was the purpose of the spells and incantations written on the walls of a king's burial chamber?* They were meant to help the king on his journey to the other world. 🔊 RI 1

p. 51 • *Why does the author write that the word* adorned *is hardly fitting for the paintings found in Egyptian tombs?* because the art was not meant to be seen *What did the figures in the paintings on the tomb walls of a powerful Egyptian represent?* They represented servants to help the powerful Egyptian in the other world. 🔊 RI 1

SECOND READ ## Analyze the Text

- Have students reread page 49. Ask: *What can you infer about the power of Egyptian rulers based on the existence of pyramids?* The rulers had to be very powerful and rich to force thousands of people to work on the pyramids for years on end. *How did common people view the rulers?* The rulers were considered divine beings. *How did this view explain the purpose of the pyramids?* The divine rulers needed soaring tombs to help them ascend back to the gods. 🔊 RI 2

- Review pages 50–51. *What is the author's critique of the sculptures found in the tombs?* The author thinks the sculptures are simple but powerful. He finds their simplicity and solemnity remote yet enduring. *What details does the author use to support his critique?* He describes how the artists focused on the basic form of the human head rather than on facial expressions. He also explains that the sculptures were not intended to be enjoyed but to serve the purpose of helping the dead person transition to the other world. 🔊 RI 5

Domain Specific Vocabulary

motif (p. 52) • decorative design

relief (p. 53) • type of sculpture with projecting details

hieroglyphs (p. 55) • pictures that represent words or sounds in ancient Egyptian writing

ENGLISH LANGUAGE LEARNERS

Use Comprehensible Input

Ask students scaffolded questions about the text, based on their abilities. For example, have beginning learners fill in sentence frames. Ask more advanced learners to answer questions in complete sentences.

RESPOND TO SEGMENT 2

Classroom Collaboration

Place students in small groups to summarize what they have read. Ask students to discuss concepts in their own words and to ask questions to clarify any concepts they don't understand.

Common Core Connection

RI 2 determine a central idea/analyze its development/provide summary; **RI 3** analyze how author unfolds an analysis or series of ideas or events; **RI 6** determine author's point of view or purpose/analyze how author uses rhetoric; **RI 9** analyze seminal U.S. documents of historical and literary significance; **RI 10** read and comprehend literary nonfiction; **W 2** write informative/explanatory texts; **W 5** develop and strengthen writing by planning, revising, editing, rewriting, or trying a new approach; **SL 4** present information, findings, and supporting evidence clearly, concisely, and logically.

Academic Vocabulary

Read each word with students and discuss its meaning.

compunction (p. 52) • a feeling of regret or hesitation

adherence (p. 53) • dogged attachment

method (p. 54) • procedure

script (p. 55) • formal handwriting

idyll (p. 57) • happy scene

FIRST READ ▸ **Think Through the Text**

Have students use text evidence and draw inferences to answer questions.

pp. 52–53 • Ask: *Why did Egyptian artists paint a full-face eye onto a side view of a face? Everything was represented from its most characteristic angle, so a head is most easily represented in side profile but an eye is most easily represented in full profile. How did this affect the way Egyptians looked in their paintings? It made them look flat and strangely contorted.* ◼RI 3

p. 55 • *What is an artistic style? It is a set of laws that the art of a people often obeys. What are some examples of the Egyptian style? Sample answer: Seated statues had to have their hands on their knees, men had to have darker skin than women, and each god was depicted in a certain way.* ◼RI 1

pp. 56–57 • *How did Egyptian art during the reign of Amenophis differ from traditional art? Pictures were less solemn and rigid and more true to life. For example, the pharaoh was sometimes portrayed as an ugly man who enjoyed playing with his family.* ◼RI 2

SECOND READ ▸ **Analyze the Text**

- Review page 52 with students. *How is an Egyptian artist's approach to painting different from that of a modern artist? An ancient Egyptian artist would want to preserve everything in a scene as clearly as possible, even if it meant drawing an overhead view of a pond with fish in profile. A modern artist would be more concerned with capturing the best angles of a scene, even if it meant leaving some details out.* ◼RI 3

- Review pages 56–57 with students. *Did Egyptian art change much over time? Why or why not? No, it did not change much over the course of 3,000 years. The best artists were considered those whose works looked the most similar to famous works of the past. So artists tried to replicate past styles rather than create new styles. Only one king, Amenophis IV, broke with this tradition, and artists reverted back to the old style not long after his death.* ◼RI 2

Academic Vocabulary

Read each word with students and discuss its meaning.

refinement (p. 58) • the state of having taste and manners

symmetry (p. 58) • the quality of being in proportion

commission (p. 59) • place an order for something

prostrate (p. 59) • lying face-down on the ground

chaff (p. 60) • seed covers separated from the seed

FIRST READ ▶ Think Through the Text

Have students use text evidence and draw inferences to answer questions.

p. 58 • *Where is Mesopotamia located?* in the valley between the two rivers: Euphrates and Tigris *Give two reasons why the art of Mesopotamia is less well-known today than the art of Egypt.* Mesopotamians did not have stone quarries, so most buildings, sculptures, and monuments weathered away. Also, Mesopotamians did not share the religious beliefs of Egyptians that the human body and its likeness must be preserved for the soul to live on, so they were not as concerned about preserving art. ▬ RI 1

p. 59 • *What is one curious fact about the picture-chronicles of King Asurnasirpal II of Assyria?* Sample answer: They show many dead or wounded soldiers in battle, but none of the dead or wounded is Assyrian. ▬ RI 1

SECOND READ ▶ Analyze the Text

• Review pages 58–60 with students. Ask: *How did the purpose of art differ between Mesopotamians and Egyptians?* Egyptians focused on the person and his or her deeds in life, with the purpose of helping the person in the afterlife. Mesopotamians focused on warlike images, with the purpose of keeping the person or the society safe. ▬ RI 9

• Review pages 59–60. Ask: *Why does the author suggest that readers take a charitable view of the artists who drew the picture-chronicles of King Asurnasirpal II?* The artists may have believed that if they painted wounded or dead Assyrians, then they would bring Assyrian soldiers bad luck. ▬ RI 6

Independent/Self-Selected Reading

Have students reread this excerpt from *The Story of Art* independently to practice analyzing the text on their own, or have them practice the skills using another book, such as:

• *Art Through the Ages* by Helen Gardner

• *History of Art* by Anthony F. Janson ▬ RI 10

Performance Task

WRITE & PRESENT

1. Have small groups of students identify and discuss the purpose and style of different types of art found in Egyptian tombs. Encourage students to refer to visuals during their discussions. ▬ RI 9

2. Have each student write a short essay describing the purpose and style of ancient Egyptian art. Tell students to cite text evidence and to include illustrations in their work. ▬ W 2

3. Have students exchange their work with partners and offer suggestions for revising and editing. Students should edit their writing based on these critiques. ▬ W 5

4. Have students share their final writing with the class. Stress that students should present the information clearly and concisely. ▬ SL 4

See Copying Masters, pp. 212–215.

STUDENT CHECKLIST

Writing

☑ Identify purpose and style of ancient Egyptian art.

☑ Use text evidence and illustrations to support writing.

☑ Use complete sentences and revise writing as needed.

Speaking & Listening

☑ Read writing aloud with a clear, audible voice.

☑ Listen respectfully to others and ask questions for clarification.

▶ OBJECTIVES

- Recount cause-and-effect relationships in history
- Identify influences on economic growth
- Describe the relationship between humans and their environment
- Analyze text using text evidence

Cod: A Biography of the Fish That Changed the World is broken into three instructional segments.

SEGMENTS

Options for Reading

Independent Students read the book independently or with a partner and then answer questions posed by the teacher.

Supported Students read a segment and answer questions with teacher support.

Common Core Connection

RI 1 cite textual evidence to support analysis of what the text says explicitly as well as inferences drawn; **RI 2** determine a central idea/analyze its development/provide summary; **RI 3** analyze how author unfolds an analysis or series of ideas or events; **RI 5** analyze how author's ideas or claims are developed and refined

Cod: A Biography of the Fish That Changed the World

by Mark Kurlansky

SUMMARY Due to its ease of preservation, the Atlantic cod fueled early European ship crews on their journeys of exploration and colonization. Cod-fishing then helped develop the economies of countries such as Iceland. Technology-aided fishing techniques have now depleted the worldwide cod supply.

ABOUT THE AUTHOR Mark Kurlansky was born in Hartford, Connecticut. After working as a playwright and at various other jobs, he became a journalist and the author of twenty-four books.

Discuss Genre and Set Purpose

INFORMATIONAL TEXT Remind students that informational texts about history or social studies subjects tell facts about events in human history. Discuss why the author might have chosen to focus his history text on an animal.

SET PURPOSE Help students set a purpose for reading, such as to find out why cod has always been considered valuable to humans.

▲ TEXT COMPLEXITY RUBRIC

Overall Text Complexity		Cod: A Biography of the Fish That Changed the World INFORMATIONAL TEXT
		COMPLEX
Quantitative Measure	Lexile	1200L
Qualitative Measures	Text Structure	organization of main ideas and details is highly complex
	Language Conventionality and Clarity	sophisticated descriptions
	Knowledge Demands	specialized knowledge required
	Purpose/Levels of Meaning	multiple topics

Academic Vocabulary

Read each word with students and discuss its meaning.

moratorium (p. 3) • a temporary ban on an activity

microcosm (p. 5) • a place or thing that demonstrates the qualities of something larger

commodity (p. 24) • a valuable good to trade or sell

bier (p. 79) • a stand on which a coffin is placed

Domain Specific Vocabulary

skiff (p. 1) • a small open boat with a flat bottom

fathoms (p. 6) • multiple units of length, each equal to 6 ft.

anglers (p. 33) • people who fish with rods and lines

dorsal (p. 38) • on the upper side or back of an animal

FIRST READ Think Through the Text

Have students use text evidence and draw inferences to answer questions.

pp. 1–14 • *What moratorium has Newfoundland instituted? How does it affect the fishermen in the prologue?* It is a moratorium on groundfishing in surrounding waters. The fishermen do work for the government, tracking the cod population to see if it increases. Otherwise, they would not be able to earn a living trying to fish. ◖RI 2

pp. 32–45 • *What qualities that help cod survive does the text describe?* Sample answer: Page 42 describes how cod make a protein that helps them live in freezing water. Page 45 tells how cod lay many eggs and can adapt their diet to their environment to eat almost anything. ◖RI 1

pp. 48–60 • *Why did cod-fishing become strategic for countries to control?* Fish was the main fuel for the military on boats. Also, trade issues around fish and salt affected relations between countries. ◖RI 2

SECOND READ Analyze the Text

• Review page 40 with students. Ask: *The Icelandic chef says that they don't eat money. What does he mean?* Selling cod to other countries brings a large amount of money into Iceland's economy. It makes financial sense for Icelandic people to eat other kinds of fish and sell off their cod supply. ◖RI 2

• Review pages 72–74. Ask: *How did climate and fishing affect New England and Newfoundland colonization differently?* Prime fishing time in New England is opposite its farming season, while prime fishing time coincides with farming season in Newfoundland. Because people in New England could split their time over the course of the year both fishing and farming, many colonists settled there, and New England developed into a wealthier area with more people. ◖RI 3

• Review pages 92–94. *Why does the author think that cod was an issue behind the American Revolution?* New Englanders were proud of their ability to rise to the middle class because of industries like cod-fishing. The author states that this part of their identity fueled their desire to break free of English economic control. ◖RI 5

ELL ENGLISH LANGUAGE LEARNERS

Use Sentence Frames

Guide students to paraphrase some of the major events in the segment. Guide them with sentence frames such as the following:

Vikings traveled to _____. Iceland, Greenland, and Newfoundland *Traders from New England sent cod* _____, *to the West Indies*

RESPOND TO SEGMENT 1

Classroom Collaboration

Have partners create a summary of the major events of this segment. Then have students make a statement or statements generalizing about the importance of cod.

Cod: A Biography of the Fish That Changed the World • **159**

Domain Specific Vocabulary

dories (p. 114) • small rowboats

trawler (p. 117) • a boat used for fishing with nets

buoys (p. 119) • floats used to mark locations

 ENGLISH LANGUAGE LEARNERS

Use Comprehensible Input

Ensure students understand the importance of historical developments by asking questions such as *What were the "Cod Wars"?* and *What inventions changed the fishing industry?*

RESPOND TO SEGMENT 2

 Classroom Collaboration

Have small groups work together to summarize what they have read. Have them ask questions about what they don't understand.

 Common Core Connection

RI 1 cite textual evidence to support analysis of what the text says explicitly as well as inferences drawn; **RI 2** determine a central idea/analyze its development/provide summary; **RI 5** analyze how author's ideas or claims are developed and refined; **RI 6** determine author's point of view or purpose/analyze how author uses rhetoric; **RI 10** read and comprehend literary nonfiction; **W 2** write informative/explanatory texts; **W 5** develop and strengthen writing by planning, revising, editing, rewriting, or trying a new approach; **SL 4** present information, findings, and supporting evidence clearly, concisely, and logically

Academic Vocabulary

Read each word with students and discuss its meaning.

subsidize (p. 118) • to support financially

prophetic (p. 133) • predicting something proved later to be correct

finite (p. 144) • having limits

subsistence (p. 151) • the act of being just able to support oneself

sovereignty (p. 166) • power or authority over something

FIRST READ Think Through the Text

Have students use text evidence and draw inferences to answer questions.

pp. 111–118 • *What general challenges do fishermen face? Among other things, fishermen face hard physical labor, dangerous weather conditions like fog and storms, tough competition, and uncertainty.* ⬤ RI 1

pp. 125–134 • *How did technology affect the cod-fishing industry? The steam engine made fishing and transporting fish faster, and freezing techniques allowed cod to be transported far inland.* ⬤ RI 2

pp. 166–173 • *What was the European 200-mile zone? How did this affect Iceland and England? Fishery limits for European countries were extended to 200 miles from shorelines. Iceland's and England's fishing territories overlap under this rule, and England felt it was losing control of the best cod-fishing territory.* ⬤ RI 2

SECOND READ Analyze the Text

- Have students revisit pages 144–173. Ask: *How has cod-fishing changed people's lifestyle in Iceland in the last century? Why are they so protective of the industry? Iceland went from an almost primitive country that basically survived on fish to a modern European country that can export fish and develop the economy in other areas. Icelanders don't have many other natural resources, so they want to keep control of the industry that allowed them to modernize.* ⬤ RI 2

- Ask: *Recall the moratorium mentioned in the prologue. What connection can you draw between technological advances in cod fishing and the state of the Newfoundland fishing industry today? The steam engine, large boats, and freezing technology made it so easy to catch and sell cod that the fish's population must have been decreasing. The demand for the fish would be up because so many people suddenly had access to it, which would also put a strain on the supply. Newfoundland must have set the moratorium when the supply got too low.* ⬤ RI 2

Academic Vocabulary

Read each word with students and discuss its meaning.

referendum (p. 178) • a vote on a specific question

conglomerate (p. 181) • different parts that create a whole

rhetoric (p. 209) • persuasive speaking or writing

FIRST READ Think Through the Text

Have students use text evidence and draw inferences to answer questions.

p. 196 • *Why have people turned to farm fishing?* It is an artificial way to increase the cod population. *What new problems might farm fishing cause?* Since people don't always select the right cod to set free, they might introduce bad genetic traits. RI 1

pp. 223–231 • *How have the United States and Canada handled unemployment among fishermen differently?* Canada subsidizes the fishermen's salaries, while the U.S. tries to direct them to other trades. *How are the communities similar and different today?* The fishermen have lost their traditional way of life, and the economies of the towns have suffered. The Canadian fishermen, however, have outlets for practicing their trade, while fewer Americans are able to learn it. RI 2

SECOND READ Analyze the Text

- Review the recipes throughout the book. Ask: *What do these recipes tell you about cod's effect on people and why do you think the author included them?* Sample answer: The recipes are from all around the world and from different ages. The author included them to show how cod has been an important part of many cultures for a long time. RI 5

- Ask: *Why do you think the author subtitled this book "A Biography of the Fish That Changed the World"?* Sample answer: Cod allowed major changes like sea exploration and colonization. It developed economies in many previously undeveloped areas. All countries of Western Europe and North America were affected. RI 6

Independent/Self-Selected Reading

Have students reread *Cod: A Biography of the Fish That Changed the World* independently to practice analyzing the text on their own, or have them practice the skills using another book, such as:

- *Salt: A World History* by Mark Kurlansky

- *Banana: The Fate of the Fruit that Changed the World* by Dan Koeppel RI 10

Performance Task

WRITE & PRESENT

1. Have students think about and discuss cause-and-effect relationships in the book. RI 2

2. Have each student write a short essay explaining direct and indirect effects that cod had on one of the following: New England, Newfoundland, or Iceland. Encourage students to cite text evidence to defend their ideas. W 2

3. Have students share their work with partners and offer suggestions for revising and editing. Students edit their writing based on these suggestions. W 5

4. Have students present their final writing to their classmates. Ask students to comment on the causes and effects their classmates chose to explore and how they are further linked. SL 4

See Copying Masters, pp. 212–215.

STUDENT CHECKLIST

Writing

☑ Identify major changes in one geographic region.

☑ Explain the cause-and-effect relationships that led to those changes.

☑ Use complete sentences and developed paragraphs to structure writing.

Speaking & Listening

☑ Read writing aloud with a clear, audible voice.

☑ Present ideas in a meaningful way.

▶ OBJECTIVES

- Identify the use of primary sources by the author
- Analyze the information and examples presented in a text
- Explain the differing points of view of writers of history

Black, Blue & Gray is broken into three instructional segments.

SEGMENTS

Options for Reading

Independent Students read the book independently and then answer questions posed by the teacher.

Supported Students read smaller segments within each section with teacher support.

 **Common Core Connection**

RI 1 cite textual evidence to support analysis of what the text says explicitly as well as inferences drawn; **RI 4** determine the meaning of words and phrases, including figurative, connotative, and technical meanings/analyze impact of word choices; **RI 5** analyze how author's ideas or claims are developed and refined; **RI 6** determine author's point of view or purpose/analyze how author uses rhetoric

Black, Blue & Gray: African Americans in the Civil War

by Jim Haskins

SUMMARY This book explains the contributions of African Americans during the Civil War. Through letters, news stories, speeches, and other sources, Haskins emphasizes the value of African Americans in the Civil War and Reconstruction era.

ABOUT THE AUTHOR Jim Haskins wrote over 100 books for adults and young adults. His books often highlight the contributions of African Americans to society, including *The Story of Stevie Wonder* and *Lena Horne*.

Discuss Genre and Set Purpose

INFORMATIONAL TEXT Explain that informational texts about history present the facts about people and events from the past. In this book, the writer discusses the exclusion of African Americans' contribution to the Union victory in the Civil War in previous histories of the event.

SET PURPOSE Help students set a purpose for reading, such as to find out the attitude of white soldiers toward their African American counterparts during the Civil War.

◢ TEXT COMPLEXITY RUBRIC

Overall Text Complexity		Black, Blue & Gray: African Americans in the Civil War NONFICTION, HISTORY COMPLEX
Quantitative Measure	Lexile	1280L
Qualitative Measures	Text Structure	complex concepts, historical context
	Language Conventionality and Clarity	complex sentence structure
	Knowledge Demands	fairly complex theme
	Purpose/Levels of Meaning	multiple levels of meaning

Academic Vocabulary

Read each word with students and discuss its meaning.

seceded (p. 1) • formally withdrew from an alliance

ratified (p. 6) • confirmed by formal sanction or consent

chattel (p. 7) • an article of personal property; a slave

eloquence (p. 10) • using language with fluency or aptness

abstraction (p. 23) • an impractical idea; something visionary or unrealistic

Domain Specific Vocabulary

artillery (p. 3) • large arms, such as cannons

 ENGLISH LANGUAGE LEARNERS

Use Props

Supply students with blank maps of the United States, with states outlined. As they read the introduction and first two chapters of the book, ask them to label the states that seceded from the Union.

FIRST READ ## Think Through the Text

Have students use text evidence and draw inferences to answer questions.

p. 3 • *Why does the author quote Woodward saying that African Americans became free without their own effort?* He is showing how much history had been rewritten by the 1930s. *What is one reason Haskins wrote this book?* He wanted to set the historical record straight about the role of African Americans in the Civil War. RI 5, RI 6

pp. 13–14 • *What were the circumstances and the outcome of the Dred Scott case?* Dred Scott was a slave who sued for the right to buy his freedom, but the court decided that he was not a citizen and so was not allowed to sue in court. RI 1

p. 23 • *Why did African Americans feel suspicious of whites in the South and the North?* They knew that whites mistreated African Americans in both the South and the North; even though slavery existed in the South, African Americans experienced much discrimination in the North, too. RI 1

SECOND READ ## Analyze the Text

- Review the photograph on page 26. *The photo on this page shows how African Americans supported the Union troops earlier in the Civil War. What is the person in the photo doing?* He is cooking for the troops. *What are some other jobs done by African Americans?* building fortifications and other support roles RI 4

- Review pages 25–27. Ask: *How were African Americans essential to the Confederate army?* The Confederate army needed to use slaves as support personnel so that they could free up as many white soldiers as possible for combat. RI 1

- Review pages 28–30 with students. Then ask: *Why does the author include the report from Lt. Churchill?* Sample answer: This report shows that the Union army saw African Americans working in support roles for the Confederate army. It is an eyewitness account. RI 1

RESPOND TO SEGMENT 1

 Classroom Collaboration

Have partners discuss the different sources of information the writer uses to determine what happened (letters, government reports, photographs, newspaper accounts, personal accounts, etc.). Ask partners to evaluate the reliability of each source.

Domain Specific Vocabulary

blockade (p. 47) • obstruction of passage

munitions (p. 46) • materials, weapons, and ammunition

enlistee (p. 48) • a person who enlists in the military

mustered (p. 54) • to assemble troops

cavalry (p. 60) • troops on horseback

 ENGLISH LANGUAGE LEARNERS

Comprehensible Input

Ask yes/no questions for students with beginning language skills and provide sentence frames for more advanced speakers. Sample sentence frame:
The Union used ships to _____ the Confederate boats. blockade

 RESPOND TO SEGMENT 2

Classroom Collaboration

Have small groups work together to summarize what they have read. Have them ask questions about what they do not understand.

 Common Core Connection

RI 1 cite textual evidence to support analysis of what the text says explicitly as well as inferences drawn; **RI 2** determine a central idea/analyze its development; **RI 4** determine the meaning of words and phrases; **RI 5** analyze how author's ideas or claims are developed and refined; **RI 6** determine author's point of view or purpose/analyze how author uses rhetoric; **W 2** write informative/explanatory texts; **W 5** develop and strengthen writing by planning, revising, editing, rewriting, or trying a new approach; **SL 4** present information, findings, and supporting evidence clearly, concisely, and logically

Academic Vocabulary

Read each word with students and discuss its meaning.

disavowed (p. 53) • denied, rejected

deploying (p. 58) • spreading out to form a strategic line

fugitives (p. 70) • people who ran away or fled

urbanites (p. 75) • residents of a city

light-complected (p. 83) • fair-skinned

FIRST READ ▶ Think Through the Text

Have students use text evidence and draw inferences to answer questions.

pp. 59–60 • *What did the Emancipation Proclamation do, and how did the slaves learn about it?* It freed the slaves in the Confederacy; the slaves who could read found out about it in the newspapers, and others heard by word of mouth. ▬ RI 1

p. 63 • *What did the secretary of war do when the Emancipation Proclamation was signed?* He began the process of organizing African American regiments for the Union army. ▬ RI 4

p. 67 • *Why was enlisting in the army so dangerous for African Americans (more so than whites)?* The Confederacy issued an order to immediately kill any African American person found with a weapon, which meant that anyone fighting for the Union would be subject to murder, not just taken prisoner. ▬ RI 1

pp. 78–80 • *Give one example of how conditions were different for white and African American troops in the Union army.* The African Americans were paid ten dollars but no clothing allowance, while white soldiers got thirteen dollars and money to replace worn uniforms. ▬ RI 1

SECOND READ ▶ Analyze the Text

- Have students review page 48. Ask: *What did Robert Smalls manage to do in spite of high odds against him?* He escaped from the Confederate side by hijacking a boat and running to the Union blockade near Charleston Harbor. ▬ RI 1

- Review pages 61–63 with students. Ask: *What did Frederick Douglass do when he learned of the Emancipation Proclamation?* He took it as a clear invitation for African Americans to join the military to fight for freedom. He published calls for enlistment in his newspaper. *What did Douglass advertise about the enlistment drive?* African American soldiers would receive equal treatment with the white soldiers. ▬ RI 1

- Review pages 71–74 with students. Ask: *What caused the food shortages in the South during 1863–1864?* Sample answer: ruined agricultural economy, Union blockades of Southern ports, needs of soldiers ▬ RI 4

Academic Vocabulary

Read each word with students and discuss its meaning.

casualties (p. 109) • lost through death, wounds, sickness, or capture

evinced (p. 109) • shown clearly, proven

Reconstruction (p. 115) • reorganization of the Confederacy, 1865–1877

vanguard (p. 118) • foremost division or part of the army; at the front line

rigging (p. 120) • manipulating fraudulently

Medal of Honor (p. 126) • highest military honor for bravery above and beyond the call of duty

WRITE & PRESENT

1. Have small groups discuss what this book suggests about how and why race relations have changed over time. ▬RI 1

2. Ask students to write an informative essay explaining how the book shows that the perspective of the writer can affect how history is learned and remembered. Students should provide examples from the text in their essays. ▬W 2

3. Have students share their work with partners and suggest revisions and edits. Students edit their writing based on these suggestions. ▬W 5

4. Have students present their final essays to the class by giving an oral presentation. ▬SL 4

See Copying Masters, pp. 212–215.

FIRST READ ## Think Through the Text

Have students use text evidence and draw inferences to answer questions.

pp. 100–105 • *How did the role of African Americans in the Union army change over time?* *The number of regiments grew to 140, and the African American soldiers were fighting with extraordinary courage, not just working in support roles.* ▬RI 4

pp. 120–121 • *The writer quotes Frederick Douglass on his feelings about Reconstruction. Why is Douglass so disappointed?* *He was disappointed that the government had not found ways to support former slaves after their emancipation so that they could live a better life and enjoy true equality.* ▬RI 2

SECOND READ ## Analyze the Text

• Review pages 109–112. Ask: *Why did the Confederacy finally agree to arm slaves?* *In spite of long-standing opposition, the leaders of the Confederacy realized that they could not win the war without arming the slaves to help them fight.* ▬RI 6

• Review pages 127–135. Ask: *In Chapter 7, the author writes that the roles of African American soldiers were forgotten in the years after the Civil War. Why was this the case and how did it change?* *War monuments did not include black soldiers; the military did not encourage blacks to reenlist and discharged the African American units. As African Americans won more equality by the end of the twentieth century, more historical research was done on their role in the Civil War.* ▬RI 2, RI 5

Independent/Self-Selected Reading

Have students reread *Black, Blue & Gray* independently to practice analyzing the text on their own, or have them practice the skills using another book, such as:

• *Narrative of the Life of Frederick Douglass* by Frederick Douglass

• *Undying Glory: The Story of the Fifty-Fourth Regiment* by Clinton Cox ▬RI 5

STUDENT CHECKLIST

Writing

☑ Analyze what the text implies about how and why history changes.

☑ Write an essay with examples from the text.

☑ Strengthen writing by revising it.

Speaking & Listening

☑ Present ideas in an organized and logical way.

☑ Demonstrate command of formal spoken English.

OBJECTIVES

- Describe the structure of ideas and series of events in a text
- Determine meanings of technical and domain-specific vocabulary
- Analyze text using text evidence

The Longitude Prize is broken into three instructional segments.

SEGMENTS

Options for Reading

Independent Students read the book independently and then answer questions posed by the teacher.

Supported Students read a segment and answer questions with teacher support.

Common Core Connection

RI 1 cite textual evidence to support analysis of what the text says explicitly as well as inferences drawn; **RI 4** determine the meanings of words and phrases, including figurative, connotative, and technical meanings/analyze impact of word choices

The Longitude Prize
by Joan Dash

SUMMARY Early navigation was dangerous and often deadly because of the inability to determine a ship's longitude. In 1714, the British Parliament offered a large monetary prize to whoever could invent a device to fix longitude. Self-educated commoner John Harrison not only succeeded in inventing a seagoing watch to mark longitude but also fought the prejudice of the upper-class scientific community to claim the prize.

ABOUT THE AUTHOR Joan Dash is a published author of several notable books for young adults as well as children, including biographies of Benjamin Franklin and Helen Keller. She won the Horn Book Award and several other awards for *The Longitude Prize*.

Discuss Genre and Set Purpose

INFORMATIONAL TEXT Have students study the cover, the table of contents, and the illustrations to see what information they will read about in this book. Discuss how, like many informational texts, the book includes a glossary, index, and timeline at the back to help readers keep track of important terminology and events.

SET PURPOSE Help students set a purpose for reading, such as to find out information about why the prize was offered and what was needed to win it.

TEXT COMPLEXITY RUBRIC

Overall Text Complexity		*The Longitude Prize* INFORMATIONAL TEXT
		COMPLEX
Quantitative Measure	Lexile	1160L
Qualitative Measures	Text Structure	more than one text structure
	Language Conventionality and Clarity	some unfamiliar or academic words
	Knowledge Demands	some specialized knowledge required
	Purpose/Levels of Meaning	clear or implied but easy to identify

Academic Vocabulary

Read each word with students and discuss its meaning.

execute (p. 26) • to carry out

precision (p. 32) • exactness

designated (p. 45) • specified

counteracted (p. 49) • opposed and lessened the effect of

FIRST READ ## Think Through the Text

Have students use text evidence and draw inferences to answer questions.

pp. 10–19 • *What evidence is there that John Harrison had an analytical, scientific mind?* Sample answers: He taught himself clock-making by taking clocks apart and putting them back together. He noticed that metals expand and contract at different rates and measured and compared the rates to determine the best combination for pendulum rods.  RI 1

pp. 31–32 • *How was Harrison's idea for a device to measure longitude different from what others were attempting?* Others were trying to use the "celestial clock," or heavenly bodies and charts that related their positions to time. Harrison's idea was to use an actual seagoing clock. RI 1

pp. 61–62 • *What was the most important outcome of the test of Harrison's clock?* It showed that the clock would work at sea. RI 1

SECOND READ ## Analyze the Text

• Reread pages 3–7 with students. Ask: *How did a navigator sail the parallel?* He kept his ship on a particular line of latitude, or parallel, to hold a steady east-west course. *How did a navigator use dead reckoning?* To measure longitude, he measured how long his ship took to pass a wooden chunk, figured the ship's speed, and then determined the number of miles sailed each day from a spot whose longitude he knew. *Why was latitude much easier to measure than longitude?* Latitude could be determined by observing the position of the sun or the North Star above the horizon; it could be done with the naked eye or using instruments like an astrolabe or, later, a quadrant. Longitude is related to time and has no reference point; some methods could be used on land but not at sea. *How do these terms reflect social aspects of history?* Sample answer: These terms were used in the literature of the day, including the account of the shipwreck and works by Shakespeare. RI 4

Domain Specific Vocabulary

quadrant (p. 4) • an instrument used to measure the angle between a heavenly body and the horizon

astrolabe (p. 5) • an ancient instrument used to determine latitude by measuring the altitude of a heavenly body; forerunner of the quadrant

meridian (p. 28) • a line of longitude

ELL ### ENGLISH LANGUAGE LEARNERS

Use Props

Use a map or a globe to point out lines of latitude and longitude, or meridians. Use Internet or encyclopedia photos of a quadrant and astrolabe. Have students use the props to explain the terms in their own words.

RESPOND TO SEGMENT 1
Classroom Collaboration

Have groups create a summary of the events in this segment. Encourage them to include the technical vocabulary that has been used.

ENGLISH LANGUAGE LEARNERS

Use Cognates

Point out the English/Spanish cognates to aid comprehension: *navigate/navega; latitude/latitud; longitude/longitud; galleon/galeón*. Have students use the words in sentences related to the text.

RESPOND TO SEGMENT 2

Classroom Collaboration

Have small groups work together to summarize events in this segment. Encourage them to ask and answer questions to clarify understanding.

 Common Core Connection

RI 1 cite textual evidence to support analysis of what the text says explicitly as well as inferences drawn; **RI 3** analyze how author unfolds an analysis or series of ideas or events; **RI 4** determine the meanings of words and phrases, including figurative, connotative, and technical meanings/analyze impact of word choices; **RI 10** read and comprehend literary nonfiction; **W 2** write informative/explanatory texts; **W 5** develop and strengthen writing by planning, revising, editing, rewriting, or trying a new approach; **SL 4** present information, findings, and supporting evidence clearly, concisely, and logically

Academic Vocabulary

Read each word with students and discuss its meaning.

erratic (p. 72) • irregular; with no pattern or course

circumnavigators (p. 79) • persons who sail around the world

skeptics (p. 90) • persons who question or doubt

compensate (p. 91) • to make up for

ascertained (p. 92) • determined for sure

substantial (p. 105) • having substance; real

FIRST READ **Think Through the Text**

Have students use text evidence and draw inferences to answer questions.

pp. 64–67 • *Why did Harrison make additional clocks?* He wanted to correct defects in the previous clocks. *What does this suggest about Harrison?* He wanted the clock to be perfect before he tried it at sea. **RI 1**

pp. 80–85 • *What was the lunar method of determining longitude?* using the position of the moon to determine time and therefore latitude *Why did Harrison say his third clock was ready to be tested?* The tables of the moon's position that were needed for the lunar method were being worked on, and that method rivaled Harrison's clock. **RI 4**

pp. 110–123 • *What were the Board's objections to the first Indies trial of Harrison's watch, and what might have been more legitimate objections?* The Board faulted the longitude used for Jamaica, doubted that the watch lost only five seconds, and pointed out they knew nothing about the watch's mechanisms. Legitimate objections could be that the watch was too expensive to be practical, and other watchmakers needed to know how to construct more watches so that many ships could use them. **RI 1**

SECOND READ **Analyze the Text**

• Review pages 68–79 with students. Ask: *Why does the author include this recounting of George Anson's voyage?* It emphasized the need for a device to measure longitude, especially now that ships were circumnavigating the globe. **RI 3**

• *Why does the author feel there was bias toward the lunar method?* The basic principles of the lunar method had been known for centuries; it was noble; Isaac Newton supported it; Harrison's personality and fiery temper as well as his common background worked against acceptance of his watch. **RI 3**

Academic Vocabulary

Read each word with students and discuss its meaning.

evaded (p. 131) • avoided; eluded

stipulated (p. 136) • specified or demanded as a condition

miscellaneous (p. 138) • made up of various different elements

replica (p. 138) • exact copy

conjunction (p. 141) • combination

vindication (p. 178) • support; justification

FIRST READ ⟩ ## Think Through the Text

Have students use text evidence and draw inferences to answer questions.

pp. 128–129 • *How did Parliament change the rules of the awarding of the prize?* It said Harrison would receive half the award if he explained how his watch was made, took it apart before experts, and turned it over along with his three clocks. He would receive the other half only if he made more watches. ⟨RI 1⟩

pp. 149–159 • *Why was King George III motivated to help John Harrison?* The king was educated in science and interested in astronomy and in timekeepers. ⟨RI 1⟩

p. 176 • *Did Harrison actually win the Longitude Prize? Explain.* He was given the money but never acknowledged as the winner. ⟨RI 1⟩

SECOND READ ⟩ ## Analyze the Text

• Review pages 163–173 with students. Ask: *Why does the author include this recounting of Captain Cook's voyage?* It proved that Harrison's watch worked and could be used to measure longitude reliably. This was especially important because Cook had been a believer in the lunar method. ⟨RI 3⟩

• Ask: *What new name was given to Harrison's clock?* marine chronometer *How else is Harrison remembered?* A research group formed that was named for him. He is referred to as "Longitude." ⟨RI 4⟩

Independent/Self-Selected Reading

Have students reread *The Longitude Prize* independently to practice analyzing the text on their own, or have them practice the skills using another book, such as:

• *Where on Earth Am I?* by Robert Gardner

• *The Remarkable Voyages of Captain Cook* by Rhoda Blumberg ⟨RI 10⟩

WRITE & PRESENT

1. Have small groups determine the meaning of words such as *quadrant, astrolabe, equator line,* and *horizon* as well as phrases such as *dead reckoning* and *sailing the parallel*. Discuss how the words reflect social aspects of history. ⟨RI 4⟩

2. Ask students to write an informative essay that explains how the words reflect social aspects of history. ⟨W 2⟩

3. Have students exchange drafts of their essays and peer-review for revising. Then have them edit their revised drafts. ⟨W 5⟩

4. Have students present their final essays in small groups before submitting them. ⟨SL 4⟩

See Copying Masters, pp. 212–215.

STUDENT CHECKLIST

Writing

☑ Write an informative essay.

☑ Use content-related terms.

☑ Use complete sentences and developed paragraphs to structure writing.

Speaking & Listening

☑ Read writing aloud with a clear, audible voice.

☑ Present information clearly and concisely.

OBJECTIVES

- State main idea and supporting details
- Determine how an author structures text
- Interpret information presented in encyclopedic form
- Interpret information presented visually
- Analyze text using text evidence

This excerpt from *The Illustrated Book of Great Composers* is broken into three instructional segments.

Options for Reading

Independent Students read the book independently or with a partner and then answer questions posed by the teacher.

Supported Students read a segment and answer questions with teacher support.

 Common Core Connection

RI 1 cite textual evidence to support analysis of what the text says explicitly as well as inferences drawn; **RI 2** determine a central idea/analyze its development/provide summary; **RI 5** analyze how an author's ideas are developed and refined

from *The Illustrated Book of Great Composers*

by Wendy Thompson

SUMMARY This illustrated encyclopedia provides a short overview of the history of music composition, followed by a guide to the lives and works of the greatest classical composers from the Middle Ages to the post–World War II period.

ABOUT THE AUTHOR **Wendy Thompson** is a musician as well as a writer, who studied violin at the Royal College of Music in London. She has written many other books on musical subjects, including several biographies of composers such as Handel, Mozart, and Beethoven.

Discuss Genre and Set Purpose

ENCYCLOPEDIA Help students identify characteristics of informational texts: table of contents, headings, epigraphs, primary source illustrations, captions, fact boxes, glossary, and index.

SET PURPOSE Help students set a purpose for reading, such as to find out information about composers who lived during different periods.

TEXT COMPLEXITY RUBRIC

Overall Text Complexity		from *The Illustrated Book of Great Composers* ENCYCLOPEDIA
		COMPLEX
Quantitative Measure	Lexile	1400L
Qualitative Measures	Text Structure	more difficult social studies concepts
	Language Conventionality and Clarity	some academic language and words
	Knowledge Demands	some specialized knowledge required
	Purpose/Levels of Meaning	explicitly stated

Academic Vocabulary

Read each word with students and discuss its meaning.

medium (p. 8) • the means by which a sensory effect is transmitted

standardized (p. 11) • matching an established set of conventions

recreational (p. 12) • for fun

individualism (p. 14) • a belief in the primary importance of the individual

derivative (p. 17) • copied from or based on a previous source

FIRST READ ## Think Through the Text

Have students use text evidence and draw inferences to answer questions.

pp. 8–13 • *What tells you the main subject of each page or spread?* the heading at the top *What are the subheadings on page 12?* Music and drama, Oratorio, and Instrumental forms *What information does each subheading tell you?* Each tells what topic will be discussed in the next section of text. ▬ RI 1

pp. 14–15 • *What is the general topic of these pages?* These pages talk about changes in musical composition during the Romantic era of the nineteenth century. *What kinds of details can you learn about the topic?* Details include information about class and culture of the era. For example, the middle class was growing, so there was a growing market for private music that could be played at home. New instruments were added to the orchestra. With the rise of nationalism, many composers began mixing elements of the native folk music of their cultures with more traditional music genres. ▬ RI 2

SECOND READ ## Analyze the Text

• Show students the visuals on pages 10–11. Explain that publishers include illustrations to help readers picture and understand important information. Ask: *How do these visuals support the text?* Each visual provides an example of one of the styles of notation described by the text. *How do the captions help you better understand what each visual is showing?* The captions label the visuals, explaining the origin of each sheet of music. ▬ RI 5

• Review page 12. Ask: *What is the relationship between the epigraph and the text that follows?* The epigraph gives an example of a way people at the time described the musical genre of opera. The text that follows describes developments in opera, such as the addition of recitatives and arias, and explains popular trends in opera written at the time. The epigraph catches the reader's attention and provides another viewpoint on the information covered in this section. ▬ RI 5

Domain Specific Vocabulary

composition (p. 8) • the act of arranging elements into a work of art

notation (p. 8) • a set system of written symbols picked to represent information

pitch (p. 8) • how high or low the tone of a note is

harmony (p. 9) • an often pleasing combination of notes or other sounds

 ENGLISH LANGUAGE LEARNERS

Use Visuals

Use the illustrations in the text to develop students' oral language. Help students restate the information in each caption, using their own words. Then have students use complete sentences to describe each illustration.

RESPOND TO SEGMENT 1

💬 **Classroom Collaboration**

Have small groups summarize what they have read so far. Invite them to share their summaries. Have them ask questions about things they don't yet understand.

ENGLISH LANGUAGE LEARNERS

Use Visuals and Sentence Frames

To explain the information contained in each fact box, have students point to various fact boxes throughout the section. Prompt students to use the following sentence frames to interpret the information in each fact box: *S/he was from the nation of _____. S/he was born in _____. S/he died in _____. The genre(s) of his/her work was/were _____. One of his/her major achievements was _____.*

 RESPOND TO SEGMENT 2

Classroom Collaboration

Have partners work together to create and present a verbal summary and to answer questions about what was presented in the text.

 Common Core Connection

RI 1 cite textual evidence to support analysis of what the text says explicitly as well as inferences drawn; **RI 2** determine a central idea of a text/analyze its development/and provide a summary; **RI 5** analyze how an author's ideas are developed and refined; **RI 10** read and comprehend literary nonfiction; **W 2** write informative/explanatory texts; **W 5** develop and strengthen writing by planning, revising, editing, rewriting, or trying a new approach; **SL 4** present information, findings, and supporting evidence clearly, concisely, and logically

---

Academic Vocabulary

Read each word with students and discuss its meaning.

sacred (p. 22) • devoted to or meant for spiritual purposes

secular (p. 22) • pertaining to worldly things

contemporary (p. 26) • belonging to the same time period

enhancing (p. 30) • bringing forth greater worth or beauty

adapting (p. 33) • changing to take into account new circumstances

FIRST READ **Think Through the Text**

Have students use text evidence and draw inferences to answer questions.

p. 24 • *What kinds of works did Hildegard of Bingen write?* She wrote descriptions of her mystical experiences, books about natural history and medicine, lyric and dramatic poetry, liturgical poetry, and a morality play. ▬RI 1

p. 29 • *What was remarkable about the works Josquin des Prez composed?* He was among the first composers to match words to the notes of his compositions, establishing a relationship between text and music. ▬RI 1

SECOND READ **Analyze the Text**

- Work with students to identify examples of some different kinds of visuals used in this section. Ask: *What kinds of information do the different visuals offer the reader? Use text examples to support your ideas.* Sample answer: Contemporary portraits of the composers shown on pages 26 and 27 show how artists of the time portrayed them. Pictures of patrons such as the painting of Charles VIII on page 28 or of Queen Elizabeth I on page 33 show who supported the composers' work. The picture of the virginal on page 34 shows what one popular instrument of the time looked like. The songs shown on pages 36 and 37 show what sheet music looked like. ▬RI 5

- Have students reread page 33. Say: *Summarize the main idea of this entry and explain it using supporting details.* Sample answer: Although the composer Thomas Tallis retained his Catholic identity during a dangerous time for Catholics, he was able to live and work by adapting his style to suit the tastes of different monarchs and by not attracting too much attention to himself. His epitaph declares that he was able to live and die peacefully because he lived a mild, quiet life. The text notes that his talent and mildness enabled a long career serving four different monarchs. ▬RI 2

SEGMENT 3 pp. 38–67

Academic Vocabulary

Read each word with students and discuss its meaning.

pejorative (p. 40) • insulting

ornamental (p. 40) • decorative

significance (p. 42) • importance

amalgamated (p. 44) • joined together

prolific (p. 52) • productive

FIRST READ **Think Through the Text**

Have students use text evidence and draw inferences to answer questions.

pp. 48–49 • *What instrument was promoted by Italians and why?* violins; The best violin makers of the time were Italian. **RI 1**

pp. 56–59 • *How did the way people felt about J. S. Bach's music change over time?* During his lifetime, he was better known as an organist than as a composer. Immediately after his death, people thought of his music as old-fashioned, so it was not very popular or influential. During the nineteenth century, his music was rediscovered, and today he is one of the world's most popular and well-known composers. **RI 1**

SECOND READ **Analyze the Text**

• Help students note the structure of the text and compare its organization to *The Story of Art* or another informational text. Ask: *What is alike about the organization of the two books?* Sample answer: Both tell facts about a particular subject, in order, over time from the past to the present. Both use color illustrations to support the text. **RI 3**

• Reread pages 50–51. Ask: *What is the main idea of this section?* Henry Purcell did not live long, but his work brought great glory to England. *What are some of the details that support the main idea?* The epigraph says that after a long search, the country has finally found an Englishman who is as talented as composers from other countries. Purcell's genius was to write appealing melodies, with elements of music from other countries, and to combine them with English words. **RI 2**

Independent/Self-Selected Reading

Have students reread this excerpt from *The Illustrated Book of Great Composers* independently to practice analyzing the text on their own, or have them practice the skills using another book, such as:

• *The Great Composers* by Jeremy Nicholas

• *The Encyclopedia of Music: Musical Instruments and the Art of Music-Making* by Max Wade-Matthews and Wendy Thompson **RI 10**

WRITE & PRESENT

1. Have small groups refer to different entries in the text to explain how an author uses the text structure of main idea and details to describe the history of musical composition and the lives and works of several great composers. **RI 2**

2. Have individual students choose one entry from the encyclopedia and write a paragraph that describes how the author uses the text structure of main idea and details to convey information. Have them cite text evidence to support their ideas. **W 2**

3. Have students share their work with partners and edit their writing based on the suggestions they receive. **W 5**

4. Have students present their final paragraphs to the class. **SL 4**

See Copying Masters, pp. 212–215.

STUDENT CHECKLIST

Writing

☑ Explain how an author uses main ideas and details to give information.

☑ Provide reasons supported by facts and details from the text.

☑ Use correct language conventions.

Speaking & Listening

☑ Logically present claims and findings.

☑ Cite text evidence to support ideas.

▶ OBJECTIVES

- Describe the central ideas of a nonfiction book
- Analyze how an author develops a series of ideas
- Analyze how an author's claims are developed and refined
- Analyze text using text evidence

This excerpt from *1491* is broken into three instructional segments.

Options for Reading

Independent Students read the book independently or with a partner and then answer questions posed by the teacher.

Supported Students read a segment and answer questions with teacher support.

COMMON CORE Common Core Connection

RI 1 cite textual evidence to support analysis of what the text says explicitly as well as inferences drawn; **RI 2** determine a central idea/analyze its development/provide summary; **RI 3** analyze how author unfolds an analysis or series of ideas of events; **RI 5** analyze how author's ideas are developed and refined

from *1491*

by Charles C. Mann

SUMMARY *1491* is subtitled "New Revelations of the Americas Before Columbus." The book uses archaeological and anthropological findings to imagine the Western Hemisphere immediately before Europeans arrived. The book considers that there may have been more people living in the Americas than in Europe in 1491—people living in greater cities than any in Europe at the time, and who may have transformed the American continents into giant "gardens" that sustained their societies.

ABOUT THE AUTHOR **Charles C. Mann** is a journalist and author who specializes in scientific topics. Published in 2006, *1491* won the National Academy of Sciences Keck Award for the best book of the year.

Discuss Genre and Set Purpose

INFORMATIONAL TEXT Explain that *1491* is a work of nonfiction that uses current archaeological and anthropological evidence to speculate about life in the Western Hemisphere before Europeans began to colonize the region. Point out that evidence-based speculation is not the same as fictionalizing real events.

SET PURPOSE Help students set a purpose for reading, such as to learn what life might really have been like here before Columbus arrived.

▲ TEXT COMPLEXITY RUBRIC

Overall Text Complexity		from *1491* INFORMATIONAL TEXT
		COMPLEX
Quantitative Measure	Lexile	1210L
Qualitative Measures	Text Structure	somewhat complex science concepts
	Language Conventionality and Clarity	many unfamiliar or high academic words
	Knowledge Demands	specialized knowledge required
	Purpose/Levels of Meaning	multiple purposes and topics

Academic Vocabulary

Read each word with students and discuss its meaning.

proclivity (p. 4) • tendency, natural habit

putative (p. 14) • supposed

garrulous (p. 34) • overly talkative

incursions (p. 38) • invasions

Domain Specific Vocabulary

indigenous (p. 14) • native to a place

Neolithic (p. 17) • referring to the last part of the Stone Age

FIRST READ ## Think Through the Text

Have students use text evidence and draw inferences to answer questions.

pp. 8–10 • *How does the author's examination of "Holmberg's mistake" set the tone for the rest of the segment?* Sample answer: The author uses Holmberg as an example of how historians' views of the people in the ancient Americas were wrong and deeply flawed. This establishes the idea that we will learn new things about those people. **RI 3**

pp. 17–30 • *How long ago might people have migrated to the Western Hemisphere?* The exact time is unknown. However, scientific estimates range from fifty thousand years ago to around twenty thousand years ago. **RI 1**

pp. 42–47 • *What sources does the author use to describe life among the natives of the Massachusetts coastal areas in the 1500s?* The information comes from accounts by English colonists of the time. **RI 5**

SECOND READ ## Analyze the Text

• Review pages 3–16 with students. Ask: *What concept does the author call "Holmberg's Mistake?"* Sample answer: Holmberg's Mistake is the idea that the people living in the Americas lived "without history"—that they lived without affecting nature. **RI 2**

• Ask: *What is an example of Holmberg's Mistake cited by the author?* Sample answer: On page 37, the author describes the traditional but erroneous view of the Plymouth Colony, noting that a variation of Holmberg's Mistake dated back to the Pilgrims themselves. **RI 1**

• Have students review pages 47–61. Ask: *How populous was the New England coast when Verrazzano arrived around 1523?* On page 48, Verrazzano's own description says it was very densely populated. *How did other European sailors describe the coast at the end of the 1500s and beginning of the 1600s?* On page 52, the author notes that the coast was so full of people that colonies could not be established there. *How had conditions changed by 1620?* Everything had changed: the coastal villages were gone, and a contemporary account (page 59) says the coast was empty of people. **RI 2**

ENGLISH LANGUAGE LEARNERS

Use Visuals

Have student pairs work together to describe the maps, photographs, and illustrations in this segment, and relate the visual aids to the information presented in the text.

RESPOND TO SEGMENT 1

Classroom Collaboration

Have small groups of students outline the information they have read so far. Encourage them to list possible theses that the author is presenting and the evidence he is using to support his arguments.

ENGLISH LANGUAGE LEARNERS

Use Peer Supported Learning

Have pairs of students review the history of the Inkan Empire described in this segment. Monitor as they review to be sure students understand the purpose of the details the author has included.

 RESPOND TO SEGMENT 2

Classroom Collaboration

Have small groups work together to summarize the historically quick rise and fall of the Inkan Empire. Have them ask questions about what they don't understand.

 Common Core Connection

RI 1 cite textual evidence to support analysis of what the text says explicitly as well as inferences drawn; **RI 2** determine a central idea/analyze its development/provide summary; **RI 3** analyze how author unfolds an analysis or series of ideas of events; **RI 5** analyze how author's ideas are developed and refined; **RI 10** read and comprehend literary nonfiction; **W 1** write arguments to support claims; **W 5** develop and strengthen writing by planning, revising, editing, rewriting, or trying a new approach; **SL 4** present information, findings, and supporting evidence clearly, concisely, and logically

---

Academic Vocabulary

Read each word with students and discuss its meaning.

foray (p. 69) • quick raid

demography (p. 69) • the science of social statistics, such as births, deaths, and population ages

succumbed (p. 70) • gave way to a superior force

cosmology (p. 79) • branches of philosophy and/or astronomy that consider the origin and structure of the universe

metallurgy (p. 91) • the science of working with metals

FIRST READ ## Think Through the Text

Have students use text evidence and draw inferences to answer questions.

pp. 90–93 • *What are some examples of advanced technology among the Inka? Sample answer: On page 91, Inkan metallurgy is shown to be advanced; on page 92, examples of suspension bridges and ocean-going ships made of fibers are mentioned.* **Why does the author focus on these technologies?** *The author is comparing Inkan technology to European technology to show that the Inkans were equally advanced.* ◼RI 3

pp. 100–103 • *How many times did conquistadors try to conquer Florida between 1510 and 1560 (page 101)?* six times *Why does the author consider this significant?* *The repeated failure to conquer Florida suggests that the native populations were able to resist European invasion when it did not include introducing disease. When disease was introduced in the Americas, it weakened and fragmented the native population, making it vulnerable to conquest.* ◼RI 1

SECOND READ ## Analyze the Text

• Review pages 71–100 with students. Ask: *How are the Inka Empire and the Wampanoag different and alike? Sample answer: They differ in scope—the Inka were the world's largest empire at the time, while the Wampanoag were a loose confederation with fewer people. They differ also in location, and in which European cultures they faced. They are similar in that European diseases wiped out a huge percentage of their people and fragmented their societies.* ◼RI 1

• Review pages 101–106 with students. Say: *Epidemic diseases arrived among the American Indians before the Europeans successfully established colonies.* Ask: *What bearing does this have on our understanding of the rest of the continent? Sample answer: Because epidemics may have spread all across the Americas before Europeans ever reached all regions, we have no way of truly knowing what those cultures were like.* ◼RI 2

Academic Vocabulary

Read each word with students and discuss its meaning.

deleterious (p. 114) • harmful or causing injury

homogeneity (p. 114) • sameness; made of the same parts

disparate (p. 115) • basically different and distinct

internecine (p. 123) • conflict or struggle within a group

FIRST READ ## Think Through the Text

Have students use text evidence and draw inferences to answer questions.

pp. 107–108 • *What did de Soto's party encounter along the Mississippi River around 1540?* On page 108, the author says de Soto's troops were met by thousands of Indian warriors and saw almost countless towns and communities. *What is important about this fact?* Sample answer: It is significant because the next time Europeans were in the same location, the countryside was almost empty. ◼ RI 1

pp. 116–121 • *What does the author suggest could have led to the colonies losing the American War of Independence?* On pages 119–120, he recounts a smallpox epidemic that crippled the Revolutionary forces. *Why does the author use this example?* Sample answer: The author is drawing a parallel with what the American Indians experienced with smallpox and other European diseases. ◼ RI 5

SECOND READ ## Analyze the Text

• Have students reread pages 143–148. Ask: *What happened to the population of what is now Mexico after Cortez arrived in 1519?* On page 143, the author speculates that more than ninety percent of the inhabitants died over the next century. *Does the author assign blame for this loss of life?* The author's opinion is that the tragedy was unintentional. ◼ RI 3

• Ask: *Why do you think the author includes the insights of Las Casas at the end of this segment?* Sample answer: Las Casas wrote in 1542, just fifty years after Columbus first arrived in the Western Hemisphere. Such a contemporaneous account adds great weight to the author's thesis. ◼ RI 5

Independent/Self-Selected Reading

Have students reread the first 148 pages of *1491* independently to practice analyzing the text on their own, or have them practice the skills using other texts, such as:

• *1491* by Charles C. Mann (Parts 2, 3, and the Coda)

• *1493: Uncovering the New World Columbus Created* by Charles C. Mann ◼ RI 10

Performance Task

WRITE & PRESENT

1. Have student groups discuss the arguments, evidence, and conclusions about the sophisticated cultures of the Americas that are presented in each segment. ◼ RI 2

2. Ask students to analyze the main thesis of the entire reading. Have them write a radio editorial either supporting or disagreeing with Mann's thesis about the impact of European diseases in the Western Hemisphere. Encourage them to cite evidence from the text to develop their content. ◼ W 1

3. Have students share their work with partners and offer suggestions for revising and editing. Students edit their writing based on these suggestions. ◼ W 5

4. Have students orally present their final editorials to their classmates. Ask students to respond to the ideas from each student's writing. ◼ SL 4

See Copying Masters, pp. 212–215.

STUDENT CHECKLIST

Writing

☑ Identify the book's main thesis.

☑ Summarize the supporting arguments using text evidence from the book.

☑ Argue for or against the conclusions presented by the author.

Speaking & Listening

☑ Present ideas in a meaningful way.

from *Elements*
by Euclid

OBJECTIVES

- Analyze how ideas are presented and analyzed
- Determining the meanings of words and phrases
- Determine the author's purpose
- Read and comprehend literary nonfiction

This excerpt from *Elements* is broken into three instructional segments.

Options for Reading

Independent Students read the book independently or with a partner and then answer questions posed by the teacher.

Supported Students read a segment and answer questions with teacher support.

SUMMARY *Elements* is a collection of thirteen mathematical textbooks written over 2,300 years ago. As in most textbooks, the ideas presented are not solely those of the author. Instead, they are a set of ideas known at that time about geometry, proportions, and number theory. *Elements* starts from just five postulates and five unproved assumptions, called *common notions*. It has been used and acclaimed for so long because it presents a clear progression of concepts based on these postulates.

ABOUT THE AUTHOR Euclid was born around 300 B.C.E in Alexandria, Egypt, but almost nothing is known about his life. In the mid-400s C.E, the Greek philosopher Proclus wrote a commentary in which he notes that Euclid taught mathematics in Alexandria at its famous library.

Discuss Genre and Set Purpose

INFORMATIONAL TEXT Remind students that an informational text conveys information about a topic and often includes an argument or claim. Explain that the author supports his or her argument or claim with facts, details, and opinions. It is up to the reader to evaluate the information presented in order to come to his or her own conclusions.

SET PURPOSE Help students set a purpose for reading, such as understanding the methods by which Euclid presents his propositions.

▲ TEXT COMPLEXITY RUBRIC

Overall Text Complexity		from *Elements* INFORMATIONAL TEXT
		COMPLEX
Quantitative Measure	Lexile	1140L
Qualitative Measures	Text Structure	complex mathematics concepts
	Language Conventionality and Clarity	more complex descriptions
	Knowledge Demands	specialized knowledge required
	Purpose/Levels of Meaning	implied, but easy to identify from context

COMMON CORE

Common Core Connection

RI 3 analyze how author unfolds an analysis or series of ideas or events; **RI 4** determine the meaning of words and phrases, including figurative, connotative, and technical meanings/ analyze impact of word choices; **RI 10** read and comprehend literary nonfiction

SEGMENT 1 pp. 1–2

Academic Vocabulary

Read each word with students and discuss its meaning.

extremities (p. 1) • the farthest parts or ends of an object

inclination (p. 1) • act of slanting toward something

terminated (p. 1) • met the end or limit of

axiomatic (p. 1) • based on a system of statements accepted as true

coincide (p. 2) • occur at the same point or time

FIRST READ ## Think Through the Text

Have students use text evidence and draw inferences to answer questions.

p. 1 • *Explain in your own words how Euclid defines a right angle.* Sample answer: Draw two straight lines that intersect so that the adjacent angles they form are equal. These angles are right angles. **How does he define an obtuse and an acute angle?** An angle is obtuse if it is greater than a right angle and acute if it is less than a right angle. ● RI 4

p. 2 • *What six types of trilateral figures does Euclid define?* equilateral triangle, isosceles triangle, scalene triangle, right-angled triangle, obtuse-angled triangle, and acute-angled triangle **Which of these has exactly two equal sides?** isosceles triangle ● RI 10

p. 2 • *How does the author define an oblong?* It is a quadrilateral figure that has right angles but is not equilateral. ● RI 4

p. 2 • *What two things must be true about two lines in order for them to be parallel?* They must be in the same plane. If they are in the same plane and extend indefinitely in both directions, they do not meet. ● RI 10

SECOND READ ## Analyze the Text

- Have students review the definitions on page 1. Ask: *Why it is important that Euclid begins by defining the most basic concepts in geometry, a point and a line?* The rest of his definitions, as well as his proofs, use and rely upon these definitions. ● RI 3

- Draw students' attention to definitions 5–7 on page 1. Ask: *How does the author's definition of a surface differ from his definition of a plane surface?* A surface has extremities that are lines. A plane surface continues outward past the lines. ● RI 4

- Draw students' attention to definition 9 on page 1. Ask: *In your own words, what does the author mean by a rectilineal angle?* Sample answer: A rectilineal angle is an angle formed where two straight lines meet. ● RI 4

Domain Specific Vocabulary

breadthless (p. 1) • without breadth (width) or depth

plane (p. 1) • a flat surface

circumference (p. 1) • the outer boundary of a circle

bisects (p. 1) • divides into two parts

postulates (p. 1) • true statements that do not need to be proved and can be used as the basis for making other statements

finite (p. 2) • having an end

ELL ### ENGLISH LANGUAGE LEARNERS

Use Peer Supported Learning

Have students work with a partner to read through the text. Instruct students to stop after each definition or paragraph and discuss the meaning.

RESPOND TO SEGMENT 1

 Classroom Collaboration

Have partners create a summary of important ideas presented in this segment. Then have them determine the meanings of important words and phrases.

Domain Specific Vocabulary

subtend (p. 5) • are opposite to; end at

random (p. 6) • without a plan or conscious choice

 ENGLISH LANGUAGE LEARNERS

Use Visuals

Use the diagram associated with each proposition to help students understand the details. Help students identify the part of the diagram being described for each sentence of the proposition. Then have them describe each diagram using their own words.

RESPOND TO SEGMENT 2

 Classroom Collaboration

Have small groups work together to summarize what they have read. Have them ask questions about what they don't understand.

 Common Core Connection

RI 3 analyze how author unfolds an analysis or series of ideas or events; **RI 4** determine the meaning of words and phrases, including figurative, connotative, and technical meanings/analyze impact of word choices; **RI 6** determine author's point of view or purpose/analyze how author uses rhetoric; **RI 8** delineate the argument and specific claims in a text; **RI 10** read and comprehend literary nonfiction; **W 2** write informative/explanatory texts; **W 5** develop and strengthen writing by planning, revising, editing, rewriting, or trying a new approach; **SL 4** present information, findings, and supporting evidence clearly, concisely, and logically

Academic Vocabulary

Read each word with students and discuss its meaning.

proposition (p. 3) • a statement that is offered for discussion and that can be deduced from postulates

construct (p. 3) • draw or form from parts

literally (p. 3) • actually in reality

respectively (p. 5) • one after the other

absurd (p. 7) • ridiculous; untrue

FIRST READ   Think Through the Text

Have students use text evidence and draw inferences to answer questions.

p. 3 • _What is the purpose of Proposition 1?_ to describe how to construct an equilateral triangle on the line AB, a finite straight line _Which of the common notions does Euclid use in this proposition?_ common notion 1   ◗ **RI 6**

p. 5 • _In Proposition 4, what three things does Euclid say must be true if two sides and the angle between them of one triangle are equal to two sides and the angle between them of another triangle?_ The bases of the triangles must be equal. The triangles are equal. The remaining angles of the triangles are equal.   ◗ **RI 8**

pp. 6–7 • _What does Euclid mean in the eighth line of Proposition 6 by the word_ common? Line BC is part of both triangles ABC and ACB.   ◗ **RI 4**

SECOND READ   Analyze the Text

• Review Proposition 3 on pages 4–5. Ask: _What starting details are given in Proposition 3?_ two unequal straight lines _What does Euclid show how to do in the proposition?_ how to cut a part off from the longer of the lines that is equal to the length of the shorter of the two lines   ◗ **RI 8**

• Review Proposition 6 on pages 6–7. Say: _At the top of page 7, Euclid assumes that_ AB _is unequal to side_ AC. _Why does he later say that this is absurd?_ Sample answer: His purpose is to prove that AB is equal to AC. He assumes the opposite and then shows that the two cannot be unequal, proving that AB must be equal to AC.   ◗ **RI 6**

• Have students review Proposition 7 on page 7. Point out that Euclid first describes the lines _AC_ and _CB_ drawn on the line _AB_. Ask: _What are the other two lines Euclid describes drawn on the line_ AB? lines AD and DB _What contradiction does Euclid end with that completes the proof?_ He shows that angle CDB must be equal to angle DCB but it must also be greater than it.   ◗ **RI 3**

Academic Vocabulary

Read each word with students and discuss its meaning.

adjacent (p. 10) • next to; sharing a vertex and common side

vertical angles (p. 12) • opposite angles made by two intersecting lines

porism (p. 13) • related proposition

manifest (p. 13) • obvious

interpolation (p. 13) • something introduced between other parts

---

FIRST READ ## Think Through the Text

Have students use text evidence and draw inferences to answer questions.

pp. 9–10 • *What is the purpose of Proposition 11?* to draw a straight line at right angles to a given straight line at a certain point *According to the proof, what must be true in order for the angles on either side of the point to be right angles?* The adjacent angles must be equal to one another. ⬛RI 6

pp. 12–13 • *According to Proposition 15, how are vertical angles constructed?* by two straight lines that cut or cross one another *What is true about the vertical angles?* They are equal. *What does the porism after Proposition 15 say must also be true if two straight lines cut one another?* They make angles at the point where they meet that are equal to four right angles. ⬛RI 10

SECOND READ ## Analyze the Text

- Review Proposition 8 on page 8. Ask: *What does Euclid prove cannot be true?* He shows that it cannot be true that if BC is applied to EF, the sides BA, AC do not coincide with EF, DF. *What method does he use to prove this?* He assumes that the opposite must be true and then shows that his assumption is impossible. ⬛RI 3

- Review Proposition 10 on page 9. Ask: *What does Euclid show how to do in this proposition?* bisect (cut in half) a finite straight line *What process does he use to show this?* Draw an equilateral triangle with the line as its base. Draw a line bisecting the triangle. This line also bisects the base line. ⬛RI 3

Independent/Self-Selected Reading

Have students reread this excerpt from *Elements* independently to practice analyzing the text on their own, or have them practice the skills using another book, such as:

- *The Babylonian Theorem* by Peter S. Rudman

- *Geometry: Euclid and Beyond* by Robin Hartshorne ⬛RI 10

WRITE & PRESENT

1. Have small groups review Proposition 2 and discuss how Euclid presents the steps of his proof. ⬛RI 3

2. Have each student write a short essay explaining the general method Euclid uses to present steps in his propositions. Instruct students to cite text evidence from several of the propositions to support their explanations. ⬛W 2

3. Have students share their work with a partner and offer suggestions for revising and editing their essays. Then have students edit their essays based on these suggestions. ⬛W 5

4. Have students present their final essays to their classmates. Ask students to respond to the ideas from each student's writing. ⬛SL 4

See Copying Masters, pp. 212–215.

STUDENT CHECKLIST

Writing

- ☑ Analyze how the author develops ideas.

- ☑ Include specific text references.

- ☑ Use complete sentences and developed paragraphs to structure writing.

Speaking & Listening

- ☑ Engage effectively in collaborative conversations.

- ☑ Read writing aloud with a clear, audible voice.

- ☑ Present ideas in a meaningful way.

DOMAIN: Science
LESSON TOPIC: Stars

▶ OBJECTIVES

- Identify a central idea
- Evaluate supporting evidence
- Analyze text using text evidence

"Classifying the Stars" is broken into three instructional segments.

SEGMENTS

Options for Reading

Independent Students read the text independently or with a partner and then answer questions posed by the teacher.

Supported Students read a segment and answer questions with teacher support.

"Classifying the Stars"

by Annie J. Cannon

SUMMARY In this radio address, Annie J. Cannon explains the importance of the scientific discovery that light is made up of a spectrum of colors, or a rainbow. This spectrum is used as the basis for classifying stars.

ABOUT THE AUTHOR Annie J. Cannon was born in Delaware in 1863. As a young girl, Cannon's mother taught her about constellations and encouraged her interest in astronomy. Cannon went on to study physics and astronomy at Wellesley College. In 1896, she was hired by Edward Pickering at the Harvard College Observatory. She worked with Pickering and his all-female team to index and classify stars by their spectra.

Discuss Genre and Set Purpose

INFORMATIONAL TEXT Remind students that an informational text conveys the author's ideas about a topic. Have students determine the topic of the text and identify notable text features.

SET PURPOSE Help students set a purpose for reading, such as to identify Cannon's central idea and the evidence used to support it.

▲ TEXT COMPLEXITY RUBRIC

Overall Text Complexity		"Classifying the Stars" INFORMATIONAL TEXT
		COMPLEX
Quantitative Measure	Lexile	1300L
Qualitative Measures	Text Structure	more difficult science concepts
	Language Conventionality and Clarity	less straightforward sentence structure
	Knowledge Demands	specialized knowledge required
	Purpose/Levels of Meaning	implied, but easy to identify from context

 Common Core Connection

RI 1 cite textual evidence to support analysis of what the text says explicitly as well as inferences drawn; **RI 2** determine a central idea/analyze its development/provide summary; **RI 3** analyze how author unfolds an analysis or series of ideas or events; **RI 6** determine author's point of view or purpose/analyze how author uses rhetoric

Academic Vocabulary

Read each word with students and discuss its meaning.

dispersed (p. 101) • spread out; separated

myriad (p. 101) • a very great number of things

omnipresent (p. 102) • ever present

FIRST READ ## Think Through the Text

Have students use text evidence and draw inferences to answer questions.

p. 101 • *How does Cannon connect the idea of radio waves and light waves?* Radio waves travel with the speed of light. ⬤RI 1

p. 101 • *What example does Cannon use to illustrate that light is made up of many colors?* a rainbow ⬤RI 3

p. 102 • *What is the main purpose of Cannon's radio address?* Its purpose is to explain the way in which astronomers have divided, or classified, the stars into families and learned about their positions in the sky. ⬤RI 6

SECOND READ ## Analyze the Text

• Review pages 101–102. Ask: *How would you summarize Cannon's explanation of starlight?* Starlight is made up of light waves of various lengths. These light waves can be separated into a spectrum, or rainbow, when passed through a prism. ⬤RI 2

• Ask: *Based on Cannon's introduction, what prediction can you make about how astronomers classify the stars?* The stars are classified by their spectra of light. *What text evidence supports your prediction? Sample answer: Cannon explains light waves and light spectra in her introduction. She says that the understanding of the nature of stars dates back to the experiments of Isaac Newton, in which he passed sunlight through a prism to create a spectrum, or rainbow.* ⬤RI 1

Domain Specific Vocabulary

prism (p. 102) • a transparent solid body used for dispersing light into a spectrum

spectrum (p. 102) • the band of colors produced when sunlight is passed through a prism

ELL **ENGLISH LANGUAGE LEARNERS**

Use Visuals

Assist students in understanding the basic concept that light is made up of a spectrum of colors. Use a prism, if available, to capture and disperse sunlight or show an illustration of sunlight passing through a prism to create a spectrum.

RESPOND TO SEGMENT 1

 Classroom Collaboration

Have partners create a summary of the main ideas and important details in this segment.

Domain Specific Vocabulary

spectroscope (p. 103) • an optical device for producing and observing a spectrum of light

compounds (p. 104) • composed of two or more elements

 ENGLISH LANGUAGE LEARNERS

Use Peer Supported Learning

Pair students to read and discuss the text. Have them take turns paraphrasing the main points of each paragraph to their partners.

RESPOND TO SEGMENT 2

 Classroom Collaboration

Have small groups work together to summarize what they have read. Have them ask questions about what they don't understand.

 Common Core Connection

RI 1 cite textual evidence to support analysis of what the text says explicitly as well as inferences drawn; **RI 2** determine a central idea/analyze its development/provide summary; **RI 5** analyze how author's ideas or claims are developed and refined; **RI 6** determine author's point of view or purpose/analyze how author uses rhetoric; **RI 10** read and comprehend literary nonfiction; **W 2** write informative/explanatory texts; **W 5** develop and strengthen writing by planning, revising, editing, rewriting, or trying a new approach; **SL 4** present information, findings, and supporting evidence clearly, concisely, and logically

Academic Vocabulary

Read each word with students and discuss its meaning.

penetrate (p. 104) • to pierce or pass through

rarefied (p. 106) • of, or belonging to, a select group

FIRST READ ## Think Through the Text

Have students use text evidence and draw inferences to answer questions.

p. 103 • *What evidence does Cannon use to explain the connection between the sun and Earth's elements? The spectrum of the sun has the same defining features as the spectrum of salt—yellow lines cut out by two black lines. The sun's spectrum also has two thousand black lines that have been traced to iron and all common substances found on Earth.* ◼ RI 1

pp. 103–104 • *What evidence does Cannon use to explain the discovery that all stars are suns? When viewed through a spectroscope, starlight mimics the spectrum of the sun, with all of the colors of the rainbow and the same dividing black lines.* ◼ RI 1

p. 106 • *What is the life cycle of a star? Stars begin as gigantic and red. They become blue and hot. Then, at the end of their life, they shrink and become red again.* ◼ RI 2

SECOND READ ## Analyze the Text

• Have students review page 104. Ask: *What role did photography play in the first efforts of classifying the stars by spectra? With the use of a prism and telescope, the spectrum of bright stars could be photographed, compared, and classified.* ◼ RI 1

• Review pages 105–106 with students. Ask: *Explain the alphabet classification system in your own words. Sample answer: The letters B, A, F, G, K, M stand for the six major divisions in the classification system. The letters represent the stars according to decreasing temperatures and increasing redness.* ◼ RI 2

• Review the last paragraph on page 106. Ask: *What two important scientific conclusions were scientists able to make by understanding the stars' compounds? Stars differ in temperature rather than in composition. Scientists also believe that all of the substances known on Earth can be accounted for in the stars; there is no new kind of matter to be found in the universe.* ◼ RI 2

Academic Vocabulary

Read each word with students and discuss its meaning.

beneficent (p. 107) • doing good or causing good to be done

epochs (p. 108) • periods of time marked by distinctive features or events

FIRST READ ## Think Through the Text

Have students use text evidence and draw inferences to answer questions.

p. 107 • *What discovery did astronomers make about the location of stars like the sun, in Class G?* Class G stars seem to be scattered throughout the universe. *What is the nearest Class G star?* Alpha Centauri *What does Cannon infer about Alpha Centauri and other Class G stars?* They may have their own solar systems. **RI 5**

p. 107 • *What facts does Cannon convey about the Great Nebula of Andromeda?* It is a Class G star. It belongs to a separate system, outside our universe of suns. It is about a million light years away. *What are astronomers able to learn by looking at very distant stars?* Astronomers are able to see what stars were like hundreds of thousands of years ago. *What are astronomers not able to know about distant stars?* Astronomers do not know what the stars are like presently. **RI 2**

SECOND READ ## Analyze the Text

- Review page 107 with students. Ask: *What conclusion were astronomers able to make about the location of different types of stars, such as B and A stars?* Many stars of a particular classification seem to be found in specific locations in the universe. *Provide one example that supports this conclusion.* Sample answer: Nearly all of the stars represented by the letter B, which are extremely hot stars in the high point of their lives, can be found in the Milky Way. **RI 1**

- Review the concluding paragraph with students. Ask: *What is Cannon's final message to her radio audience?* Sample answer: Pay attention to the stars in the sky. Take the time to observe them. Observing them is more important than hearing about them. **RI 6**

Independent/Self-Selected Reading

Have students reread "Classifying the Stars" independently to practice analyzing the text on their own, or have them practice the skills using another text, such as:

- "Wonders of Science" speech by Albert Einstein

- "The Discovery of Radium" by Marie Curie **RI 10**

WRITE & PRESENT

1. Have students think about and discuss the scientific importance of the discovery that light is composed of many colors, citing specific text evidence from Cannon's radio address. **RI 2**

2. Have students independently write a short essay analyzing the scientific importance of this discovery, including precise details from the text. **W 2**

3. Have students share their work with partners and offer suggestions for revising and editing. Students edit their writing based on these suggestions. **W 5**

4. Have students present their final writing to their classmates. Ask students to respond to the ideas from each student's writing. **SL 4**

See Copying Masters, pp. 212–215.

STUDENT CHECKLIST

Writing

☑ Identify at least one significant scientific outcome that is based on the discovery that light is composed of many colors.

☑ Include specific text details to support analysis.

☑ Use complete sentences and developed paragraphs to structure writing.

Speaking & Listening

☑ Read writing aloud with a clear, audible voice.

☑ Present ideas in a meaningful way.

"Classifying the Stars" • **185**

▶ OBJECTIVES

- Describe how ideas develop over the course of a nonfiction article
- Identify the main idea of a nonfiction article
- Summarize conclusions about scientific information
- Analyze text using text evidence

"Amusement Park Physics" is broken into three instructional segments.

SEGMENTS

Options for Reading

Independent Students read the text independently or with a partner and then answer questions posed by the teacher.

Supported Students read a segment and answer questions with teacher support.

"Amusement Park Physics"

by Jearl Walker

SUMMARY "Amusement Park Physics" comes from a 1985 *Scientific American* article that was subtitled "Thinking about physics while scared to death (on a falling roller coaster)." Using accessible technical terms, the article presents the principles of physics that make amusement park rides so much fun (or so terrifying, depending on point of view).

ABOUT THE AUTHOR Jearl Walker is a physics professor at Cleveland State University. He received his B.S. in physics from the Massachusetts Institute of Technology in 1967 and his Ph.D. in physics from the University of Maryland in 1973. In 1975, he published the popular book *The Flying Circus of Physics*. He spent years doing physics-related stunts, such as lying on a bed of nails and walking on hot coals for audiences, in order to make the science enjoyable and accessible for nonscientists.

Discuss Genre and Set Purpose

INFORMATIONAL TEXTS Point out that "Amusement Park Physics" is an article from a *Scientific American* series called The Amateur Scientist. The article was designed to explain the science of physics using the everyday examples on display in any amusement park.

SET PURPOSE Help students set a purpose for reading, such as to understand the physics that make a roller coaster work.

Common Core Connection

RI 1 cite textual evidence to support analysis of what the text says explicitly as well as inferences drawn; **RI 2** determine a central idea/analyze its development/provide summary; **RI 3** analyze how author unfolds an analysis or series of ideas or events; **RI 5** analyze how author's claims or ideas are developed and refined

TEXT COMPLEXITY RUBRIC		"Amusement Park Physics" INFORMATIONAL TEXT
Overall Text Complexity		COMPLEX
Quantitative Measure	Lexile	1080L
Qualitative Measures	Text Structure	complex science concepts
	Language Conventionality and Clarity	some unfamiliar language
	Knowledge Demands	some specialized knowledge required
	Purpose/Levels of Meaning	multiple topics, but explicitly stated

Academic Vocabulary

Read each word with students and discuss its meaning.

rotational (p. 1) • circular motion

symmetrically (p. 1) • balanced equally on two or more sides

negligible (p. 2) • insignificant or not worth noticing

FIRST READ ## Think Through the Text

Have students use text evidence and draw inferences to answer questions.

p. 1 • *What makes a roller coaster function? The fourth paragraph states that it functions because of transfers of energy. Where does a roller coaster's energy come from? Gravity—the cars gain and store gravitational potential energy when they are pulled to the top of a high hill. This energy is transferred into kinetic energy as the cars descend the hill.* RI 2

pp. 1–2 • *Summarize why the choice of seat makes a difference in the ride on a roller coaster. On the first descent, the front seats start more slowly than the back seats. The riders in the back feel the momentum force more strongly because momentum is greater in the rear. But at the bottom of the hill, the greatest momentum force is felt in the front of the coaster. This is reversed as the cars pass through the valley and ascend the next hill.* RI 3

p. 2 • *Why does the author say that roller coaster passengers who don't hold on to the safety bar are brave? The forces on a roller coaster can make the riders feel they will be thrown free, which may seem more dangerous. Riders will be thrown if no safety bar holds them in place, so it is important to hold on.* RI 1

SECOND READ ## Analyze the Text

- Review pages 1–2 with students. Ask: *At what point early in a roller coaster ride does acceleration increase? Acceleration increases as more cars follow the front car onto the downward slope; when all of the cars are on the slope, acceleration is greatest.* RI 1

- Ask: *How does the author explain this phenomenon? Sample answer: Acceleration is the product of gravitational force and the steepness of the track; therefore the steeper the slope, the greater the acceleration.* RI 5

- Have students review page 2. Ask: *What three forces appear to be at work when a roller coaster goes into a loop? Sample answer: the rider's weight pushing downward; the force from the seat; an apparent centrifugal force downward Which force does the author say is not really occurring? He says the centrifugal force is not occurring.* RI 3

Domain Specific Vocabulary

potential energy
(p. 1) • energy that can be used but has not yet been used

kinetic energy
(p. 1) • the energy of objects in motion

centrifugal
(p. 2) • a force directed away from a central point

ELL ### ENGLISH LANGUAGE LEARNERS

Use Visuals

Have students work with an English-proficient partner to examine the illustrations that accompany the article. As needed, assist in understanding the language and concepts that are illustrated by the diagrams.

RESPOND TO SEGMENT 1

Classroom Collaboration

Have the class as a whole recount amusement park experiences they have had that relate to the concepts explored in the first segment of the article. Have they been in the front of a roller coaster? The back? What sensations did they have that are explained by the author?

Domain Specific Vocabulary

centripetal (p. 3) • a force directed toward a central point

coefficient (p. 3) • a constant for a substance that is a measure of a property

 ENGLISH LANGUAGE LEARNERS

Use Peer Supported Learning

Have teams of students review the basic principles of motion that the author is discussing. Have them work together to identify a term, such as *acceleration*, and find the example the author uses to illustrate it in the article.

RESPOND TO SEGMENT 2

 Classroom Collaboration

Have small groups work together to summarize the differences between the physics of the Rotor and a roller coaster. Have them ask questions about what they don't understand.

 Common Core Connection

RI 1 cite textual evidence to support analysis of what the text says explicitly as well as inferences drawn; **RI 2** determine a central idea/analyze its development/provide summary; **RI 3** analyze how author unfolds an analysis or series of ideas or events; **RI 5** analyze how author's claims or ideas are developed and refined; **RI 10** read and comprehend literary nonfiction; **W 2** write informative/explanatory texts; **W 9** draw evidence from informational texts; **SL 1** initiate/participate in a range of collaborative discussions

Academic Vocabulary

Read each word with students and discuss its meaning.

intervening (p. 3) • coming between or interrupting

radially (p. 3) • going out from the center like rays

illusory (p. 3) • not real, like an illusion

FIRST READ ## Think Through the Text

Have students use text evidence and draw inferences to answer questions.

p. 3 • *What is the difference between the Double Loop roller coaster and the Corkscrew?* The coasters are similar except that the Corkscrew has helical loops, meaning the coaster moves in a corkscrew fashion. The major difference is the direction of the apparent centrifugal force. *Why does this matter?* It is the changing direction of the apparent centrifugal force that makes the Corkscrew so popular. ◼RI 1

pp. 3–4 • *What makes a rider stick to the wall in the Rotor?* friction *Why does the author explain the forces in the Rotor in such detail?* Sample answer: He is using this as a good example of how the apparent centrifugal force of the rides is not real, but only appears real. ◼RI 3

SECOND READ ## Analyze the Text

• Review page 3 with students. Ask: *What is the main idea the author wants to examine regarding the roller coaster, the water slide, and the Gold Rush Log Flumes?* Sample answer: All three rides operate according to the same principle, that gravitational potential energy is converted into kinetic energy, which is what makes the rides exciting. ◼RI 2

• Ask: *What is an everyday example that you could use to demonstrate the same principle?* Sample answers: riding a bicycle down a hill without pedaling; riding a skateboard up and down the slopes in a skating park; riding a snowboard in a halfpipe ◼RI 3

• Have students revisit page 4. Ask: *The author mentions three forces that seemed to affect him on the swing. What are they?* his weight, the chair and its suspension chains, and the apparent centrifugal force *What earlier explanation is echoed here?* Sample answer: On page 2, the author discussed the three forces sensed when a roller coaster enters a loop. ◼RI 5

Academic Vocabulary

Read each word with students and discuss its meaning.

augment (p. 6) • add to or make larger

cusps (p. 6) • the points where two branches of a curve meet

superposed (p. 6) • placed one on top of another

dissipated (p. 6) • scattered or dispersed

discontinuities (p. 7) • irregularities

FIRST READ ## Think Through the Text

Have students use text evidence and draw inferences to answer questions.

p. 5 • *What does the author conclude will deliver the most fun on a ride like the Calypso or the Scrambler?* On page 5, he states that the best ride will come if the arms rotate at different rates. ● **RI 1**

p. 5 • *How do the diagrams reinforce the author's claims about boring versus exciting rides?* Sample answer: The diagrams make it clear that acceleration and speed will be greater if the arms are of unequal length and rotating in opposite directions. ● **RI 3**

pp. 6–7 • *How does the Tilt-a-Whirl compare with the other rides the author analyzes?* It provides three types of motion, but in this case, he can influence the motion by shifting his weight. *What was the result of his influence?* He was able to make the compartment spin rapidly, making the experience very similar to the Calypso and the Scrambler. ● **RI 1**

SECOND READ ## Analyze the Text

• Have students review pages 5–6. Ask: *What conclusion does the author draw about the rides?* Sample answer: The forces experienced are basically the same on all of the rides. ● **RI 2**

• Have students reread the Notes, pages 6–7. Ask: *How do these notes enhance your understanding of the main article? How can they help a reader make a similar analysis of his or her own experiences?* Sample answers: The responses from teachers and students in different parts of the country give additional examples that help explain the concepts of physics the author is presenting. ● **RI 3**

Independent/Self-Selected Reading

Have students reread "Amusement Park Physics" independently to practice analyzing the text on their own, or have them practice the skills using another text, such as:

• *The Flying Circus of Physics* by Jearl Walker

• *Physics in the Real World* by Keith Lockett ● **RI 10**

Performance Task

WRITE & PRESENT

1. Have students analyze how Jearl Walker explains the phenomenon of acceleration in order to write an explanation of the physics of something they experience frequently, such as riding in a car or bus, on a train or plane, or on an amusement park ride. ● **RI 5**

2. Ask students to summarize his conclusions regarding the physics of roller coasters as they explain the physics of, for example, another carnival ride. ● **W 2**

3. Have students include an account that traces how Walker incorporates supporting details about the processes of rotational dynamics and energy conversion in his explanation. ● **RI 1, W 9**

4. Have students present their final writing to their classmates. Ask students to respond to the themes and ideas from each student's writing. ● **SL 1**

See Copying Masters, pp. 212–215.

STUDENT CHECKLIST

Writing

☑ Determine how Walker clarifies the phenomenon of acceleration.

☑ Summarize his conclusions.

☑ Trace supporting details.

Speaking & Listening

☑ Present ideas in a meaningful way.

☑ Integrate multiple sources of information.

► OBJECTIVES

- Describe how ideas develop over the course of a nonfiction story
- Identify the main idea of a nonfiction story
- Analyze word choices and structure in a story
- Analyze text using text evidence

This excerpt from *The Hot Zone* is broken into three instructional segments.

SEGMENTS

Options for Reading

Independent Students read the book independently or with a partner and then answer questions posed by the teacher.

Supported Students read a segment and answer questions with teacher support.

Common Core Connection

RI 1 cite textual evidence to support analysis of what the text says explicitly as well as inferences drawn; **RI 2** determine a central idea/analyze its development/provide summary; **RI 3** analyze how author unfolds an analysis or series of ideas or events; **RI 6** determine author's point of view or purpose/analyze how author uses rhetoric

from *The Hot Zone*
by Richard Preston

SUMMARY *The Hot Zone* is subtitled "A Terrifying True Story." Called a "nonfiction thriller," the 1994 book concentrates on the origins and potential danger of the Ebola virus, a Biosafety Level 4 agent that is related to other filoviruses. Ebola is believed to kill ninety percent of the people it infects. The section read here is the first section of the book, which examines the history of the filoviruses and presents the consequences of Ebola infection in great detail.

ABOUT THE AUTHOR **Richard Preston** is a writer for *The New Yorker* who expanded his 1992 article "Crisis in the Hot Zone" into the bestselling book excerpted here. He has written a number of novels and nonfiction books. He became interested in dangerous viruses and global pandemics after witnessing medical epidemics in Africa.

Discuss Genre and Set Purpose

INFORMATIONAL TEXT Point out that *The Hot Zone* is a work of nonfiction that reads like a science fiction thriller.

SET PURPOSE Help students set a purpose for reading, such as to learn how a deadly virus can rapidly spread throughout the world.

▲ TEXT COMPLEXITY RUBRIC

Overall Text Complexity		from *The Hot Zone* INFORMATIONAL TEXT
		COMPLEX
Quantitative Measure	Lexile	1030L
Qualitative Measures	Text Structure	more difficult science concepts, implicit compare/contrast text structure, genre traits less common to informational text
	Language Conventionality and Clarity	some unfamiliar language and academic words, longer descriptions
	Knowledge Demands	some specialized knowledge required
	Purpose/Levels of Meaning	implied, but easy to identify from context

SEGMENT 1 pp. 1–36

Academic Vocabulary

Read each word with students and discuss its meaning.

culminating (p. 5) • reaching the highest point

warrens (p. 11) • crowded areas with many people living in a limited space

scarp (p. 16) • a line of cliffs

fulminating (p. 22) • exploding, as if a bomb has detonated

abscess (p. 23) • a collection of pus in body tissues

Domain Specific Vocabulary

gurney (p. 19) • a table or stretcher on wheels

 ENGLISH LANGUAGE LEARNERS

Use Peer Supported Learning

Have partners work together to summarize the nonfiction story so far. Have them outline events in order to work through the nonlinear way the author is telling the story. As they outline, have partners use specific page numbers from the segment to create reference points.

FIRST READ ## Think Through the Text

Have students use text evidence and draw inferences to answer questions.

pp. 5–9 • *What location does Monet visit on Mount Elgon (page 8)?* Monet and a friend visit Kitum Cave. *Why does the author focus so much attention on this location?* It may have been the place where Monet picked up the Marburg virus. The author is using a simple example to show how a terrifying disease could enter the population. ◼ RI 2

pp. 12–16 • *How far from the United States is the Marburg virus, according to the author?* On page 12, Preston says that a deadly tropical virus is within a 24-hour plane ride of every city on Earth. ◼ RI 1

pp. 11–21 • *How long did it take Monet to die after the virus entered his body?* On page 11, we learn that headaches began on January 8, seven days after exposure to a viral agent. January 15 is given as the date of death (pages 19–21); so the virus killed him in fifteen days. *What does the author tell us about the disease in those pages?* We learn of the horrific effects the Marburg virus has on the human body. ◼ RI 3

RESPOND TO SEGMENT 1

Classroom Collaboration

Have small groups of students create a hand-drawn map to compare the route of the Marburg virus to Germany and the potential similar arrival of the same virus or the Ebola virus in the United States.

SECOND READ ## Analyze the Text

• Review pages 3–6 with students. Ask: *Why do you think the author starts with background about Charles Monet on these pages?* Sample answer: The background information about a specific individual humanizes the disease victim while also emphasizing that a terrible epidemic can start with a single case of a disease. RI 3

• Have students review pages 11–22. Ask: *Why are the effects of the disease told in such detail?* Sample answer: The author is building a sense of horror and suspense. ◼ RI 6

• Have students review pages 25–36. Ask: *What virus related to Ebola is discussed in this section?* On page 26, Marburg virus is named. *How did the Marburg virus reach Europe?* It was carried by laboratory monkeys from Africa. *Why is this significant?* Sample answer: It shows two things—that unscrupulous traders can send terrifying diseases all over the world, and that extremely dangerous human diseases can come from animals. ◼ RI 1

Domain Specific Vocabulary

hemostat (p. 62) • an instrument used to clamp shut blood vessels to prevent bleeding

Academic Vocabulary

Read each word with students and discuss its meaning.

paroxysm (p. 40) • sudden, energetic or possibly violent outburst

wizened (p. 40) • withered or shriveled up

amulets (p. 56) • small charms worn for protection

necropsy (p. 62) • examination of a body after death

breached (p. 70) • broke through or ruptured

 ENGLISH LANGUAGE LEARNERS

Use Visuals

Have pairs of students review the seven pages at the beginning of the book. Ask them to use those visual aids, which replicate the process of entering a Biosafety Level 4 area, to help them describe the different procedures and precautions required by ever-higher biosafety levels.

 RESPOND TO SEGMENT 2

Classroom Collaboration

Have small groups work together to summarize the precautions taken in a Biosafety Level 4 facility. Have them ask questions about what they don't understand.

 Common Core Connection

RI 1 cite textual evidence to support analysis of what the text says explicitly as well as inferences drawn; **RI 2** determine a central idea/analyze its development/provide summary; **RI 3** analyze how author unfolds an analysis or series of ideas or events; **RI 5** analyze how author's claims or ideas are developed and refined; **RI 10** read and comprehend literary nonfiction; **W 1** write arguments to support claims; **SL 4** present information, findings, and supporting evidence clearly, concisely, and logically

FIRST READ ## Think Through the Text

Have students use text evidence and draw inferences to answer questions.

pp. 37–42 • *Why does the author spend so much time on Nancy Jaax's background?* *The background humanizes the character, while implying, by noting her job as an Army veterinarian, that she may be connected to research being done on Ebola.* ■ **RI 3**

p. 42 • *What happens to Jaax on page 42?* *She cuts the palm of her hand.* *Why does the author present this detail at this point?* *The author is foreshadowing a danger to Jaax from the injury on her hand; it helps build tension in the pages that follow.* ■ **RI 5**

SECOND READ ## Analyze the Text

• Review pages 45–47 with students. Ask: *Why was Nancy Jaax only allowed to work in Level 4, which contains the most dangerous diseases?* *She could not work in the other levels because she reacts poorly to vaccines. She could work in Level 4 because no vaccines were available for Level 4 disease agents.* ■ **RI 1**

• Have students revisit pages 48–51. Ask: *How great is the risk of a pandemic caused by the Ebola virus? Why?* *The fear of a pandemic is high because Ebola kills its victims very quickly, and it kills such a high percentage of the people it infects. However, the risk seems comparatively small, because the disease has not yet broken out into the human population.* ■ **RI 2**

• Review pages 65–71 with students. Ask: *What frightening incidents does the author reveal in these pages?* *Sample answers: on pages 67–70, when Jaax is afraid the Ebola-tainted monkey blood might have reached her cut hand; on page 70, where Jaax reveals that Ebola can travel through air* ■ **RI 1, RI 3**

Academic Vocabulary

Read each word with students and discuss its meaning.

incarnation (p. 76) • form or type

agonals (p. 79) • death throes

necrosis (p. 81) • death of a certain portion of tissue

vector (p. 85) • a carrier or transporter of a disease

mutable (p. 91) • constantly changing

FIRST READ ## Think Through the Text

Have students use text evidence and draw inferences to answer questions.

pp. 72–75 • *How does the author create tension in this segment?* He creates tension by detailing the "index case" of the unknown virus in stark terms—not only of the virus's effects, but also how easily and rapidly it could spread. *What frightening fact about the new strain of Ebola virus distinguishes it from Marburg virus (page 75)?* Sample answer: The Sudan strain is more than twice as lethal as Marburg virus, killing fifty percent of its victims. ▄ RI 2

pp. 76–82 • *What disease is described on these pages?* Ebola Zaire *Why does the author describe the effects of Ebola Zaire so dispassionately?* Sample answer: A clinical description of the effects of the disease is so frightening that any attempt to write dramatically might be distracting. ▄ RI 5

SECOND READ ## Analyze the Text

- Have students review the chapters that begin on pages 72 and 99. Ask: *What is the main difference between these two chapters?* The first chapter is set in 1976; the next chapter begins in 1987. *Why do you think the author is jumping so far forward in time?* Sample answer: He is building suspense by using the time gap to suggest that viruses like Ebola are hiding, or lying in wait, ready to erupt at any time. ▄ RI 3

- Have students reread pages 102–113. Ask: *Why did the researchers send an expedition to Kitum Cave?* They were trying to find the source of the Marburg virus. ▄ RI 2

Independent/Self-Selected Reading

Have students read the rest of *The Hot Zone* independently to practice analyzing the text on their own, or have them practice the skills using another book, such as:

- *The Demon in the Freezer: A True Story* by Richard Preston

- *Flu: The Story of the Great Influenza Pandemic of 1918* by Gina Kolata
  ▄ RI 10

Performance Task

WRITE & PRESENT

1. Have student teams prepare an "intelligence report" that summarizes the spread of Ebola virus as described in this excerpt from *The Hot Zone*. ▄ RI 2

2. Ask students to analyze how the author develops a sense of tension through the order of events and the pacing of his writing. ▄ RI 3

3. Have students develop a summary that describes how Ebola first began to spread in Africa. ▄ RI 2

4. Then have students add a paragraph to the "intelligence report" that gives their idea of how to prevent the spread of Ebola or a similar disease. ▄ W 1

5. Have students present their final writing to their classmates. Ask students to respond to the themes and ideas from each student's writing. ▄ SL 4

See Copying Masters, pp. 212–215.

STUDENT CHECKLIST

Writing

☑ Identify the main ideas of the excerpt.

☑ Summarize these ideas using evidence from the excerpt.

☑ Present and explain a possible solution in a logical, organized way.

Speaking & Listening

☑ Participate effectively in a collaborative discussion.

☑ Present ideas in a meaningful way.

☑ Read report aloud with a clear, audible voice.

▶ **OBJECTIVES**

- Identify and analyze the central idea of text
- Describe evidence in a text to support analysis
- Analyze how ideas are developed

This excerpt from *Life by the Numbers* is broken into three instructional segments.

Options for Reading

Independent Students read the book independently or with a partner and then answer questions posed by the teacher.

Supported Students read a segment and answer questions with teacher support.

COMMON CORE **Common Core Connection**

RI 1 cite textual evidence to support analysis of what the text says explicitly as well as inferences drawn; **RI 2** determine a central idea/analyze its development/provide summary; **RI 3** analyze how author unfolds an analysis or series of ideas or events; **RI 5** analyze how author's ideas or claims are developed and refined; **RI 8** delineate/evaluate the argument and specific claims in a text/identify false statements

from *Life by the Numbers*

by Keith Devlin

SUMMARY Mathematics is viewed by many people as complicated, but *Life by the Numbers* explores the beauty of mathematics. Each chapter focuses on a different and creative application of math. Examples include special effects for movies, performance in sports, and order in nature.

ABOUT THE AUTHOR Keith Devlin is a mathematician at Stanford University and senior researcher at the Center for the Study of Language and Information. He has written over thirty books. He is also the "Math Guy" on National Public Radio.

Discuss Genre and Set Purpose

INFORMATIONAL TEXT Remind students that an informational text conveys information about a topic and often includes an argument or claim. Explain that the author supports his or her argument or claim with facts, details, and opinions. It is up to readers to evaluate the information presented in order to come to their own conclusions. Discuss how the author expresses his ideas by describing applications of mathematics in the world.

SET PURPOSE Help students set a purpose for reading, such as identifying reasons why the author describes mathematics as beautiful.

TEXT COMPLEXITY RUBRIC

Overall Text Complexity		from *Life by the Numbers* INFORMATIONAL TEXT
		COMPLEX
Quantitative Measure	Lexile	1160L
Qualitative Measures	Text Structure	more difficult mathematics concepts
	Language Conventionality and Clarity	some figurative language
	Knowledge Demands	some specialized knowledge required
	Purpose/Levels of Meaning	implied, but easy to identify from context

Academic Vocabulary

Read each word with students and discuss its meaning.

maneuver (p. 4) • a movement that requires skill

collaborating (p. 7) • working together for a common goal

virtual (p. 7) • having the effect of being real without being real

FIRST READ ## Think Through the Text

Have students use text evidence and draw inferences to answer questions.

pp. 6–7 • *How does graphic artist Donna Cox use mathematics to help the scientists at the University of Illinois?* She represents the numbers with pictures. *Why is this helpful for the scientists?* The numbers represent the early moments of the universe. The scientists can understand the numbers by seeing and experiencing these early moments. **RI 1**

p. 8 • *What types of maps does geographer Dawn Wright produce?* She produces undersea maps from data obtained by bouncing sound waves off the ocean floor. *Why does she need mathematics for this work?* She cannot see the ocean floor directly. **RI 1**

pp. 10–11 • *What is knot theory?* the mathematical study of knots *Why is knot theory important in the study of viruses?* A DNA molecule is like a coiled string. Viruses affect DNA by tying it into knots. Scientists can understand a virus by analyzing the type of knot it makes of the DNA. **RI 1**

p. 13 • *Scientist Eugene Wigner believes that mathematics is important because it describes patterns and relationships. What are some examples the text uses to support this claim?* the symmetrical design of flowers; the area swept out by planetary orbits; a population's voting pattern **RI 8**

SECOND READ ## Analyze the Text

• Review pages 4–5. Ask: *Why does the author describe triple axels?* Skaters can only win major competitions if they can perform the triple axel. Mathematics shows them how to perform the triple axel. **RI 5**

• Point out to students that analogies are a useful way for an author to explain an idea. Review pages 17–18 with students. Ask: *How does the author use an analogy of music to explain mathematics?* Just as a musician experiences music rather than seeing just notes on a page, a mathematician experiences the simplicity and patterns of the world rather than seeing just symbols and equations. **RI 3**

• Ask: *What do you think is the central idea of this segment?* Mathematics is a tool that helps us understand our world. *How does the author develop this idea throughout the segment?* The author describes a variety of examples in science, in nature, and in everyday life for which mathematics provides explanations for complex issues. **RI 2**

 ENGLISH LANGUAGE LEARNERS

Use Visuals

Encourage students to look at the photographs as they read each section. Ask simple questions that help them relate each photograph to the ideas presented. For example, on page 9, ask: *What is in the picture?* the ocean floor *What did scientists use to make the picture?* sound waves and computers

RESPOND TO SEGMENT 1

 Classroom Collaboration

Have partners create a summary of important ideas presented in this segment. Then have them identify details that the author uses to support these ideas.

Domain Specific Vocabulary

vanishing point (p. 27) • a point in perspective art at which parallel lines seem to meet

perspective (p. 27) • a technique used in art to make things appear three-dimensional

 ENGLISH LANGUAGE LEARNERS

Use Peer Supported Learning

Have students work with a partner to read the text. Have them pause to discuss each paragraph after reading it.

RESPOND TO SEGMENT 2

 Classroom Collaboration

Have small groups work together to summarize what they have read. Have them ask questions about what they don't understand.

 Common Core Connection

RI 2 determine a central idea/analyze its development/provide summary; **RI 3** analyze how author unfolds an analysis or series of ideas or events; **RI 4** determine the meaning of words and phrases, including figurative, connotative, and technical meanings/analyze impact of word choices; **RI 10** read and comprehend literary nonfiction; **W 2** write informative/explanatory texts; **W 5** develop and strengthen writing by planning, revising, editing, rewriting, or trying a new approach; **SL 1** initiate/participate in a range of collaborative discussions; **SL 4** present information, findings, and supporting evidence clearly, concisely, and logically

Academic Vocabulary

Read each word with students and discuss its meaning.

newsreel (p. 25) • a short movie that describes a news event

array (p. 25) • a large group arranged in an orderly way

surreal (p. 27) • seeming unreal or fantastic

animate (p. 33) • to give movement to

FIRST READ # Think Through the Text

Have students use text evidence and draw inferences to answer questions.

p. 24 • *How does Doug Trumbull use mathematics to make movies more enjoyable?* He creates special effects for movies. ⬤ RI 10

p. 27 • *How does drawing lines in a painting so that they meet at the vanishing point affect the painting?* The painting will seem to have depth. ⬤ RI 10

pp. 32–34 • *What effect were mathematician George Francis and graphic artist Donna Cox able to achieve by combining their talents?* They were able to produce animated morphisms in which one image is transformed smoothly into another image. *Why did they need a supercomputer for this process?* The mathematical morphisms were complicated. ⬤ RI 10

SECOND READ # Analyze the Text

• Review pages 21–26 with students. Ask: *What is the central idea of these pages?* Mathematics can be used to produce realistic special effects in movies. *What are some ways that the author develops this idea?* On page 22, the author describes how Trumbull uses mathematics to produce a virtual reality. Trumbull uses mathematics to link the audience's motion to images on a screen to create an illusion of reality. The author also gives examples of movies in which this is done. ⬤ RI 2

• Have students review pages 26–30. Point out that the author devotes these pages to a description of how mathematics links perspective to virtual reality and special effects in movies. Ask: *According to the author, what were two key mathematical ideas that made this link possible?* One idea was projective geometry, which uses geometry to produce perspective in images. Another idea was Descartes's idea that geometry can be described by algebraic equations. ⬤ RI 3

Academic Vocabulary

Read each word with students and discuss its meaning.

melodious (p. 35) • having a musical sound

intervening (p. 38) • in between

reverberation (p. 40) • movement that continues after the source of the movement has ended

crucial (p. 43) • extremely important

concise (p. 47) • brief but complete

FIRST READ ## Think Through the Text

Have students use text evidence and draw inferences to answer questions.

pp. 35–36 • *What did mathematician Tom Banchoff and computer scientist Charles Strauss work together to develop?* *They developed a system that transforms mathematical equations into geometric figures on a computer screen.* *Using this system, what geometric object did Banchoff create?* *a hypercube* **RI 10**

p. 40 • *The author states that an interest in mathematics was responsible for the cubist movement in art. What example does he provide to support this claim?* *He explains that Pablo Picasso was trying to represent different dimensions in his cubist paintings.* **RI 1**

pp. 44–47 • *The author claims that four dimensions really exist. How does he support his position?* *Mathematics can show you what something would be like, even if it doesn't exist.* **RI 1**

SECOND READ ## Analyze the Text

- *What does Donna Cox mean on page 34 when she claims that computers have mathematicized art?* *Computers allow us to express geometric figures as numbers and then easily transform them into beautiful and unusual forms.* **RI 4**

- Have students review pages 44–47. Ask: *What is the central idea of this section?* *People can move beyond simple three-dimensional perspective drawings. They can experience them through virtual reality.* *How does the author develop this idea?* *The author describes the use of virtual environments and video goggles.* **RI 2**

Independent/Self-Selected Reading

Have students reread this excerpt from *Life by the Numbers* independently to practice analyzing the text on their own, or have them practice the skills using another book, such as:

- *The Math Gene* by Keith Devlin

- *The Math Instinct* by Keith Devlin **RI 10**

WRITE & PRESENT

1. Have small groups discuss and record the central idea of each segment they have read in *Life by the Numbers*. **RI 2, SL 1**

2. Ask students to individually think about the central idea of the entire text. Then have them write a short summary of this idea. Students should include references to the text to explain how the author develops this idea. **RI 2, W 2**

3. Have students share their views about the central idea with others in their group. Encourage students to evaluate and comment on each other's views. Then have students edit their summaries based on this feedback. **W 5**

4. Have students present their final writing to their classmates. Ask students to respond to the ideas from each student's writing. **SL 4**

See Copying Masters, pp. 212–215.

STUDENT CHECKLIST

Writing

☑ Identify a central idea of the text..

☑ Include specific text references to explain how the author supports this idea.

☑ Use complete sentences and developed paragraphs to structure writing.

Speaking & Listening

☑ Read writing aloud with a clear, audible voice.

☑ Present ideas in a meaningful way.

OBJECTIVES

- Delineate/evaluate an argument and specific claims
- Analyze how an author unfolds an analysis or series of events or ideas
- Analyze text using text evidence

The Race to Save the Lord God Bird is broken into three instructional segments.

SEGMENTS

Options for Reading

Independent Students read the selection independently or with a partner and then answer questions posed by the teacher.

Supported Students read a segment and answer questions with teacher support.

Common Core Connection

RI 1 cite textual evidence to support analysis of what the text says explicitly as well as inferences drawn; **RI 3** analyze how an author unfolds an analysis or series of ideas or events; **RI 8** delineate/evaluate the argument and specific claims in a text/identify false statements

The Race to Save the Lord God Bird

by Phillip Hoose

SUMMARY The book describes the tragedy of extinction by following the demise of the Ivory-billed Woodpecker, often called the Lord God bird. The book has won several awards, including the ALA Best Books for Young Adults and the Boston Globe Horn Book Award.

ABOUT THE AUTHOR Phillip Hoose writes books, essays, plays, songs, and magazine articles. He covers many environmentally related topics, including animals, as well as sports. Hoose is also a staff member of the Nature Conservancy. His book, *Claudette Colvin: Twice Toward Justice* won the National Book Award and was also a Newbery Medal runner-up.

Discuss Genre and Set Purpose

INFORMATIONAL TEXT Preview the selection with students. Help them identify characteristics of informational text, such as illustrations, photographs, quotations, and sidebars.

SET PURPOSE Help students set a purpose for reading, such as to find out more about the challenges facing those who wanted to save this bird.

TEXT COMPLEXITY RUBRIC

Overall Text Complexity		The Race to Save the Lord God Bird INFORMATIONAL TEXT COMPLEX
Quantitative Measure	Lexile	1160L
Qualitative Measures	Text Structure	genre traits more specific to scientific
	Language Conventionality and Clarity	some unfamiliar or academic words, more complex sentence structure and descriptions
	Knowledge Demands	some specialized knowledge required
	Purpose/Levels of Meaning	single topic, explicitly stated

Academic Vocabulary

Read each word with students and discuss its meaning.

conservationists (p. 4) • people who work to preserve things from change

mangle (p. 8) • destroy by crushing

specimen (p. 24) • an organism collected as an example

heritage (p. 31) • something passed from generation to generation

carcasses (p. 49) • dead bodies of animals

Domain Specific Vocabulary

taxidermy (p. 17) • the art of preparing, stuffing, and mounting animal skins for a lifelike appearance

ornithologist (p. 33) • someone who studies birds

FIRST READ ▶ ## Think Through the Text

Have students use text evidence and draw inferences to answer questions.

pp. 4–5 • *How did the Ivory-bill get its nickname of "Lord God bird"?* People who saw how beautiful it was gave it the name. *How do we know about the bird now?* Scientists from Cornell University recorded its call and took photographs and movies of it. ▬RI 1

pp. 14–15 • *How does the author get a sense of the bird's life?* He examines the features of the specimen and asks himself questions about the reasons for some of these features. ▬RI 1

pp. 29–31 • *Why did many forest animals begin to disappear or die out?* The forests were cut down to provide fuel and clear spaces for farming. The forest animals had no place to go. ▬RI 1

pp. 49–51 • *How was Harriet Hemenway influential in saving birds?* She founded the Massachusetts Audubon Society, which eventually became a nationwide organization dedicated to protecting birds. ▬RI 1

SECOND READ ▶ ## Analyze the Text

• Review pages 3–6. Ask: *Why was the sixth wave of extinction so different from the previous waves?* It was the first time that there was a conflict between the groups trying to destroy and those trying to preserve a creature's habitat. *How does the Ivory-bill fit into this wave?* Modern conservationists model some of their approaches on the ones that were used to try to save the Ivory-bill. ▬RI 8

• Review pages 7–11. Ask: *How does the author begin to tell the story of the Ivory-bill?* He retells an account of a man who hunted and captured one of the birds in 1809. He describes the bird's appearance and actions, using specific details. ▬RI 3

• Review pages 42–45. Ask: *Why does the author include information about Wayne and Brewster?* to explain one challenge to keeping the Ivory-bill species alive *Evaluate the author's statements about Wayne and Brewster.* Sample answer: The author asks important questions about their motives and actions, but he is not able to give definite answers supported by facts. ▬RI 8

ENGLISH LANGUAGE LEARNERS

Use Cognates

Point out the English/Spanish cognates to aid comprehension: *photograph/ fotografía; map/mapa; equipment/equipo.* Have students use the words in sentences related to the text.

RESPOND TO SEGMENT 1

Classroom Collaboration

Have partners create a summary of the main ideas in this segment. Then have students raise questions that might be answered in the next segment.

ENGLISH LANGUAGE LEARNERS

Use Visuals

Use the photographs and captions to discuss with students the actions that some people took that resulted in the death of the birds and the actions that others took to save them. Have students use their own words to describe the information provided by each visual.

 RESPOND TO SEGMENT 2

Classroom Collaboration

Have small groups work together to summarize what they have read. Have them ask questions about what they don't understand.

 Common Core Connection

RI 1 cite textual evidence to support analysis of what the text says explicitly as well as inferences drawn; **RI 3** analyze how an author unfolds an analysis or series of ideas or events; **RI 8** delineate/evaluate the argument and specific claims in a text/identify false statements; **RI 10** read and comprehend literature; **W 2** write informative/explanatory texts; **W 5** develop and strengthen writing by planning, revising, editing, rewriting, or trying a new approach; **SL 4** present information, findings, and supporting evidence clearly, concisely, and logically

---

Academic Vocabulary

Read each word with students and discuss its meaning.

strenuous (p. 59) • active and energetic

preened (p. 74) • straightened and cleaned the feathers with the beak

ravenously (p. 85) • greedily and hungrily

finicky (p. 110) • picky and particular

FIRST READ **Think Through the Text**

Have students use text evidence and draw inferences to answer questions.

pp. 59–62 • *How was Jim Tanner different from previous ornithologists? Instead of killing the birds, Tanner studied them alive as they lived in their habitats in nature.* ⬤RI 1

pp. 72–77 • *What was the importance of the Tensas swamp? Tanner found the Ivory-bill there, so Cornell's team would be able to record its voice. How was the swamp turned into a preserve? The Singer company bought the swamp and declared it a refuge so they could be the only company to cut the trees. Then the company gave the land to the Louisiana Fish and Game Department to protect it.* ⬤RI 1

pp. 102–106 • *What does the text say was Tanner's plan to figure out the way the Ivory-bill lived? The author explains on page 103 that Tanner planned to get a complete knowledge of the Singer Tract and learn about all of the plants and animals that lived in it so he could better understand the history of the Ivory-bill.* ⬤RI 1

SECOND READ **Analyze the Text**

• Review pages 59–113 with students. Ask: *How does the author portray Jim Tanner? Sample answer: He portrays Tanner as someone who cares about birds and works diligently to help preserve them in the wild as well as understand their way of life.* ⬤RI 3

• Have students review pages 92–99. Ask: *How does the author present evidence that supports his analysis that protecting the bird was challenging? Sample answer: The author gives details about Tanner's work finding the bird. He includes anecdotes about Tanner's encounters with other people and the bird. He also includes quotes from Tanner and others.* ⬤RI 8

Academic Vocabulary

Read each word with students and discuss its meaning.

penetrating (p. 118) • reaching or entering

intact (p. 121) • in one unbroken piece

ethical (p. 129) • moral

brink (p. 138) • the threshold of something dangerous happening

tantalizing (p. 153) • possessing a quality that teases or excites interest

FIRST READ ## Think Through the Text

Have students use text evidence and draw inferences to answer questions.

pp. 115–119 • *What is the actual race described in this book? The race is between the lumber company that wants to cut down the trees in the Singer Tract and the Audubon Society that wants to save the forest so that the Ivory-bills have food.* ◾ **RI 1**

pp. 120–129 • *What was the result of the Audubon Society's attempt to save the Singer Tract? It was not successful.* **What events influenced the outcome of their attempt?** *The United States entered World War II and needed the wood. Neither company was interested in preserving the Singer Tract.* ◾ **RI 1**

pp. 139–140 • *Why was Dr. Short finally allowed to go to Cuba to look for the bird? Cuban scientists hoped that his participation would help them get permission to create an area dedicated to protecting the bird.* ◾ **RI 1**

SECOND READ ## Analyze the Text

• Reread page 145. Ask: *How does the author express his opinion about the bird? He compares it to two legendary places, the Fountain of Youth and El Dorado. The existence of these places can't be proved or disproved, just like the current existence of the Ivory-bill.* ◾ **RI 3**

• Reread pages 153–155. Ask: *How does the author support his claim about the importance of the Ivory-bill? He includes a list of positive changes that have happened because of the work done on behalf of the bird.* **Can these claims be proven to be true?** *Yes, each one could be documented.* ◾ **RI 8**

Independent/Self-Selected Reading

Have students reread *The Race to Save the Lord God Bird* independently to practice analyzing the text on their own, or have them practice the skills using another book, such as:

• *Moonbird: A Year on the Wind with the Great Survivor B95* by Phillip Hoose

• *Theodore Roosevelt, the Naturalist* by Paul Russell Cutright ◾ **RI 10**

Performance Task

WRITE & PRESENT

1. Have small groups assess the extent to which the reasoning and evidence the author presents support his scientific analysis of why protecting this particular species was so challenging. ◾ **RI 8**

2. Ask students to think about the reasoning behind the author's claims and the evidence he uses to support them. Have students write a paragraph that compares the author's analysis and his evidence. Encourage students to cite text evidence to defend their ideas. ◾ **W 2**

3. Have students share their work with partners and then edit it. ◾ **W 5**

4. Have students present their final writing to their classmates. Ask students to respond to the statements and ideas from each student's writing. ◾ **SL 4**

See Copying Masters, pp. 212–215.

STUDENT CHECKLIST

Writing

☑ Analyze how the author presents his analysis.

☑ Explain how the author uses text evidence to support his analysis.

☑ Use complete sentences and developed paragraphs to structure writing.

Speaking & Listening

☑ Read writing aloud with a clear, audible voice.

☑ Present ideas in a meaningful way.

▶ **OBJECTIVES**

- Analyze how an author presents a series of ideas or events
- Determine the meaning of words and phrases
- Read and comprehend literary nonfiction

This excerpt from *The Story of Science: Newton at the Center* is broken into three instructional segments.

SEGMENTS

Options for Reading

Independent Students read the book independently or with a partner and then answer questions posed by the teacher.

Supported Students read a segment and answer questions with teacher support.

COMMON CORE **Common Core Connection**

RI 1 cite textual evidence to support analysis of what the text says explicitly as well as inferences drawn; **RI 3** analyze how author unfolds an analysis or series of ideas or events; **RI 5** analyze how author's ideas or claims are developed and refined; **RI 6** determine author's point of view or purpose/analyze how author uses rhetoric; **RI 8** delineate/evaluate the argument and specific claims in a text/identify false statements

from *The Story of Science: Newton at the Center*

by Joy Hakim

SUMMARY *The Story of Science* is a three-book series about advances in science from ancient times to the present. Each book is a set of stories that together show how scientists built upon existing knowledge to make new discoveries. *Newton at the Center,* the second book in the series, focuses on the work of Isaac Newton and also describes related advances made by other scientists before and after Newton's time.

ABOUT THE AUTHOR Joy Hakim lives in Colorado, but she grew up and went to college in Virginia. Before becoming a writer, she was an English teacher, a newspaper reporter, and an associate editor.

Discuss Genre and Set Purpose

INFORMATIONAL TEXT Remind students that an informational text conveys information about a topic and often includes an argument. Discuss how the author presents a series of ideas and events.

SET PURPOSE Help students set a purpose for reading, such as understanding how scientific discoveries were linked to each other.

▲ TEXT COMPLEXITY RUBRIC

Overall Text Complexity		from *The Story of Science: Newton at the Center* INFORMATIONAL TEXT
		COMPLEX
Quantitative Measure	Lexile	950L
Qualitative Measures	Text Structure	more difficult scientific concepts
	Language Conventionality and Clarity	some figurative language
	Knowledge Demands	some specialized knowledge required
	Purpose/Levels of Meaning	implied, but easy to identify from context

Academic Vocabulary

Read each word with students and discuss its meaning.

deposed (p. 120) • removed from power

tufted (p. 122) • gathered in a bunch

harmoniously (p. 127) • in peace and agreement

straitjacket (p. 134) • a garment that binds a person's arms

Domain Specific Vocabulary

retina (p. 120) • the back part of an eye that senses light

lens (p. 121) • a curved, transparent material that bends and focuses light rays

ellipse (p. 125) • a curved shape similar to a slightly flattened circle

FIRST READ ## Think Through the Text

Have students use text evidence and draw inferences to answer questions.

pp. 124–125 • *What important discovery did Kepler make about the planets?* The planets travel along elliptical orbits around the sun. *How was this different from Tycho Brahe's ideas?* Brahe thought the planets moved around Earth. **RI 1**

p. 130 • *What were Kepler's three laws of planetary motion?* Planets travel in an elliptical orbit around the sun. The planets travel faster when they are close to the sun and slower when they are farther away. Planets that are farther from the sun take longer to complete one orbit than those that are closer. **RI 1**

pp. 134–135 • *How do you know that the author thinks the Cartesian coordinate system had important effects on algebra and geometry?* The author points out that the Cartesian coordinate system enables us to use algebra to describe two- and three-dimensional figures. **RI 6**

pp. 136–137 • *Why does the author describe some of Descartes's ideas as dangerous?* Descartes was describing ideas in which planets moved around the sun, not Earth. The church at the time said this was against its beliefs and put his books on a prohibited list. **RI 8**

p. 137 • *According to the author, why are wrong ideas sometimes useful?* They can make people begin to think about and question important issues. **RI 5**

SECOND READ ## Analyze the Text

- Review pages 136–137. Ask: *How does the author show that Descartes's discoveries about the nature of motion are based on discoveries made by Galileo?* Descartes showed that objects, including the planets, naturally travel in a straight line at a constant velocity. The author explains that this is based on Galileo's idea that the natural tendency of objects in motion is to stay in motion. **RI 3**

- Review pages 140–143. Ask: *Why does the author describe Wiles's first mistaken claim that he had solved Fermat's last theorem, as well as his correct claim?* Sample answer: to emphasize that instead of giving up, he continued until he was able to prove the theorem **RI 3**

ELL ### ENGLISH LANGUAGE LEARNERS

Use Visuals

Make sure English language learners understand the meaning of one discovery being based on a previous discovery. Use an analogy of a building or a statue. Point out that a *base* is the bottom part of a structure that other parts rest on. Demonstrate by displaying pictures of structures with a base. Explain that, similarly, discoveries in science often "rest on" previous ideas.

RESPOND TO SEGMENT 1

 Classroom Collaboration

Have partners create a summary of important ideas presented in this segment. Then have them identify how the author explains links between scientific discoveries.

Domain Specific Vocabulary

alchemy (p. 170) • an early form of chemistry in which the scientists tried to change a common substance into a valuable one, such as gold, and they tried to produce a substance that would keep people forever young

 ENGLISH LANGUAGE LEARNERS

Use Props

Help students understand some of Newton's ideas by providing simple demonstrations. For example, when students read page 166, show them a spectrum of light by passing sunlight through a prism. Demonstrate the laws of motion on page 173 by rolling a ball across the floor.

RESPOND TO SEGMENT 2

 Classroom Collaboration

Have small groups work together to summarize what they have read. Have them ask questions about what they don't understand.

 Common Core Connection

RI 3 analyze how author unfolds an analysis or series of ideas or events; **RI 5** analyze how author's ideas or claims are developed and refined; **RI 6** determine author's point of view or purpose/analyze how author uses rhetoric; **W 2** write informative/explanatory texts; **W 5** develop and strengthen writing by planning, revising, editing, rewriting, or trying a new approach; **SL 1** initiate/participate in a range of collaborative discussions; **SL 3** evaluate speaker's point of view, reasoning, use of evidence and rhetoric; **SL 4** present information, findings, and supporting evidence clearly, concisely, and logically

Academic Vocabulary

Read each word with students and discuss its meaning.

peevishness (p. 148) • state of being easily annoyed

innate (p. 157) • a natural part of

homogeneous (p. 165) • the same throughout

heretic (p. 171) • a person who does not act in agreement with certain religious beliefs

convivial (p. 178) • friendly; pleasant

FIRST READ ▶ # Think Through the Text

Have students use text evidence and draw inferences to answer questions.

p. 147 • *What changed Newton from an uninterested student to a serious one?* He was trying to be better than a bully who was a good student. ◼ RI 10

pp. 150–151 • *What happened that provided Newton an opportunity to spend an entire year studying science independently?* There was an epidemic of the plague in London. Cambridge University had to close down for the year, and Newton went to his home. ◼ RI 10

pp. 165–166 • *What does Newton prove about white light?* He proves that it is made of different colors of light rays. *How does he prove this?* He shines light through a triangular glass prism. ◼ RI 10

pp. 173–174 • *What are Newton's three laws of motion?* A body that is not moving will stay at rest unless a force causes it to move. A body moving in a straight line at a constant speed will not change speed or direction unless a force changes its speed or direction. There is an equal and opposite reaction to every action. ◼ RI 10

SECOND READ ▶ # Analyze the Text

• Review pages 149–150. *According to the text, Newton read about the ideas of which scientists while at Cambridge?* Aristotle, Copernicus, Galileo, Kepler, Descartes, and Euclid *How were Newton's discoveries based on an idea by Descartes?* Descartes said the universe could be studied by trying to understand how each part works. ◼ RI 3

• Review pages 154–156. Ask: *What poem does the author describe in this section?* a poem by John Dryden about "the year of wonders," 1666 *What does Dryden describe as so wonderful about 1666?* England has defeated the Dutch in battle, London has survived the Great Fire, and London is recovering from the plague. *What is the author's purpose in describing this poem?* The author believes 1666 is also a "year of wonders" because it is the year that Newton makes many amazing scientific discoveries. ◼ RI 6

Academic Vocabulary

Read each word with students and discuss its meaning.

conjectures (p. 188) • expresses an opinion

pompous (p. 194) • arrogant; self-centered

steeping (p. 209) • soaking; covered with a liquid

assaying (p. 212) • testing a metal to determine what it is

FIRST READ ## Think Through the Text

Have students use text evidence and draw inferences to answer questions.

p. 187 • *How does the author use a figure to show Halley's important observation about stars?* *Halley found that the positions of stars change. The figure shows changes in position of stars of the Big Dipper.* **RI 3**

pp. 205–206 • *Why did King Augustus II imprison Johann Friedrich Böttger in his laboratory?* *Böttger had bragged that he could make gold. The king wanted him to do it.* **What did Böttger make instead?** *porcelain* **RI 10**

SECOND READ ## Analyze the Text

- Review "Prime Time for France" on page 190 with students. Ask: *What is the author's purpose in writing this?* *to tell about the Paris Observatory's origin and claim as the prime meridian and then the prime meridian's shift to Greenwich, England* **RI 6**

- Review pages 190–192. Ask: *What important measurement does Roemer make?* *He measures the speed of light.* **In what way does Roemer's observation depend on an idea by Descartes?** *Descartes stated that light was instantaneous. Roemer used this idea to predict an eclipse of Jupiter's moon, Io, but it didn't work. He realized light is not instantaneous and then measured its speed.* **RI 3**

- Review pages 210–215. Ask: *Why does the author title this chapter "Robert Boyle, Skeptic—or Airhead"?* *Boyle is a skeptic because he doesn't just follow what others believe. He tests things for himself. The author refers to him as an airhead as a play on words because of Boyle's experiments with air, such as showing that it has mass.* **RI 5**

Independent/Self-Selected Reading

Have students reread this excerpt from *The Story of Science: Newton at the Center* independently to practice analyzing the text on their own, or have them practice the skills using another book, such as:

- *The Last Sorcerers: The Path from Alchemy to the Periodic Table* by Richard Morris

- *Isaac Newton* by Gale E. Christianson **RI 10**

WRITE & PRESENT

1. Have small groups review the story of Kepler and explain how the author shows that important scientific discoveries relied on previous discoveries. **RI 3, SL 1**

2. Have individual students review the second segment in the book. Have them write a paragraph explaining how the author shows that Newton's discoveries relied on previous discoveries by other scientists. Instruct students to cite text evidence to support their explanations. **RI 3, W 2**

3. Have students share explanations with others in their group. Instruct students to evaluate each other's explanations. Then have students edit their explanations. **W 5, SL 3, SL 4**

4. Have students present their final paragraphs to their classmates. Ask students to respond to the ideas from each student's writing. **SL 3, SL 4**

See Copying Masters, pp. 212–215.

STUDENT CHECKLIST

Writing

☑ Analyze how the author develops ideas.

☑ Include specific text references.

☑ Use complete sentences and developed paragraphs to structure writing.

Speaking & Listening

☑ Engage effectively in collaborative conversations.

☑ Read writing aloud with a clear, audible voice.

☑ Present ideas in a meaningful way.

OBJECTIVES

- Determine the author's point of view and purpose
- Determine the meaning of words and phrases
- Read and comprehend literary nonfiction

from *Circumference*
by Nicholas Nicastro

This excerpt from *Circumference: Eratosthenes and the Ancient Quest to Measure the Globe* is broken into three instructional segments.

SEGMENTS

Options for Reading

Independent Students read the book independently or with a partner and then answer questions posed by the teacher.

Supported Students read a segment and answer questions with teacher support.

SUMMARY *Circumference* tells the story of how Eratosthenes, head librarian at the Museum in Alexandria, saw past the scientific misconceptions that prevailed in the 3rd century B.C.E and discovered a way to calculate Earth's circumference.

ABOUT THE AUTHOR Nicholas Nicastro was born in Astoria, New York. He has an undergraduate degree in English as well as an M.F.A. in filmmaking and an M.A. in archaeology. His literary works include short stories, travel and science articles, and both fiction and nonfiction books.

Discuss Genre and Set Purpose

INFORMATIONAL TEXT Remind students that an informational text conveys information about a topic and often includes an argument or claim. Explain that the author supports his or her argument or claim with facts, details, and opinions. It is up to reader to evaluate the information presented in order to come to their own conclusions. Discuss how the author presents a series of ideas and events.

SET PURPOSE Help students set a purpose for reading, such as understanding both the details and the importance of Eratosthenes' calculation.

Common Core Connection

RI 1 cite textual evidence to support analysis of what the text says explicitly as well as inferences drawn; **RI 6** determine author's point of view or purpose/analyze how author uses rhetoric; **RI 10** read and comprehend literary nonfiction

TEXT COMPLEXITY RUBRIC

Overall Text Complexity		from *Circumference* INFORMATIONAL TEXT
		COMPLEX
Quantitative Measure	Lexile	1360L
Qualitative Measures	Text Structure	somewhat complex science concepts
	Language Conventionality and Clarity	many unfamiliar or high academic words
	Knowledge Demands	some specialized knowledge required
	Purpose/Levels of Meaning	implied, but easy to identify from context

SEGMENT 1 pp. 1–11

Academic Vocabulary

Read each word with students and discuss its meaning.

entrepôt (p. 1) • warehouse

canonical (p. 6) • official; recognized

self-aggrandizing (p. 6) • arrogant; egotistical

obelisks (p. 8) • four-sided columns

anthropomorphic (p. 9) • human-looking

pecuniary (p. 8) • relating to money

encomium (p. 11) • expression of praise

FIRST READ ## Think Through the Text

Have students use text evidence and draw inferences to answer questions.

p. 1 • *To what city in Egypt is Eratosthenes headed?* Alexandria *What does he plan to do there?* He will be the head librarian at the Museum in Alexandria. RI 10

p. 2 • *What evidence does the author offer to support the idea that Eratosthenes booked passage on the deck of the ship and not in a cabin?* Cabins were few, small, and expensive. RI 1

p. 3 • *What does the author say was the popular explanation for the Milky Way at that time?* At that time, many people thought it was the leftover path of the sun's path through the sky. RI 10

pp. 5–6 • *What were the two meanings of* Pharos? It was Greek for Great Lighthouse, and it was the name of the island on which the lighthouse sat. *What eventually happened to the lighthouse?* It was toppled by earthquakes. RI 10

SECOND READ ## Analyze the Text

• Review pages 2–3. Ask: *What is the importance of Eratosthenes spending his time on the ship's deck rather than in a cabin?* On deck, it is likely that he saw the lighthouse when it first appeared. This experience would be important for him later in his realization that he could calculate Earth's circumference. RI 6

• Review the first paragraph on page 7. Say: *The author spends a great deal of time discussing the beacon on the lighthouse. According to this paragraph, what is the author's purpose?* The beacon demonstrates Earth's curvature. A person at sea heading toward Alexandria sees the beacon on top of the lighthouse first. If Earth were not spherical, a person would see the entire lighthouse at the same time. RI 6

ELL ENGLISH LANGUAGE LEARNERS

Use Peer Supported Learning

Have students work in small groups to read and review the segment. Have them pause after each page and take turns paraphrasing each paragraph.

RESPOND TO SEGMENT 1

Classroom Collaboration

Have partners create a summary of important ideas presented in this segment. Then have them identify the main idea of the segment.

Domain Specific Vocabulary

polymath (p. 24) • a person educated in several subjects

 ENGLISH LANGUAGE LEARNERS

Use Props

Use a map that includes a close-up of northern Egypt to show the location of Alexandria. Use terms that students will encounter in the text to point out how Eratosthenes must have sailed toward the city.

RESPOND TO SEGMENT 2

 Classroom Collaboration

Have small groups work together to summarize what they have read. Have them ask questions about what they don't understand.

 Common Core Connection

RI 1 cite textual evidence to support analysis of what the text says explicitly as well as inferences drawn; **RI 2** determine a central idea/analyze its development/provide summary; **RI 4** determine the meaning of words and phrases, including figurative, connotative, and technical meanings/analyze impact of word choices; **RI 6** determine author's point of view or purpose/analyze how author uses rhetoric; **RI 10** read and comprehend literary nonfiction; **W 2** write informative/explanatory texts; **W 5** develop and strengthen writing by planning, revising, editing, rewriting, or trying a new approach; **SL 3** evaluate speaker's point of view, reasoning, use of evidence and rhetoric; **SL 4** present information, findings, and supporting evidence clearly, concisely, and logically

Academic Vocabulary

Read each word with students and discuss its meaning.

ascension (p. 12) • rising

ephemeral (p. 13) • short-lived

aesthete (p. 13) • a person who greatly appreciates beauty

razed (p. 17) • demolished

benign (p. 17) • not harmful

salubrious (p. 20) • healthy

warren (p. 20) • a maze of connected underground tunnels

abayas (p. 21) • a long, black robe worn by some Muslim women

FIRST READ ## Think Through the Text

Have students use text evidence and draw inferences to answer questions.

p. 13 • *What does the author mean by the phrase* bait and switch *in the last paragraph? Euergetes convinced the government of Athens to lend him some great plays. He used a deposit to get the plays but then kept them for himself.* RI 4

pp. 14–15 • *What was the problem with the calendar in Eratosthenes' time? A year wasn't exactly correct—short by six hours; so over time holidays were celebrated at the wrong time of year.* **Who was able to fix this problem by developing a calendar that was the basis of the calendar we use today?** *Julius Caesar* RI 10

p. 20 • *What does the author say about main roads in big cities? The main roads often were also main roads long ago.* **What evidence does he offer?** *He describes Broadway in Manhattan.* RI 1

pp. 24–25 • *Why do we know about Eratosthenes' accomplishment only from a successor and not from Eratosthenes himself? The account by Eratosthenes has been lost, but the successor, Cleomedes, left a description.* RI 10

SECOND READ ## Analyze the Text

- Review pages 16–21. Say: *The author spends several pages describing his personal visit to Alexandria.* **What is the purpose of this personal account?** *The author is describing how the city has changed since Eratosthenes' day.* RI 6

- Review the top of page 25. Ask: *What is the author's opinion of Eratosthenes' calculation of Earth's circumference? He thinks it is extraordinary—greater than other discoveries at that time.* RI 6

COMMON CORE

Academic Vocabulary

Read each word with students and discuss its meaning.

limpid (p. 26) • clear

conflagration (p. 31) • overwhelming fire

prosaic (p. 36) • common; ordinary

chthonic (p. 46) • related to gods and spirits living underground

interlopers (p. 54) • intruders; trespassers

FIRST READ Think Through the Text

Have students use text evidence and draw inferences to answer questions.

pp. 27–28 • *Why was it important that Eratosthenes used angles observed on the solstice for his calculations?* The sun is directly overhead Syene and makes no shadow there. The angle of the shadow made on that day in Alexandria can be used to calculate Earth's curvature. ▬RI 10

p. 30 • *What does the author mean when he describes the Babylonians' idea of science as a black-box approach?* They wanted to describe things they saw and experienced, not necessarily to explain things. ▬RI 4

p. 35 • *What was an Apollonius's epicycle?* a time period during which heavenly bodies revolved around Earth *How did Ptolemaeus build on this idea?* He developed the idea of an Earth-centered universe. ▬RI 10

SECOND READ Analyze the Text

• Review pages 32–33. Ask: *What is the author's purpose in describing the Pythagoreans?* Unlike many scholars of the day, they were willing to consider that Earth was round. ▬RI 6

• Review pages 52–58. Ask: *What is the author's purpose on page 52?* The author describes benefits and drawbacks of having foreigners versus natives serve as laborers in Egypt. *What effect did the separation of Greek and Egyptian populations have?* Two distinct and antagonistic societies developed: one wealthy and urban in Alexandria, the other was poor and rural. ▬RI 2

Independent/Self-Selected Reading

Have students reread the excerpt from *Circumference* independently to practice analyzing the text on their own, or have them practice the skills using another book, such as:

• *The History of Science from the Ancient Greeks to the Scientific Revolution* by Ray Spangenburg

• *The Usborne Book of Scientists: From Archimedes to Einstein* by Struan Reid ▬RI 10

Performance Task

WRITE & PRESENT

1. Have students work in small groups to review the author's comments and identify his points of view about science on pages 39–40. ▬RI 6

2. Have individual students write a paragraph explaining the author's purpose in describing Eratosthenes' calculation of Earth's circumference. Instruct students to identify the author's point of view and cite text evidence to support their explanations. ▬RI 6, W 2

3. Have students share explanations with others in their group. Instruct them to evaluate each other's explanations. Then have students edit their explanations. ▬W 5, SL 3, SL 4

4. Have students present their final paragraphs to their classmates. Ask students to respond to the ideas from each student's writing. ▬SL 3, SL 4

See Copying Masters, pp. 212–215.

STUDENT CHECKLIST

Writing

☑ Analyze the author's point of view and purpose

☑ Include specific text references.

☑ Use complete sentences and developed paragraphs to structure writing.

Speaking & Listening

☑ Engage effectively in collaborative conversations.

☑ Read writing aloud with a clear, audible voice.

☑ Present ideas in a meaningful way.

Options for Reading

Independent Students examine the selection independently or with a partner and then answer questions posed by the teacher.

Supported Students examine the graphic map and then the chart and answer questions with teacher support.

Recommended Levels of Insulation

by U.S. Environmental Protection Agency/U.S. Department of Energy

SUMMARY This document uses a color-coded map of the United States as well as a chart to give information about the levels of insulation that are needed to provide older homes with new insulation.

ABOUT THE AUTHOR The United States Environmental Protection **Agency (EPA)** is an agency of the United States government. Its purpose is to protect the health of the citizens and their environment. The agency offers free information to individuals, businesses, communities, and local and state governments.

Discuss Genre and Set Purpose

INFORMATIONAL TEXT Preview the selection with students. Help them identify characteristics of graphic informational text, such as maps and charts.

SET PURPOSE Help students set a purpose for reading, such as to find information about the recommended levels of insulation that apply to specific locations.

Common Core Connection

RI 1 cite textual evidence to support analysis of what the text says explicitly as well as inferences drawn; **RI 2** determine a central idea/analyze its development/provide summary; **RI 3** analyze how author unfolds an analysis or series of ideas or events; **RI 10** read and comprehend literature; **W 2** write informative/explanatory texts; **W 5** develop and strengthen writing by planning, revising, editing, rewriting, or trying a new approach; **SL 4** present information, findings, and supporting evidence clearly, concisely, and logically

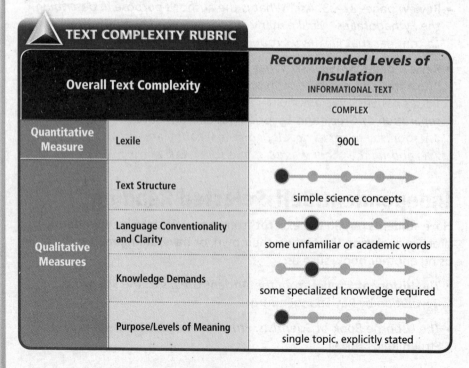

TEXT COMPLEXITY RUBRIC		Recommended Levels of Insulation INFORMATIONAL TEXT
Overall Text Complexity		COMPLEX
Quantitative Measure	Lexile	900L
Qualitative Measures	Text Structure	simple science concepts
	Language Conventionality and Clarity	some unfamiliar or academic words
	Knowledge Demands	some specialized knowledge required
	Purpose/Levels of Meaning	single topic, explicitly stated

Academic Vocabulary

Read each word with students and discuss its meaning.

insulation • material that prevents the passage of heat

resist • withstand

thermal • heat retaining

retrofitting • modifying with new parts

sheathing • protective covering

siding • material covering the outside of a building

WRITE & PRESENT

1. Have small groups analyze how the EPA author presents the information in the document. Have them pay particular attention to the order in which the points are made and how the graphics are used. ◗ RI 3

2. Ask students to describe the structure the EPA author used to present the information. Have them each write a paragraph that evaluates what is most and least effective about the presentation. Encourage students to cite text evidence to defend their ideas. ◗ W 2

3. Have students share their paragraphs with partners and offer suggestions for revising and editing. Students can edit their writing based on these suggestions. ◗ W 5

4. Invite students to present their final writing to their classmates. Ask listeners to respond to the themes and ideas from each student's writing. ◗ SL 4

See Copying Masters, pp. 212–215.

STUDENT CHECKLIST

Writing

☑ Analyze how the EPA author presents information.

☑ Explain the structure by which the document presents information.

☑ Use complete sentences and developed paragraphs to structure writing.

Speaking & Listening

☑ Read writing aloud with a clear, audible voice.

☑ Present ideas in a meaningful way.

FIRST READ ## Think Through the Text

Have students use text evidence and draw inferences to answer questions.

- *What is the function of the map?* The map shows the levels of insulation appropriate to zones of the United States. ◗ RI 3

- *What is the function of the chart?* The chart indicates how to add insulation to given buildings in each zone so that insulation levels are useful and cost-effective. ◗ RI 3

- *What does the text explain?* The text explains what kind of insulation to install and how and where to install it. ◗ RI 3

SECOND READ ## Analyze the Text

- Ask: *What is the purpose of this document?* The document provides guidelines for people who want to make sure their homes are properly insulated. ◗ RI 2

- Ask: *What inference can you make by looking at the map and reading the chart?* Sample answer: Colder climates, such as those in northern and mountainous areas, need the insulation with higher R-values with better thermal performance. ◗ RI 1

Independent/Self-Selected Reading

Have students reread *Recommended Levels of Insulation* independently to practice analyzing the text on their own, or have them practice the skills using other EPA resources, such as the following:

- *Protect Your Family from Asbestos—Contaminated Vermiculite Insulation.* http://www.epa.gov/asbestos/vermiculite.html

- *Best Practice: Wind Baffles: Attic Insulation.* http://www.epa.gov/indoorairplus/technical/moisture/wind_baffles.html ◗ RI 10

"Loveliest of Trees"

by A. E. Housman (1920)

Loveliest of trees, the cherry now
Is hung with bloom along the bough,
And stands about the woodland ride
Wearing white for Eastertide.
Now, of my threescore years and ten,
Twenty will not come again,
And take from seventy springs a score,
It only leaves me fifty more.
And since to look at things in bloom
Fifty springs are little room,
About the woodlands I will go
To see the cherry hung with snow.

"Sonnet LXXIII"

by William Shakespeare (1609)

That time of year thou mayst in me behold
When yellow leaves, or none, or few, do hang
Upon those boughs which shake against the cold,
Bare ruin'd choirs, where late the sweet birds sang.
In me thou see'st the twilight of such day
As after sunset fadeth in the west;
Which by and by black night doth take away,
Death's second self, that seals up all in rest.
In me thou see'st the glowing of such fire,
That on the ashes of his youth doth lie,
As the death-bed, whereon it must expire,
Consum'd with that which it was nourish'd by.
This thou perceiv'st, which makes thy love more strong,
To love that well, which thou must leave ere long.

"Ozymandias"

by Percy Bysshe Shelley (1892)

I met a traveler from an antique land
Who said: Two vast and trunkless legs of stone
Stand in the desert … Near them, on the sand,
Half sunk, a shattered visage lies, whose frown,
And wrinkled lip, and sneer of cold command,
Tell that its sculptor well those passions read
Which yet survive, stamped on these lifeless things,

The hand that mocked them, and the heart that fed:
And on the pedestal these words appear:
'My name is Ozymandias, king of kings:
Look on my works, ye Mighty, and despair!'
Nothing beside remains. Round the decay
Of that colossal wreck, boundless and bare
The lone and level sands stretch far away.

Academic Vocabulary

from *The Odyssey*

assail
beguiled
brandish
burnished
chided
flouting
libations
malinger
muster
overweening
ramparts
slander
staunchly
suppliants
unscathed
waft

from *Metamorphoses*

aspect
chaos
deceptive
fame
fate
founded
immortality
metamorphoses
mortal
oath
penalty
pledged
sacrilegious
semblance
soul

"The Nose"

averse
blackguard
conspicuous
disreputable
edifying
futile
incomprehensible
indignation
instigator

invective
mercenary
olfactory
preposterous
prosaic
retaliation

Candide

circumspection
convalescence
corsair
countenance
Dervish
farthing
impertinence
ingenuous
lackey
mercantile
moiety
mongrel
obeisance
provisions
shrewdly
traverse
valet
wary

Fathers and Sons

adjudicate
archaic
averred
cynicism
deferentially
disabuse
languor
liveried
magnanimous
obtuse
propriety
sallies
subaltern
surreptitiously
timorously

"The Gift of the Magi"

appertaining
chaste
coveted
depreciate
discreet
ecstatic
hysterical
mendicancy
meretricious
parsimony
prudence
ransacking
ravages
vestibule

The Metamorphosis

abraded
harbinger
hearsay
implacably
lucid
multifarious
pallidly
propulsion
relinquish
retrenchments
stenography
swoonlike

The Grapes of Wrath

cantankerous
corrugated
demure
dissipated
flailing
gauged
greasewood
paralytic
pellagra
reedy
rivulet
skirling
truculent
vagrant
wrath

Fahrenheit 451
abstract
bewilderment
centrifuge
gout
illumination
incinerator
incomprehensible
infinite
insidious
nuzzling
phosphorescent
profusion
scapegoat
sieve

I Stand Here Ironing
anonymity
articulate
convalescent
convulsing
corroding
denunciations
dredging
engulfed
fluted
frailer
fretted
hashing
ravaged
somber
sterner
tormented
WPA

Things Fall Apart
abomination
despair
destiny
dispensation
exile
high-handed
improvident
kites
missionary
oracle

proverb
scorched
suitor
zeal

To Kill a Mockingbird
appoint
compassion
condescension
cynical
defend
despise
evidence
grudge
humiliation
intimidation
malevolent
mob
pity
testify
values

The Killer Angels
abide
dapper
declaiming
doctrine
foraging
glowered
ineradicable
inscrutable
interpose
languid
mutineers
polyglot
pontifically
repulsed
secession

The Joy Luck Club
adversary
benevolently
character
circumstances
concessions
consulate

dialect
dowry
intention
kowtowed
malignant
meager
ritual

In the Time of the Butterflies
admonishes
anguish
commemorations
desecrating
empathetic
gallant
impertinent
mandatory
perforce
posthumous
sanctioned
swarthy
tenuous
vehemence
volition

The Book Thief
appalled
auspicious
caustic
epitome
gratuitous
hiatus
illustrious
immutable
innocuous
ludicrous
malignant
miscreants
morose
profanity
prolific
raucous
vindication

Oedipus Rex
contagion
defilement
execrable
goad
grave
lustration
malediction
parricide
perquisites
primal
sepulchre
sphinx
wretched

The Tragedy of Macbeth
accompt
bedlams
bodements
broil
composition
contriver
corporal
eminence
filthy witness
gospl'd
hurlyburly
knell
palpable
perchance
perturbation
'scap'd

A Doll's House
capricious
constrained
crestfallen
gruesome
Neopolitan
notice
obstinate
petty
prodigal

The Glass Menagerie
automatism
emulate
expressionism
imminent

immutable
intimated
jalopy
nostalgia
novelty
ominous
paragon
patronage
rejuvenated
slackening
vivacity

Rhinoceros
capitulating
caprice
chivalry
dissociation
intuitive
opiate
pachyderm
pedant
sublimating
syllogism
wretched

"Master Harold" ... and the boys
audacity
barbaric
daunted
deportment
despot
fiasco
flotsam and jetsam
hiding
hunky-dory
Inquisition
intrepid
lenient
oscillate
perpetual
shambles
undeterred

"Sonnet LXXIII"
choirs
doth
expire

"Song"
befell
cleft
pilgrimage

"Ozymandias"
colossal
pedestal
visage

"The Raven"
dirges
melancholy
ominous
surcease

"We Grow Accustomed to the Dark"
accustomed
alters
disclose

"Loveliest of Trees"
bough
Eastertide
score
threescore

"Lift Every Voice and Sing"
chastening
harmonies
resounding

"Yet Do I Marvel"
catechism
fickle
quibble

"Musée des Beaux Arts"
forsaken
martyrdom
ploughman
reverently

"Women"
battered
stout

"I Am Offering This Poem"
dense
hogan
mature

"Speech to the Second Virginia Convention"
apt
arduous
comports
subjugation
supplication

"Farewell Address"
actuated
apprise
delineated
insidious
maxims
solicitude

"Gettysburg Address"
consecrate
devotion
endure
fourscore
proposition
vain

"Second Inaugural Address"
avert
engrosses
expiration
impending
ventured

"State of the Union Address"
abiding
acquiesce
antithesis
appropriations
dupes
millennium
partisanship
peril
propaganda

stamina
stimulating
tyranny
unprecedented
vindicate

The "Spirit of Liberty" Speech
affirm
aspirations
bias
conviction
oppression

"Declaration of Conscience"
calumny
deliberative body
impute
national condition
rendezvous
vilification

"Letter from Birmingham Jail"
advocate
alternative
conformity
moderate
status quo

"I Have a Dream"
degenerate
legitimate
promissory
urgency

I Know Why the Caged Bird Sings
affluent
anachronism
aphorisms
blasphemous
cajoled
chifforobe
clemency
commensurate
filial
heinous

metamorphosis
onerous
rancor
sobriquet
solicitous
traverse

"Hope, Despair and Memory"
aberration
abhorrence
incumbent
propitious
repugnant
xenophobia

"Speech at Moscow State University"
cudgel
ingenious
monopoly
unintrusive

"A Quilt of a Country"
coalescing
improbable
pluralistic
tenuously

from *Bury My Heart at Wounded Knee*
alliance
annuities
barricade
circular
destitute
dialects
dictum
expedition
extinction
genuinely
neutral
obsequious
rations
relinquish
tenacious

from Son of the Morning Star: Custer and the Little Big Horn

acerbic
circuitous
circumspect
contemptuous
dubious
ensconced
fortuitously
impetuous
incorruptible
malicious
palimpsest
preposterous
reticent
sinister

from The Story of Art

adherence
chaff
commission
compunction
elaborate
fleeting
idyll
incantations
method
prostrate
refinement
script
symmetry
train
weathered

Cod: A Biography of the Fish That Changed the World

bier
commodity
conglomerate
finite
microcosm
moratorium
prophetic
referendum
rhetoric
sovereignty
subsidize
subsistence

Black, Blue & Gray: African Americans in the Civil War

abstraction
casualties
chattel
deploying
disavowed
eloquence
evinced
fugitives
light-complected
ratified
Reconstruction
rigging
seceded
urbanites
vanguard

The Longitude Prize

ascertained
circumnavigators
compensate
conjunction
counteracted
designated
erratic
evaded
execute
miscellaneous
precision
replica
skeptics
stipulated
substantial
vindication

from The Illustrated Book of Great Composers

adapting
amalgamated
contemporary
derivative
enhancing
individualism
medium
ornamental
pejorative
prolific

recreational
sacred
secular
significance
standardized

from 1491

cosmology
deleterious
demography
disparate
foray
garrulous
homogeneity
incursions
internecine
metallurgy
proclivity
putative
succumbed

from Elements

absurd
adjacent
axiomatic
coincide
construct
extremities
inclination
interpolation
literally
manifest
porism
proposition
respectively
terminated
vertical angles

"Classifying the Stars"

beneficent
dispersed
epochs
myriad
omnipresent
penetrate
rarefied

"Amusement Park Physics"
augment
cusps
discontinuities
dissipated
illusory
intervening
negligible
radially
rotational
superposed
symmetrically

from The Hot Zone
abscess
agonals
amulets
breached
culminating
fulminating
incarnation
mutable
necropsy
necrosis
paroxysm
scarp
vector
warrens
wizened

from Life by the Numbers
animate
array
collaborating
concise
crucial
intervening
maneuver
melodious
newsreel
reverberation
surreal
virtual

The Race to Save the Lord God Bird
brink
carcasses
conservationists
ethical
finicky
heritage
intact
mangle
penetrating
preened
ravenously
specimen
strenuous
tantalizing

from The Story of Science: Newton at the Center
assaying
conjectures
convivial
deposed
harmoniously
heretic
homogeneous
innate
peevishness
pompous
steeping
straitjacket
tufted

from Circumference: Eratosthenes and the Ancient Quest to Measure the Globe
abayas
aesthete
anthropomorphic
ascension
benign
canonical
chthonic

conflagration
encomium
entrepôt
ephemeral
interlopers
limpid
obelisks
pecuniary
prosaic
razed
salubrious
self-aggrandizing
warren

Recommended Levels of Insulation
insulation
resist
retrofitting
sheathing
siding
thermal

Name _____

Grades 9–10 Writing Checklist

In my writing, did I . . .

Argument	Informative	Narrative
☐ introduce my topic?	☐ clearly introduce my topic?	☐ engage the reader by setting out the story line?
☐ introduce my claim(s) and present clear relationships among claims?	☐ develop my topic using sufficient facts, clear definitions, and concrete details and/or quotes?	☐ clearly introduce characters and point(s) of view?
☐ develop my claim(s) and counterclaims fairly with evidence for each?	☐ use a variety of appropriate transitions to link the sections of the text?	☐ use techniques such as dialogue, description, and multiple plot lines to develop the narrative?
☐ use transitions to create organization and flow?	☐ use exact language and specific vocabulary?	☐ use a variety of techniques to sequence events?
☐ use a formal style and an objective and fair tone?	☐ use a formal style and an objective tone?	☐ use precise words and phrases and sensory language to convey a vivid picture of the narrative?
☐ write a concluding statement that supports the argument?	☐ write a concluding statement that supports the information presented?	☐ write a logical and satisfying conclusion?

Other
☐
☐
☐

Name _____

Grades 9–10 Speaking and Listening Checklist

In my speaking, did I . . .

☐ come to discussions prepared?
☐ use my preparation to stimulate thoughtful discussions?
☐ advance conversations by asking and answering relative questions?
☐ respond thoughtfully to different perspectives?
☐ actively include others in the discussion?
☐ adapt my speech to the context?

In my listening, did I . . .

☐ work with my peers to set rules, goals, deadlines, and assign roles?
☐ advance conversations by asking and answering relative questions?
☐ evaluate the speaker's point of view?
☐ evaluate the speaker's use of evidence?
☐ summarize points of agreement?

Other

☐
☐
☐

Performance Rubric

Use this rubric to evaluate writing, listening, and speaking tasks.

	Advanced	**Competent**
DEVELOPMENT	• The introduction creates a strong impression and clearly presents a well-focused controlling idea. • Relevant details and evidence support the writer's points. • The concluding section summarizes the key points and leaves readers with something to think about.	• The introduction identifies a controlling idea but could do more to grab the reader's interest. • One or two key points could use more support. • The concluding section summarizes most of the key points but could be developed more.
ORGANIZATION	• The organization is effective for the purpose and audience; ideas progress logically. • Transitions successfully show the relationships between ideas.	• The organization is confusing in a few places. • A few more transitions are needed to clarify the relationships between ideas.
LANGUAGE	• The writing reflects a formal style. • Use of language is lively and precise. • Sentence beginnings, lengths, and structures vary and have a rhythmic flow. • Spelling, capitalization, and punctuation are correct. • Grammar and usage are correct.	• The style is informal in a few places. • Most language is precise. • Sentence beginnings, lengths, and structures vary somewhat. • Several spelling, capitalization, and punctuation mistakes occur. • Some grammatical and usage errors are repeated in a few places.

	Limited	Emerging
DEVELOPMENT	• The introduction is commonplace; it only hints at a controlling idea. • Details and evidence support some key points but are often too general. • The concluding section does not completely summarize or wrap up the main ideas.	• The introduction is missing. • The writer's points lack specific support. • The concluding section is missing.
ORGANIZATION	• The organization is logical in some places but often doesn't follow a pattern. • More transitions are needed throughout to explain the relationships between ideas.	• An organizational pattern is not apparent; ideas are presented randomly. • The transitions are ineffective or are missing.
LANGUAGE	• The style is overly casual. • Language is repetitive or too general at times. • Sentence structures barely vary, and some fragments or run-on sentences are present. • Spelling, capitalization, and punctuation are often incorrect but do not interfere with the reader's understanding of the work. • Grammar and usage are incorrect in many places, but the writer's ideas are still clear.	• The style is inappropriate for the purpose and audience. • Language is inaccurate, repetitive, and too general. • Repetitive sentence structure, fragments, and run-on sentences make the writing hard to follow. • Spelling, capitalization, and punctuation are incorrect throughout. • Many grammatical and usage errors change the meaning of the writer's ideas.

Bibliography

Achebe, Chinua. *Things Fall Apart.* New York: Anchor Books, 1994. (1959)

Alvarez, Julia. *In the Time of the Butterflies.* Chapel Hill: Algonquin Books of Chapel Hill, 2010. (1994)

Angelou, Maya. *I Know Why the Caged Bird Sings.* New York: Random House, 2009. (1969)

Auden, Wystan Hugh. "Musée des Beaux Arts." *The Collected Poetry of W. H. Auden.* New York: Random House, 1967. (1945)

Baca, Jimmy Santiago. "I Am Offering This Poem." *Immigrants in Our Own Land.* Baton Rouge: Louisiana State University Press, 1979.

Bradbury, Ray. *Fahrenheit 451.* New York: Simon & Schuster, 2012. (1951)

Brown, Dee. *Bury My Heart at Wounded Knee.* New York: Picador, 2007. (1970)

Cannon, Annie J. "Classifying the Stars." *The Universe of Stars.* Edited by Harlow Shapley and Cecilia H. Payne. Cambridge: The Observatory, 1926.

Connell, Evan S. *Son of the Morning Star: Custer and the Little Bighorn.* New York: North Point Press, 1997. (1984)

Cullen, Countee. "Yet Do I Marvel." *The Norton Anthology.* By Henry Louis Gates Jr. and Nellie Y. McKay. New York: W. W. Norton & Company, Inc., 1997.

Dash, Joan. *The Longitude Prize.* Pictures by Dusan Petricic. New York: Farrar, Straus and Giroux, 2000.

Devlin, Keith. *Life by the Numbers.* New York: John Wiley & Sons, Inc., 1998.

Dickinson, Emily. "We Grow Accustomed to the Dark." *The Complete Poems of Emily Dickinson.* Edited by Thomas H. Johnson. Boston: Little, Brown and Company, 1960. (1890)

Donne, John. "Song." *The Love Poems of John Donne.* Edited by Charles Fowkes. New York: St. Martin's Press, 1982.

Euclid. *Euclid's Elements.* Translated by Thomas L. Heath. Santa Fe: Green Lion Press, 2003.

Fugard, Athol. *"Master Harold" ... and the boys.* New York: Vintage Books, 1998.

Gogol, Nikolai. "The Nose." *Diary of a Madman and Other Stories.* Translated by Ronald Wilks. New York: Penguin Books, 1972.

Gombrich, E. H. *The Story of Art.* London: Phaidon Press, 2006. (1950)

Hakim, Joy. *The Story of Science: Newton at the Center.* Washington, D.C.: Smithsonian Books, 2005.

Hand, Learned. "The 'Spirit of Liberty' Speech" presented in 1944 during "I AM an American Day." *The Providence Forum.* October 2012. *http://www.providenceforum.org/spiritoflibertyspeech*

Haskins, Jim. *Black, Blue & Gray: African Americans in the Civil War.* New York: Simon & Schuster Books for Young Readers, 1998.

Henry, O. "The Gift of the Magi." Illustrated by P. J. Lynch. Somerville: Candlewick Press, 2008. (1903)

Henry, Patrick. "Speech to the Second Virginia Convention." *The American Reader: Words That Moved a Nation.* Edited by Diane Ravitch. New York: HarperCollins, 2000. (1990)

Homer. *The Odyssey.* Translated by Robert Fagles. New York: Penguin Books, 1996.

Hoose, Phillip. *The Race to Save the Lord God Bird.* New York: Farrar, Straus and Giroux, 2004.

Housman, A. E. "Loveliest of Trees." *The Collected Poems of A. E. Housman.* Hertfordshire: Wordsworth Editions Ltd., 2005. (1994)

Ibsen, Henrik. *A Doll's House and Other Plays.* Penguin Classics, 1983.

Ionesco, Eugene. *Rhinoceros.* New York: Grove Press, 1960.

Johnson, James Weldon. "Lift Every Voice and Sing." *Complete Poems.* Edited by Sondra Kathryn Wilson. New York: Penguin Books, 2000.

Kafka, Franz. *The Metamorphosis and Other Stories.* Translated by Stanley Appelbaum. New York: Dover Publications, Inc., 1996.

King, Martin Luther, Jr. "I Have a Dream." *Letter from Birmingham Jail/"I Have a Dream" Speech.* Logan: Perfection Learning Corporation, 1990.

King, Martin Luther, Jr. "Letter from Birmingham Jail." *Letter from Birmingham Jail/"I Have a Dream" Speech.* Logan: Perfection Learning Corporation, 1990.

Kurlansky, Mark. *Cod: A Biography of the Fish That Changed the World.* New York: Penguin Books, 1998. (1997)

Lee, Harper. *To Kill a Mockingbird.* New York: Grand Central Publishing, 1960.

Lincoln, Abraham. "Address at Gettysburg, Pennsylvania." *Lincoln: Speeches and Writings: 1859–1865.* Selected by Don E. Fehrenbacher. New York: The Library of America, 1989. (1953, 1974)

Lincoln, Abraham. "Lincoln's Second Inaugural Address." *Lincoln's Gettysburg Oration and First and Second Inaugural Addresses.* Forgotten Books, 2012. (1907)

Mann, Charles C. *1491: New Revelations of the Americas Before Columbus.* New York: Vintage Books, 2006. (2005)

Nicastro, Nicholas. *Circumference: Eratosthenes and the Ancient Quest to Measure the Globe.* New York: St. Martin's Press, 2008.

Olsen, Tillie. "I Stand Here Ironing." *Tell Me a Riddle.* New York: Delacorte Press/Seymour Lawrence, 1961. (1956)

Ovid. *The Metamorphoses of Ovid.* Translated by Allen Mandelbaum. New York: Houghton Mifflin Harcourt, 1993.

Poe, Edgar A. "The Raven." *Master Thoughts of Master Minds in Poem, Prose and Pencil.* Kessinger Publishing, 2010.

Preston, Richard. *The Hot Zone: A Terrifying True Story.* New York: Anchor Books, 1994.

Quindlen, Anna. "A Quilt of a Country." *The Daily Beast.* September 26, 2001. http://thedailybeast.com/newsweek/2001/09/27/a-quilt-of-a-country.print.html

Reagan, Ronald. "Speech at Moscow State University." *The American Reader: Words That Moved a Nation.* Edited by Diane Ravitch. New York: HarperCollins, 2000. (1990)

Roosevelt, Franklin Delano. "State of the Union Address." Hard Press, 2012.

Shaara, Michael. *The Killer Angels.* New York: Ballantine Books, 2003. (1975)

Shakespeare, William. "Sonnet LXXIII." *Shakespeare's Sonnets.* CreateSpace Independent Publishing Platform, 2011.

Shakespeare, William. *The Tragedy of Macbeth.* Middlesex: The Echo Library, 2006.

Shelley, Percy Bysshe. "Ozymandias." *Shelley: Selected Poetry.* Selected by Isabel Quigly. London: Penguin Books, 1956.

Smith, Margaret Chase. "Declaration of Conscience." Margaret Chase Smith Library. June 1950. http://www.mcslibrary.org/program/library/declaration.htm

Sophocles. *Oedipus Rex. The Oedipus Cycle.* Translated by Dudley Fitts and Robert Fitzgerald. New York: Houghton Mifflin Harcourt, 1977.

Steinbeck, John. *The Grapes of Wrath.* New York: Penguin Books, 1996. (1939)

Tan, Amy. *The Joy Luck Club.* New York: Penguin Books, 2006. (1989)

Thompson, Wendy. *The Illustrated Book of Great Composers.* London: Lorenz Books, 2009. (2001)

Turgenev, Ivan. *Fathers and Sons.* Translated by Peter Carson. London: Penguin Classics, 2009. (1862)

U.S. Environmental Protection Agency. *Recommended Levels of Insulation.* Energy Star. http://www.energystar.gov/index.cfm?c=home_sealing.hm_improvement_insulation_table

Voltaire. *Candide.* CreateSpace Independent Publishing Platform, 2012. (1759)

Walker, Alice. "Women." *Her Blue Body Everything We Know: Earthling Poems, 1965–1990 Complete.* New York: Harcourt, 2003. (1968)

Walker, Jearl. "Amusement Park Physics." *Roundabout: The Physics of Rotation in the Everyday World: Readings from "The Amateur Scientist" in Scientific American.* New York: W. H. Freeman and Company, 1985.

Washington, George. "Farewell Address." *George Washington's Farewell Address.* Bedford: Applewood Books, 1999. (1796)

Wiesel, Elie. "Hope, Despair and Memory." *Nobel Lectures in Peace (1981–1990).* Singapore: World Scientific Publishing Co. Pte. Ltd., 1997.

Williams, Tennessee. *The Glass Menagerie.* New York: Penguin Group, 1987. (1945)

Zusak, Markus. *The Book Thief.* Illustrated by Trudy White. New York: Alfred A. Knopf, 2005.

Internet Resources

Use the following websites to locate additional resources for teaching the exemplar texts. Check the website for your state's department of education for specific information on the implementation of the Common Core State Standards.

http://aasl.jesandco.org/

http://www.achieve.org/achieving-common-core

http://www.achievethecore.org/

http://www.ascd.org/common-core-state-standards/common-core.aspx

http://www.ccsso.org/documents/2012/common_core_resources.pdf

http://www.corestandards.org/

http://www.engagingeducators.com/

http://www.ncte.org/standards/commoncore

http://www.ode.state.or.us/wma/teachlearn/commoncore/ ela-publishers-criteria.pdf

http://www.parcconline.org/

http://www.reading.org/Resources/ResourcesByTopic/ CommonCore-resourcetype/CommonCore-rt-resources.aspx

http://www.smarterbalanced.org/

https://www.teachingchannel.org/videos?categories=topics_common-core